TRIALS
AND
TRIUMPHS

by

Fannie Ada (Chupp) Miller

Order from:

Fannie Ada Miller
RR 1, Box 212
Leon, IA 50144

About the Author

Born the eighth of nine children, Fannie Miller grew up an Old Order Amish farm girl near Chouteau, Oklahoma.

She and her husband, Andy Jr. and their four children and sixteen grandchildren presently live near Leon, Iowa.

Fannie enjoys interacting with people and began collecting her storehouse of information during her first visit to Phoenix, Arizona, nearly thirty years ago. It was then that she and her husband and two daughters spent some time with her father Menno I. Chupp, whom she hadn't seen for thirty-two years. Fannie also gained new insights into her past by visiting with other relatives during that time, whom she'd never met before.

I personally have always enjoyed sitting and listening to "Aunt" Fannie tell stories, and thus, her heart and love for her heritage will be revealed as you read this remarkable true story.

Written by Karen (Bontrager) Miller

(She is presently engaged in prison ministry with her husband Tim in Atmore, Alabama.)

TRIALS AND TRIUMPHS

ISBN 1-896199-38-0

Printed in Canada - PrairieView Press, Rosenort, Manitoba.

Preface

Down through the years, I have been interested in my heritage. I never met my paternal grandparents as they were both gone into eternity before I was born. When I met an older person who remembered them, I always asked what kind of people they were. I never heard a bad word about them, much more of their strong faith and fairness. I found out my grandmother became a young widow with four little children at the age of twenty-six. The youngest daughter died six months later which left her with many trials to face. I do remember my Dad's half brothers and sister from that marriage and appreciated them. It was always a highlight when they came to visit.

Reading in a genealogy book of her second marriage to my grandpa Isaac Chupp, a single boy, and his ability to have a close relationship with her children from her first husband is also commendable. The sorrows they experienced in having a number of babies and young children lowered into their graves were not easy. Then also two grown daughters passed away. Taking a motherless baby into their home and nurturing her as one of their very own was a deed not just anyone would do. As a young girl, I worked for Aunt Deemy, as we always called her, who was that baby. She told me she never saw them lose their temper or be unkind to anyone. Isaac was an ordained minister in the Amish church. His wife Mattie faithfully stood by him.

Isaac passed away in his forties, and again, Grandma was left alone to face more trials. My father, Menno, the youngest was a young child and grew up without the guidance of a father.

Later Grandma met and married my maternal great-grandpa, Daniel Bontrager, a widower and also a deacon in the Amish church near Yoder, Kansas. It was through this that my mother, Barbara, grandchild of Daniel, met my father, Menno I. Chupp. He was the youngest child of my paternal grandparents, Isaac and Mattie Chupp. Mother was the oldest child of Andrew F. And Fannie Bontrager. Fannie was Daniel's oldest daughter.

My parents got married, and Mother, being the oldest child in a family of fourteen, was taught to shoulder much responsibility. So I have also included about her family and home life in this book. Father, being the youngest in his family and able to outsmart his mother at a young age, made for trials in their marriage. Nine children were born into their home, and times were hard. When he got deeply into debt during the depression years, he saw no way out except to leave the area and change his name. You will read all about their life in this book.

I want to thank all who gave me information down through the years. Many of them have passed on to their reward. Also to older cousins and my own siblings. Being the next to the youngest in the family, I'm sure I didn't experience the severity of the trials my older brothers and sisters did.

My niece, Karen, daughter of Salina and Joe Bontrager, whose house joined Mother's, often spent an evening with Mother and asked questions about her life. Karen jotted these memories into a notebook which she so graciously shared with me for this book. Many things Mother never related to us children. I also found some highlights in Salina's and my diaries of happenings in Mother's sunset years that are included.

I was often encouraged to write these experiences into a book so, with much prayer, I, in my weakness, undertook the task. I feel future generations can take a lesson from it all. My eyes often filled with tears as I wrote.

I started this book three years ago, writing in longhand. When our oldest grandson, Matthew Miller, saw what I was doing, he encouraged me to get a computer, and I give him credit for setting it up for me. Having no computer knowledge myself, I often called upon him when I ran into a snag.

One of our twelve-year-old twin granddaughters, Janice Stoltzfus, designed the cover for this book and chose a very appropriate verse to expose in the open Bible. Thanks again, Janice.

Our daughter, Carol (Mrs. Noah Yoder), gets the credit of spending many hours proofreading this manuscript and making corrections.

Last, but not least, I will give my dear husband, Andy, credit for supporting me as I gathered information, visiting people and cemeteries, making phone calls, etc. to get more information. I have tried to the best of my knowledge to write the accounts accurately in this book. However, at times in the forepart, I had to imagine how things were done in those early years. Also my memory might not always quite coincide with those of my older siblings. I apologize for any errors.

Fannie Ada Miller

Contents

Chapter 1 1877—Widowhood 7
Chapter 2 Sad Ride to Train-Glad Return 14
Chapter 3 Son Born-Died-Motherless Baby 18
Chapter 4 More Children Bless Their Home 20
Chapter 5 Grandparents Visit From Ohio-Enos Weds 27
Chapter 6 Into Eternity-First Grandchild-Shem Weds 30
Chapter 7 Drought-Depression-A Birth and Death 33
Chapter 8 Sarah's Wedding-Land Scouting in the South 36
Chapter 9 Menno Born-Mississippi Move-Nathan's Death 39
Chapter 10 Getting Established-Building 42
Chapter 11 Katie's Wedding-Trials-Deemy Weds 45
Chapter 12 Isaac-Mattie-Menno to Ohio 50
Chapter 13 Sickness-Death-Move to Kansas 53
Chapter 14 Isaac's Farewell-Changes Take Place 55
Chapter 15 1908 Shem's Wife Dies-More Trials 63
Chapter 16 New Babies-Menno's Wisdom-Weddings 64
Chapter 17 Romance-Twin Dies-More Trials 68
Chapter 18 1911-More Babies-Enos' Move Back 74
Chapter 19 Visitors in Church-Mattie's Letter 77
Chapter 20 Preparations for Wedding-More Moves 80
Chapter 21 Meet Daniel's Daughter-Fannie's Family 83
Chapter 22 Grain Hauled to Hutchinson-Move to Oklahoma 86
Chapter 23 Move Back to Kansas-Getting Settled 90
Chapter 24 Barbara Sews-More Siblings Born 92
Chapter 25 Menno in Reno County-Singing-Barbara's Date 97
Chapter 26 Menno and Barbara Wed-Own Home 100
Chapter 27 Buying Mother's Farm-Move to Garnett 103
Chapter 28 First Time Parents-Homesick-Train Ride 105
Chapter 29 Three New Matties Born All Cousins 109
Chapter 30 New Buildings on New Farm-The New Car 111
Chapter 31 Three Orphans-Menno's Move-Baby Girl 114
Chapter 32 Storm Hits-Runaway Boys 117
Chapter 33 Siblings Go Mennonite-Number Fourteen Born 120
Chapter 34 Seafer's Farm-Son Born-Flood-Bootleggers 123
Chapter 35 Menno to Prison-Family Moves to Reno County 126
Chapter 36 Andy's Third Wife-Levi's Move to Illinois 130
Chapter 37 Shem Goes to Menno's Bail-Menno Works for Shem 132
Chapter 38 Mattie's Final Farewell-Doddy's Death 136
Chapter 39 Special Son Born-Move to Chouteau, Oklahoma 139
Chapter 40 A Daughter Born-The Rich's-Menno Bales Hay 142
Chapter 41 Haying-Sad Accident-Baby Girl Born 1934 146
Chapter 42 Surgery-Death-Loneliness-A Pony 149
Chapter 43 Outdated Shoes-Weddings-Cows Starving 152

Chapter 44 Warrants-Menno's Escape-Foreclosure 155
Chapter 45 Dannie to Kansas-Girls' Jobs-Man Behind Tree 158
Chapter 46 First Grandchild-Mary and John Marry-Big Fire 160
Chapter 47 Repairing House etc.-Move to Mazie 161
Chapter 48 Births and Deaths 1939-1940 165
Chapter 49 Big Auction-War-Enos Drafted 168
Chapter 50 Dan Married-A Trip-New Grandchild 171
Chapter 51 Barbara's Roomers-Grandma Marries-Andy Drafted 173
Chapter 52 Picnic-Barnyard News-Many Problems 178
Chapter 53 Runaway-Atomic Bomb-War Ends-Andy Across 180
Chapter 54 Breaking Heifers-Andy Home-Makes Repairs 182
Chapter 55 Florida Boys-Willie's Barn-The Fall-Wedding 185
Chapter 56 Romance-Marriage-Sad News from Oklahoma 189
Chapter 57 Amelia Married-House Fire-Stillborn 192
Chapter 58 Andy Married-Barbara Seriously Ill-Babies 194
Chapter 59 Search for Menno-Boys to California-Met Dad 197
Chapter 60 Fannie's Letter-Salina's New Job-Deaths 1954 202
Chapter 61 Voluntary Service-Wedding-On Willie's Dairy Farm 205
Chapter 62 Dan's Family Visits Dad-Babies-Moves 207
Chapter 63 Mother's New House-Levi's Move to Missouri 209
Chapter 64 Mother Sells Farm-Move to Kalona-Much Sickness 211
Chapter 65 Trip to Arizona-Confession-Cousins Meet 214
Chapter 66 More Visits With Dad-Grandma's and Dad's Deaths 219
Chapter 67 Quilt Friends-Visits-1973-1974-1975-Joys and Sorrow 224
Chapter 68 Twins-Travels-Modern Convenience-1977-Reunion 228
Chapter 69 Wedding-Aunt Dies-Christmas in Leon-Merle Weds 234
Chapter 70 1980 Three Weddings-Ailments-Family Visits 236
Chapter 71 To Oklahoma-Wedding Visits-Reunion in Leon 240
Chapter 72 Ill Health-Girls Visit-More Visits-Reunion 243
Chapter 73 Twin Girls-Eighty-ninth Birthday-Joe Sick 247
Chapter 74 Corn Planted-Sudden Departure-Blackout 250
Chapter 75 Isaac Chupp Reunion-Tragedy-Poor Health 253
Chapter 76 Mother's Maud-Ninety-one Now-Family Visitors 256
Chapter 77 Very Sick-Children Come and Go-To Hospital 259
Chapter 78 Home-Wedding-Ninety-two Now-Karen Home 263
Chapter 79 1988 Maud Quits-February in Leon-Improves and Visits 266
Chapter 80 To Hospital-Home Again-Ninety-three Now-Chupp Reunion 268
Chapter 81 Hot Weather-Move to Parkview-Cousins Visit 271
Chapter 82 Mother's Outing-Triumph at Last-Funeral 274
Chapter 83 Memories and Tribute to Mother 278

Chapter 1
1877 — Widowhood

Mattie Yoder looked out her kitchen window and noticed the trees were nearly bare. The leaves had fallen early in October, 1877. Having just seen her dear husband David's body lowered into the grave, she wondered how she could go on with life. In her heart, she knew the Lord would guide her through her grief. She must carry on for the sake of her four little children. She could not help feeling as the trees looked, so much of her was gone.

At times, her thoughts wandered to the day David had gone swimming. Although it was plenty chilly, he loved to go swimming with his two little boys and felt it was his last chance before the weather turned colder. Soon afterward, he developed a chronic cold. He tried to keep busy with his fall work until he was too sick. Eventually it settled on his lungs and developed into pneumonia. Mattie made onion poultices and herb teas in an effort to help clear the congestion. However, it was to no avail, and he gradually became weaker until the Lord saw fit to call him home.

Coming back to reality, Mattie realized she needed to be courageous in order to help the children through their grief. She was in good health and was only twenty-six years old. Her parents, Bishop Shem and Anna Miller, lived near Millersburg, Ohio, as well as her five brothers. She was the only daughter and lived so far away from her parents and brothers.

Mattie had a strong faith in God which she wanted to implant in her children. Enos was a strong, stocky built boy and nearly eight years old, so he was a big help. Next was Shem; he was five and had a jolly disposition that always welcomed a challenge. Sometimes he teased his little sister Sarah. Sarah was three and truly a little sunbeam. She loved to sing and play with her baby sister Anna. Anna would be two in January. Mattie thought she was more fussy at times and knew she missed her father so much. Many evenings he had held her and rocked her.

Mattie's thoughts often wandered to the dreams she and David had shared as she gazed over the neat little farm. There was the nice red barn that David had built. Then the small white frame house with two rooms upstairs. They had so many dreams for this little farm. The buildings were not as large as many folks had; however, they were adequate for their needs. As she and the boys milked the cows and fed the horses and chickens, she wondered what the future would hold for them.

The church family assisted with any major work on the farm; otherwise, Mattie and her boys carried on the best they could.

Monday morning Mattie put a large boiler on the stove and filled it with water. Then she built a good fire and put her homemade soap into the water. Next she put the dirty laundry into the water and boiled it. It was surprising how that loosened the dirt. When the water cooled down, she used her washboard. With some extra rubbing, even the most soiled laundry became clean. On hard spots, she used extra soap. The next step was to wring out the wash and put it into a tub of clean water to rinse out the soap. After wringing the wash out of the rinse water, it was ready to hang on the line. What a satisfaction it was to see her snowy, clean wash fluttering in the breeze! When they had eaten dinner, Mattie saw that little Anna was sleepy. She rocked her and sang softly to her, and she was soon fast asleep.

Now she would quickly use the soapy laundry water and scrub the wooden kitchen floor. With the water that was left, she scrubbed the porch floor, rubbing hard with her broom. By the time she finished with that task, it was time to bring the wash in from the lines. Looking at the clock, she knew it was time to chore again. She had cooked some beans when she had a good fire going for her wash water, so they would have bean soup for supper.

Each son had his portion of the chores to do. Of course, Mattie needed to check to make sure each task was completed. They were usually pretty dependable although she was also aware that children sometimes play and forget to complete their jobs.

After supper was over, Mattie usually read Bible stories or the Bible to her children until they were sleepy. Then she prayed with them before she tucked them into bed. After the children were put to bed, Mattie had some time for quiet meditation and prayer before she herself retired for the night.

As the weather grew colder, the chores increased. There was extra feeding for the cows and horses, feeding hay, and making sure the water was not frozen. Then also, Mattie had her chickens that needed extra attention in the cold weather. She had to gather the eggs before they froze and carry water to them so they would lay better. Mattie needed all the eggs and cream she could get to take to town to trade for provisions. She churned most of the cream into butter and took it along to the general store with her eggs and cream. She could then buy groceries, cloth, and shoes. She tried to be frugal and buy only what was most necessary.

The boys were required to fill the woodbox each evening. The brethren of the church had been so kind to cut the wood for her.

Since little Anna was not well, Mattie had another concern as the winter wore on. Each evening, Mattie greased her with skunk oil. She also made various kinds of herb tea for her. During the day, she made poultices with fried onions to put on her chest. In spite of all she did, little Anna was losing out. Mattie spent many hours day and night caring for her. She thought if she could keep her going until spring, little Anna might regain her vigor.

In spite of her efforts, on April 10, 1878, just over five months after Mattie lost her dear companion, she now had to part with her sweet little Anna. This left another vacancy in their home. Mattie knew Anna was safe in the arms of Jesus which helped to ease her grief.

Communication was slow, and burial needed to be made within two days as embalming was not practiced in those days. Kind friends and neighbors helped out and extended their sympathy. Little Anna was buried beside her father David.

Later when Mattie's parents received the sad news, her father, Bishop Shem Yoder, said to his wife, "I will see about train tickets to Indiana to spend some time with our daughter and her children. Although the funeral is over, we can help and comfort her in this time of sorrow."

Mattie was glad to see her parents, and the children were very excited. Before this, they had not had much chance to get acquainted with their grandparents. Mattie's father found plenty of work to keep him busy. He repaired fences and did minor repairs on the house and barn. There was manure to haul and plowing the garden and fields.

Enos and Shem helped their grandpa with anything he asked them to do. Sarah enjoyed sitting close to her grandma and watching as she darned socks and told stories of when their mother was a little girl.

Too soon the two weeks were over, and their grandparents were packed to go back to Ohio by train. Mattie hated to see them go.

Mattie and her children took them to Mount Ayr with the spring wagon to meet the train. Tears filled Mattie's eyes as she embraced them and bid them good-bye before they boarded the train.

Mattie had taken butter, cream, and eggs to the general store to trade for necessities. As they drove home, her thoughts drifted to the suggestion her parents had given to move to Ohio with her children. If she would do that, her family could help her out. She thought of her five brothers who would gladly assist her if she were near. Oh! What should she do? As she came in sight of her cozy little home, she knew she must stay there. This is where she and David had all their dreams.

The neighbors came over and sowed oats and planted corn. Mattie was so thankful for a caring church. In spite of her courage, she had times when she felt exhausted. She tried to be brave for the sake of the children. They had first parted with their father and then later their little sister.

Early that summer, a young man by the name of Isaac Chupp arrived by train at Mount Ayr. He visited in various homes, saying he was looking for a job. When Mattie heard of it, she sent word that she would hire him. The hay was ready to mow, and corn was ready to cultivate.

Isaac took the job. He was a quiet person and seemed sincere about his work. He soon found favor in the eyes of Enos and Shem who enjoyed working with Isaac. Mattie felt a big load lifted off her shoulders. Isaac did not need to be told what to do as he had enough experience to go on his own.

Mattie was busy that summer with gardening and canning. She filled many jars with vegetables and fruit. She also dried corn and apples. She had more time to cook and bake. Mattie's sour cream cake always brought cheers from the boys. Every week, Mattie churned the cream into butter. Sarah, who enjoyed being with Mattie, could help turn the crank of the churn. In the summer, Mattie wrapped her butter in a thin cloth, put it in a bucket, and let it down into a well to keep it cool. (There were no refrigerators in those days.)

Each spring Mattie set a few hens with hatching eggs. When enough time had elapsed, these clucks would proudly parade around the place as if to show off their baby chicks. Sarah soon found that she should not get too close to these mamas or she would get pecked. She stayed close to her mother's side for the sake of safety from then on. If a rain came up, the mother hens would gather all their chicks securely under their wings. Each morning and evening, Mattie scattered grain onto the ground for her chickens. She enjoyed listening to their cackle. Then each evening, she carefully gathered the eggs.

Once a week, Mattie made her trip to town to exchange eggs, cream, and butter for groceries, and if she had enough credit she could get denim and chambray for Enos' and Shem's school clothes. She had patched their clothes until she could hardly patch more. She and Sarah could wait until later in the fall for new clothes. She had her eye on some nice navy sateen for dresses.

That fall, the barn loft was full of nice loose hay (no balers in those days). There was also a big haystack on the outside. By the time the weather turned cold, the oat bin was full of feed for the horses, cows, and chickens. She had a straw stack outside from when they had threshed the oats which was good for bedding the chickens and other animals. The corn was ready to husk. Isaac had commented that would be the next job he would need to do. After that was done, he would chop wood. Mattie knew she did not need to worry about the work. Maybe she was getting spoiled. He also knew what jobs Enos and Shem were capable of doing. They were glad to assist Isaac in any way they could.

Before cold weather set in, Mattie had managed to buy each of the boys new shoes and overshoes. Isaac had mentioned his need for new overshoes and gloves before it got cold. Mattie felt he deserved a break. She suggested he go with her and Sarah on their next trip to take produce to town. He readily accepted the offer. Isaac hitched up the horses to the wagon and loaded the produce, and they were on their way.

After they unloaded the produce and everything was figured, Mattie had enough credit left to buy Sarah a new pair of button shoes. Sarah was delighted. Mattie also purchased the navy sateen she had been wanting for some time. On the way home, Isaac said he was now ready for winter. As they were driving along, Mattie thought she detected an extra sparkle in Isaac's eyes. Oh, she must not let her mind wander! After all, he was not even a church member. She was glad, however, that he was faithful in attending church. When they would arrive at church, he always willingly unhitched the horse for her.

One evening, after Mattie had the children in bed and Isaac had also gone upstairs to retire for the night, Mattie pulled her chair close to her oil lamp to read in her German Bible. This was her time alone with the Lord when she read and meditated on the living Word of her wonderful Savior. He had sustained her thus far, and she knew He would never forsake her.

Oh, what did she hear? Was it a buggy that drove in? There was a soft knock on the door. As Mattie opened the door slowly, she saw that it was the deacon and his wife. Mattie invited them in and offered them each a chair. The deacon cleared his throat, then proceeded to say what was on his mind. "You probably wonder what we want. The church sent me to convey their concern. You have Isaac here to work for you. I'm sure you are aware that he is not a church member, and since you are a young widow, this does not look good to the people. We would ask you to dismiss him. The church realizes that you need help at times, and they would be willing to help you whenever there is a need."

Mattie's mind began to whirl. They bid her good night and left. As Mattie heard the sound of the buggy disappear, she was in deep thought. How will I manage without him? Tears blinded her eyes. Mattie went to bed, but sleep refused to come. Mattie wanted to be obedient to the wishes of the church. How would she break the news to Isaac? He seemed so much a part of their home. He had taken a load off her shoulders during the time he had worked for her. A week earlier, when Shem had celebrated his seventh birthday, Isaac had helped to make it a special occasion.

It was January, 1879, and the weather was cold with snow on the ground. Her heart was heavy the next morning as she prepared breakfast. She would wait to break the news to Isaac until the boys were off to school.

Isaac noticed a sad look on Mattie's face but hoped he had not been the cause of it. The boys discussed the sadness they had detected in their mother on the way to school. "What could be the matter?" they questioned.

Isaac went about his work as usual. The forenoon was soon gone, and Mattie called him for dinner. He noticed she still had that sad look, and she was extra quiet. When dinner was finished, Mattie cleared her throat, and with tear-filled eyes, she began to tell Isaac what was on her mind.

"Isaac, did you hear a buggy drive in last evening after you were in bed? It was the deacon and his wife. They were sent to speak about you working here. The church feels it doesn't look good since you are not a church member, and I am a widow. They want me to dismiss you."

Isaac said, "I would not want to cause you any problems. I will clean out the barn and do a few other things that need to be done. I can probably get the 11:30 train out of Mount Ayr tomorrow forenoon if I get my trunks packed in the morning."

When the boys came home from school that evening, Mattie broke the news to them. "Boys, tomorrow Isaac will get the train for home. Then we must all shoulder more responsibility. The church offered to help out when needed."

The boys said, "Oh, why can't he stay? We will miss him so much."

"Yes, boys," Mattie exclaimed, "I will also miss him!"

That evening Mattie fixed a big farewell supper of home-cured ham, mashed potatoes, dried corn, gravy, baked apples, and one of her delicious sour cream cakes. After supper, Isaac played games with the children. Even little Sarah got excited, and the boys were delighted.

The next morning the boys helped extra well with the chores, but they felt sad as they left for school. "Just think, when we get home from school, Isaac will be gone," Enos and Shem lamented to each other as they walked to school.

Chapter 2
Sad Ride to Train - Glad Return

When Isaac had the chores done, he harnessed the horses. Then he went to the house to pack his trunks. When that was done, he hitched the horses to the spring wagon and loaded his trunks. Mattie loaded her produce and bundled little Sarah up in her warmest clothes. After helping her onto the wagon, she climbed up beside her. Isaac took the lines, and they were on the road to Mount Ayr. Because of the cold, they wore their warmest clothes. They wrapped a warm cover around their legs and had a few bricks that had been heated to keep their feet warm.

Mattie was rather quiet as they drove along. As they neared Mount Ayr, she said, "Isaac, you will never know how much your help has meant to us. You have been such a good example to my boys and taught them such good manners. You will be greatly missed by all of us."

Isaac replied with a twinkle in his eyes, "I would stay and join church if you'd marry me."

Well! this really caused Mattie to do some serious thinking. "But how could we do that?"

"We could get our license today, then find a justice of peace to perform the ceremony."

After some more thought, she said, "I will."

He squeezed her hand and said, "I love you very much. You have come to mean a lot to me."

Mattie replied, "I love you, too."

Upon arriving in town, they traded out the produce. Then they purchased the license and found the justice of the peace to join them in marriage. The trunks did not need to be unloaded at the train, and a happy couple drove homeward.

When they drove into their lane, the boys were already at home from school. They saw that Isaac was with their mother and jumped up and down with glee. Isaac tied the horses to a post and proceeded to unload his trunks. The boys were beaming as they held the door open for Isaac and his trunks. They also noticed their mother seemed extra happy. Then Mattie said, "Boys, you see Isaac came home again with me. We got married today so now you can call him Dad."

Isaac gave each one a hug and said, "I'm happy to claim you boys and Sarah, along with your mother, for my family from now on." He gave each child a stick of peppermint candy. Isaac looked at Mattie and said, "I feel very blessed with such a nice family."

"Isaac, you don't need to carry your trunks upstairs. I will make room downstairs for your clothes," Mattie said. "Sarah is five years old and would like a room of her own."

Isaac said, "Well, boys, I think we'd better get busy and milk and do our other chores, don't you?"

Mattie got busy and built a fire to make supper. While Shem carried in wood to fill the woodbox, his mother was stirring vegetable soup, and the aroma filled the house. Shem said, "Oh, Mother! Will Isaac really get to stay and be our dad?" Mattie assured him that he would.

The next day, Mattie was busy moving Sarah's clothes upstairs and unpacking Isaac's clothes and putting them in their new place. She also sat down with ink and pen and started a letter to her parents to let them know they had a new son-in-law. This was all written in German, her usual way of writing.

Mail was slow in those days, and when her parents received the letter, her father was furious. He looked at his wife and said, "How could Mattie let us down like this? This marriage will have to be annulled. This Chupp is not even a church member. Oh! our only daughter letting us down like this. We must write a letter immediately that this can't be."

After his wife read the letter, she remarked, "If she had only listened to us and moved here, this may never have come to pass. I knew she was well pleased with Isaac's work, but this is something else to marry the man!"

There were some whisperings in Mattie's home community when the news got around. Isaac talked with the ministers and said he wanted to become a church member and be baptized. When people saw that he was really sincere, the shock died down. Isaac regretted that he could not read German, but Mattie was willing to help him. She also read the Scriptures to him which helped him better understand the language. Isaac's father was not born in an Amish home and never learned it well enough to pass it on to his children.

Some years later when an ordination was held in the Amish church, Isaac was chosen by lot to preach. As people had observed his honest, sincere life, they felt he was well suited for the work.

Isaac was still a poor reader in German. He felt very unworthy of his new calling, but Mattie was very willing to spend extra time with him to teach him. He was glad for her efforts. Many evenings found Mattie helping Isaac with his German reading. He was a willing student and learned quickly.

The summer of 1879, Mattie's health was not very good. Isaac and the children helped more in the garden and with canning and whatever needed to be done. Sarah was a big help to run errands and saved her mother many steps.

One evening Mattie whispered to Isaac, "You had better leave a horse in the barn as we may need a midwife before morning." He had a good fire going to keep the house warm and cozy. Soon after all was quiet in the house, Mattie nudged Isaac and said, "I think you'd better go after the midwife." He promptly hitched up the horse and drove to the home of the local granny, with whom previous arrangements had been made. Soon she was ready to go, taking along a few necessities.

When they got there, the granny went into the house while Isaac put the horse away. Mattie was relieved to see them back. In a short time, Mattie gave birth to a baby girl. For Sarah's sake, they were glad it was a girl. They decided to name her Katie, as Isaac had a deaf sister by that name who would be delighted to have a namesake. Little Katie was born October 29, 1879. The next morning when the children got up, they did not see their mother working like usual. She called the children to her bedside and showed them the baby lying beside her. Sarah's delighted response was, "Now I have a little sister again."

The midwife stayed and fixed breakfast for them and took a tray in for Mattie. After the boys were in school, Isaac went for a girl from church who would do the housework for a few weeks until Mattie regained her strength. Then he paid the midwife a few dollars and took her home. The *maud* or maid would have plenty to do with cooking and housework and doing the laundry on the washboard. Sarah was always ready to run errands. Since it was late fall, there was no garden work to do.

After a few weeks, Mattie felt strong enough to do the regular housework and cooking. So the *maud* would only need to come one day a week to do the laundry. Isaac helped out in the house when Mattie had anything strenuous to do.

Little Katie proved to be a real Godsend. Everyone enjoyed her very much. Enos and Shem enjoyed holding her and rocking her, too, when they were in the house. Of course, Sarah had more chances. Little Katie grew so fast, and before they knew it, she had her first tooth and sat alone. Next was the excitement of watching her crawl. Soon she was walking along the furniture. It was indeed a joy to see her take her first wobbly steps. The children would say words to her, and soon she was repeating them.

Chapter 3
Son Born - Died - Motherless Baby

Once again, Mattie did not feel the best. When Katie was twenty-six months old, on December 30, 1881, Mattie needed the midwife again. This time the Lord blessed them with a baby boy. Mattie told Isaac she would like to name him David if he would not object. He said he liked that name, and it was a name from the Bible. The boys were very pleased to have a baby brother, and Sarah loved to rock him and sing to him. Of course, Katie could not understand all the fuss over the new baby. However, she was not lacking for attention. She was at such a sweet age and was saying more words all the time.

Isaac enjoyed holding his little son. He thought at times he caught a faint smile on his little face. Mattie had some concerns as he seemed more fussy and not as strong as Katie was when she was a baby. She felt she had plenty of milk for him and nursed him when he demanded. But at two and a half months of age, the Lord called him home. As the family was gathered around his little body, Isaac said, "The Lord has given, and the Lord has taken him home again." The next few days were a blur as people came and extended their sympathy. After the funeral and seeing his little body lowered into the earth, they felt at peace knowing it was God's will.

Mattie felt tired and worn out as she had spent many nights caring for little David. She must count her blessings. She had kind Isaac by her side and the other children to love, and she had her Heavenly Father who was touched and concerned for each trial she faced. There were times when she would feel so uncomfortable because her breasts felt so full. Oh, her arms were so empty! She found much comfort in John 14, as well as many other Scriptures.

One day, almost a month later, Mattie was busy in the kitchen shaping her bread dough into loaves. Glancing out the window, she saw a buggy drive into the lane. She saw at once that it was not an Amish buggy, so she went on with shaping her loaves. Just as she finished, she heard Isaac come in. He said, "Mattie, there is a man out here with a tiny baby. His wife died soon after giving birth. He has tried to care for her himself, but he finds himself unable to give her the care she needs. He has four older children to see after, plus his farm. He would like for us to care for her until she's big enough for him to meet her needs."

"Oh," said Mattie as she wiped her hands on her apron. "It's from the Lord; bring her in." The father carried the baby inside, and Mattie saw how haggard he looked. He said the baby's name was Deemy. When he handed the baby to Mattie, she could not help but notice her clear blue eyes.

He said, "I will come to visit when I can. It's quite a distance so I probably won't come too often." He bid them good-bye with tears in his eyes.

When the children saw the baby, they were happy and eager to hold her. When little Katie woke up from her nap, she said, "Baby." Mattie thought the baby looked rather poorly. She nursed her and saw her grow into a chubby, healthy baby. Mattie soon noticed this baby had a shy disposition. Although she was of a shy nature, Deemy readily accepted her new parents as well as the rest of the Chupp family. She was born March 22, 1882.

Chapter 4
More Children Bless Their Home

Mattie soon realized that she was on the family way again. On February 17, 1883, Isaac went for the midwife again. The older children were in school, and Katie and Deemy were taking their naps when the baby let out his first cry. It was a boy, and they named him Levi as Isaac had a brother by that name. In those days it was popular to name a baby after a close relative. Deemy was not quite a year old yet, but that did not matter to the family as she was very much a part of them by now.

Due to the added work load at home, Sarah spent many days at home helping with the younger children. Instead of going to school, Mattie taught her many of the basics at home. Sarah often said the A B C's as she rocked a younger sibling. With a family of six, Mattie had plenty to do to keep her busy, such as cooking, cleaning, and laundry. Isaac was able to help with some of the housework since Enos and Shem were a big help with the chores and outside work. Sarah loved to play church and sing with the younger children. Levi grew so quickly, and Enos and Shem enjoyed getting down on the floor after supper and stacking the blocks up high. Then Levi delighted in knocking them down to hear the noise. These blocks were scraps left from some of their father's carpenter work.

Mattie often sat by the kerosene lamp in the evening watching the children play while she was darning socks. Isaac found this to be a good time to read his Bible and prepare his sermons for Sunday.

The summer of 1885 was hard on Mattie as she tried to tend the garden and can and dry food for the coming winter. How they loved the dried corn their mother made! The children and Isaac were a big help, putting up much food.

August 20, 1885, dawned bright and clear. Isaac got Enos started mowing hay and Shem cleaning out the stables and the barn. Isaac decided to stay near the house and help with whatever there was to do. Before long, Mattie said, "I think you had better hitch up the horse and take Sarah and the three youngest to John Yoder's house and bring the midwife here."

The children felt this was a rare treat to go to John Yoder's place. They were very cooperative in getting washed and ready to go. Isaac was soon back with the midwife or granny, as she was often called.

She went into the house while Isaac unhitched the horse. Soon after he entered the house, a baby girl was born. "Well, what shall we name her?" Mattie asked.

Isaac said, "How would you like Fannie as a namesake for my sister?"

"That sounds fine with me," Mattie agreed.

The granny stayed until later that evening to see that all was well. She prepared some toast and broth for Mattie and made sure she was comfortable. Then she fixed some food for Isaac and the boys. Toward evening, Isaac took her home and got a *maud* (maid) to help out for a few weeks. He also brought the children home. They were excited to see their little baby sister. Sarah was eleven years old and could help so much. She always scattered grain for the chickens, then she would gather the eggs into a basket. She often took Levi out with her and let him throw some grain out, too. Once, while she was gathering the eggs inside the chicken house, she suddenly heard the chickens were making quite a commotion. She quickly looked out and saw Levi chasing chickens. She said, "Come here and help me. You take hold of the handle and help me carry the eggs." Then she explained to him that he must not chase the chickens as the chickens were kind to give them eggs. Levi seemed to understand.

School would soon be starting, and Mattie decided to get the *maud* to help with some sewing. Mattie would not need school clothes for Enos, as he had finished. She hoped Sarah would be able to go more often this term. Enos may have to help her with washing clothes.

Fannie was a good baby and was growing in spite of the hot summer. Katie and Deemy were quite the pair. Where one was the other was too. They loved their little sister as she learned to crawl, then walk. At times she messed up their playthings.

Isaac was very particular with his tools, and they were neatly arranged in his tool chest. He had strictly warned the children to leave them alone. One dreary, rainy day Katie and Deemy were playing in the shop and noticed their father's tool chest sitting there. They opened it and peeked inside. Everything was in order, and they handled a few things, then put them back just like they found them. Next they found a few nails and decided to carve their initials on one end. Deemy said, "Don't you think we will get in trouble if we do that?"

“Oh,” Katie said, “I don’t think he will notice it.” So they carved their initials onto the toolbox. Their father did notice, and the next day he called Katie and Deemy to come to him. He asked, “Why did you carve your initials on my tool chest? Did you forget the rule about not meddling with my tool chest? Now I must punish you.” This broke Deemy’s heart as she felt so sorry about the misdeed.

One day Mattie had just finished shaping her bread into loaves when Isaac said, “I will need to go to town for some supplies. Mattie, would you want to go along?”

“Well,” Mattie said, “I also need some things, but what about my bread?”

“Couldn’t Sarah bake it if we make sure the outside oven is heated up well?” Isaac asked.

Mattie considered this, then said, “That might work; Sarah is pretty dependable.” The oven was already hot enough to have the hot coals scraped out. Mattie called Sarah to her and explained that as soon as the oven was so she could count to ten when she put her hand into it, it was just right to bake the bread.

Sarah said, “Sure, I can do that.” Soon Isaac and Mattie were off, and the children got to playing and having a good time. When one of the little ones wanted a drink, Sarah went to the kitchen to get one, and there, on the table, was the bread. She had forgotten all about it until now. She quickly ran out and checked the oven. “Let me see, Mom said if I can count to ten.” One, two, three, four, and on she counted, on past ten. She put the bread in and then went to play until she thought it would be done. She took the loaves out, brought them in, and set them on the table, then went back outside to join the others in their play.

When Mother and Father came home, Mattie saw the bread did not look right. “Sarah, did you put this bread in as soon as you could count to ten when you stuck your hand in the oven?”

“Oh, Mother,” Sarah answered, “I could’ve counted further then that.” Well, that solved the mystery of why the bread looked different.

On a cold winter day, February 22, 1888, Mattie felt the need for Isaac to take the younger children to John Yoder’s house and bring home the neighborhood granny again. The older boys busied themselves in the barn and shop. By now, Katie was in school, and the next year Deemy would also attend. When Katie came home from school, she was surprised to see her mother in bed with a new baby.

Isaac soon took the granny home and brought back the other children and a *maud*. This baby was another boy, and they decided to name him Andy. This made Levi really happy as he had just had his fifth birthday a few days before, and now he had a baby brother. He just beamed when he found out about his baby brother.

Sarah could do a lot of the house work by now. She could cook quite well and also make sour cream cake that was almost as good as her mother's cake. However, her brothers were still prejudiced to their mother's cakes. With all the other tasks there were to do with washing, cleaning, cooking, they felt Sarah should still have extra help. Sarah was glad for the help of the *maud*.

Isaac's parents, the Nathan Chupps, also lived nearby at this time. He had a brother, Simon and family, who also lived in the area. It was always a treat when they came to visit Isaac's family. It was so nice to have cousins to play with that attended the same church. They also liked when the grandparents came over to spend the day. They naturally had stories to tell of long ago, which captured the younger children's attention.

Little Andy was growing and learning to walk and say words. He was a busy little boy, and Katie and Deemy were to keep track of him so he would not get into mischief. Levi tried to play with him if he could keep his interest. Andy would soon have his second birthday, and Mattie decided to let him try his luck at feeding himself. Sometimes she did not know where the most food went, in his mouth or on the floor. Mattie told the girls, "That's the way they learn. It's good for Andy to be more self-sufficient as soon there will be another little one."

It was February 19, 1890, when Mattie informed Isaac that he should go get the neighborhood granny. Levi was in school now, as well as Katie and Deemy. Fannie and Andy were taking their after-dinner naps. Sarah was sixteen and could busy herself in the kitchen. When the granny got there, Mattie soon delivered a baby girl. After Isaac took the midwife home, he and Mattie discussed a name for the baby. Isaac said, "Mattie, I think we should name her after you. After all, that is also the name of my mother."

"Well, since it's also your mother's name, I will consent," said Mattie. The whole family rejoiced for a new family member. This time they did not need to get a *maud* as Sarah was very capable and, with Katie's and Deemy's help after school and on Saturdays, they did just fine. Little Fannie sometimes got to rock the baby if they fixed a pillow under her arm when the others were in school. Mother would warn her to not rock too fast or the baby could fall off.

Enos was keeping company with a young lady by the name of Sarah. She was Eli V. Yoder's daughter. He was of age and worked out to earn money for himself. He felt pretty fortunate to enjoy her company. Sunday evenings the young people usually had a hymn sing. After that, Enos would take Sarah to her home where she often fixed him a cup of tea and a piece of pie. The house was quiet as everyone else was in bed. They chatted as they sipped their tea, and, before he knew it, the clock showed time to bid farewell and go home and get some sleep. When he got home, he would put his horse away and quietly go upstairs to bed so as not to disturb anyone.

Little Mattie grew nicely and got plenty of attention from her older sisters. Before long Mattie realized she was again on the family way. There was much work, but each child had certain jobs to do. When Mattie didn't feel well, she depended a lot on the girls.

With Isaac in the ministry, he had extra responsibilities. He had to spend much time preparing for his sermons. Those times Mattie tried to keep the children out of the room where he studied.

On March 18, 1891, Mattie sent Isaac for the community midwife. All went well, and Mattie gave birth to another baby girl. After discussing various names, they finally agreed on Amelia. The family now numbered four boys and six girls. Of course, Enos worked out most of the time, and at nineteen, Shem sometimes worked out, too. Little Amelia was a chubby roly-poly baby. It wasn't long until she would give the sweetest little smiles, revealing her pretty dimples. Amelia seemed like such a long name, so soon the whole family got to calling her Millie. That name stuck, and she always went by Millie.

Soon after Millie's birth, Enos confided to his mother that Sarah and he planned to get married on November 10. "Well," Mattie said, "I'm glad you told me as that will give us time to get material for a new suit for you. I will need to find someone to sew it for you." Of course, this was to be a secret for quite a while yet. It would indeed make for a busy summer. She would need to be looking for material for new dresses for each of the girls.

Mattie asked daughter Sarah what material she would like. Sarah said, "I would like a navy cashmere, or a mohair would also be nice." Mattie felt like sateen would be more practical for the younger girls. One day when Isaac made his weekly trip to town to trade, Mattie asked Sarah if she would like to go with him and see if she could find material for her dress. Sarah felt honored to get to pick her own material for her dress.

When they got home, Sarah could hardly wait to show her mother the material. Mattie said, "I think you made a very good choice. I might go along the next time and see what I can find."

Later Isaac sold some fat hogs and was pleased with the money. He said, "Mattie, why don't you go with me next time? Then you can get some things taken care of before we get so busy with summer work."

"Well, I think I will take you up on your offer." Mattie went along on the next trip to town. After trading the eggs and cream for some groceries, Mattie went to the fabric section. First she found serge that she thought looked really nice and serviceable. So she had the storekeeper cut off the amount she needed. Then she found cashmere in a dark navy, just what she liked so well. She searched further and found sateen in navy for the other girls. Now what should she get for Levi and Andy? One thing she kept in mind was that they needed something that would take the knocks of romp and tumble boys. "Here is some moleskin," she showed Isaac. "I think that will take the knocks." Isaac felt it and admitted he didn't know much about material. However, that felt to him like it would survive some rough wear. Since it was a gray salt and pepper effect, it wouldn't show dirt so quickly. Mattie had the storekeeper cut off enough for the little boys. Then she thought, "I will need some white poplin yet for Enos' wedding shirt and some for Isaac and Shem." She hoped she had not forgotten anything. This was their first experience of preparing a son for his wedding.

The next Sunday after church, Mattie called a sister aside to see if she could make Enos a wedding suit. "Well," the sister replied, "I think I can work it in." Mattie said she would certainly be obliged and reminded her to keep it a secret.

Enos had a nice buggy and a spirited horse. Sarah could always tell from a distance by the sound of the horse's gait when Enos was coming down the road to see her. They had many plans to make this summer. It was also a busy summer at the Chupp home. Mattie and the girls filled many jars of vegetables and fruit.

Mattie often marveled how Deemy took to the younger children. They were also very fond of her. She was nine and adored little

Millie. Mattie was two, and Andy was three and needed a watchful eye on him. He was rather fine-featured, but quick as a whip. Fannie turned six that summer, and at times, she could keep Andy entertained.

Chapter 5
Grandparents Visit From Ohio - Enos Weds

The entire family eagerly awaited the arrival of their grandparents from Ohio who would be coming for the wedding. The children would ask, "How soon are Doddy and Mommy coming on the train?" Finally the great day arrived. Isaac and Mattie went to Mount Ayr to meet the train that would bring Bishop Shem Miller and his wife Anna. Mattie also had some last minute shopping she wanted to do. After the shopping was done, they went to the depot. The train whistle was blowing, and soon the train came to a stop. Soon they saw them stepping off the train with their baggage. Mattie met them, and Isaac was soon by her side to welcome them and to help with their baggage. Finally they were seated on the spring wagon and on their way home. They had so much to talk about, catching up on all the news, it seemed to be only a short ride home. When they arrived back at the tidy farm, the children stood around shyly. Doddy and Mommy shook hands with each child, and Doddy gave each child a piece of peppermint candy which dissolved some of the shyness.

November 17, 1891, arrived, and everyone got up early as that was the day Enos and his Sarah would join hands for life. Isaac took Mattie and the younger children to the Eli V. Yoder home where the bountiful dinner was being prepared. Sarah had stayed there overnight in order to be there the first thing that morning to help. She would help wait on tables at noon, as would the bride's sister Sovilla. Isaac and Doddy and Mommy would go on to Eli V.'s neighbors, who hosted the wedding church.

Many people gathered there to hear the wedding sermons. Enos and Sarah sat on some chairs with their witnesses, Shem and his girlfriend, Anna Stutzman, seated on Enos' side and Sarah's sister, Abbie, and her boyfriend by Sarah's side. As people arrived, they shook hands with the bridal party, then they sat down on some benches that were set up for the guests. When all were seated, the singing began while the ministers and the bridal couple met in a room upstairs. The ministers gave much admonition and spoke to the couple of the seriousness of marriage. Then they all went downstairs and took their seats. The singing soon ended, and Isaac stood up and preached a nice sermon on marriage. He spoke of Abraham, Isaac, and Jacob in the Bible and the beauty of their marriages, and how

God must be the center of the home in order to receive His blessings. Then he ended with a prayer. Next Bishop Shem stood to his feet and said he felt there was not much more to say but to live by what had already been said. He mentioned he was glad he could be at the ceremony of his grandson. After this, he expounded the Word of God. Soon he said, "If the young couple here today still feels the desire to be joined in holy matrimony, they may come forth." He asked the customary questions, then he pronounced them man and wife. After this, the congregation sang another song, and the bridal party got up and went outside. Three buggies, with young boys as chauffeurs, were ready to take them back to Eli V.'s home.

The cooks had worked very hard to prepare a bountiful meal of fried chicken, dressing, mashed potatoes, gravy, coleslaw, stewed prunes, puddings, mixed fruit, cakes, a few different kinds of pies, homemade bread, butter, jam, and coffee. There were tables set up all around the room, and one was built across the corner where the bride and groom, along with their witnesses, were seated. The tables had been set the day before. After the tables were filled with guests and the blessing had been asked, the servers brought bowls after bowls of food to pass around. They had three couples and a few young girls to see that everything was passed and everyone had plenty. Then those at the tables spent some time singing German songs. During this time, the cooks and servers ate. Toward evening, people left for their homes to chore. Supper was served to the young people, relatives, and close neighbors. After supper, more songs were sung. The next day the cooks and witnesses helped wash dishes. Then the tables were taken down, and life returned to normal. Enos and Sarah stayed with her parents until they had some furniture and a place of their own.

With Mattie's parents staying a few weeks longer, Mattie had a quilting to make Enos' quilt and also a comforter. She was careful to use dark colors as that would not show dirt so easily. She also thought it would not draw attention as much as brighter colors would. A quilt was not washed more often then necessary.

As Mattie's parents observed the consideration Isaac showed to his family and the sincerity of his daily walk of life, they developed a deep respect for him. They themselves had also found a warm spot in the hearts of their grandchildren. Little Mattie liked to sit on Mommy's or Doddy's lap, and Millie may have gotten a little spoiled while they were there. Andy enjoyed the extra attention he received during their visit. But all too soon the time came for them to be taken to the depot for their homeward journey.

As Mattie noticed Shem's love for Anna Stutzman growing deeper, she decided she might as well get started on his quilts and comforter before spring work began. He may soon want to establish his own home.

Enos and his wife were now settled on a farm with a small house and barn. They had a few cows, chickens, and pigs. Enos was looking for a team and plow and other items needed for spring farm work.

Winter went fast, and soon it was time to plant garden. It was a wet spring, and Mattie had to watch her chance to get some seeds into the ground. She was grateful for what little garden she did get planted. Isaac remarked that the oats he sowed had drowned out, and he would probably need to sow again. When he talked to others, they felt it was too late, and they talked of sowing buckwheat instead. Isaac decided to do likewise. It was so wet that Isaac didn't get any corn planted.

Another concern that spring was daughter Fannie's deteriorating health. She had no appetite, lost weight, and seemed so listless. She enjoyed watching little Millie toddling around, walking along furniture, and sometimes taking a few steps alone. Fannie didn't play, preferring to sit on the rocker or lay down. Isaac and Mattie heard cod liver oil sometimes helped children, so they tried some on Fannie, but to no avail.

Chapter 6
Into Eternity - First Grandchild - Shem Weds

On June 8, 1892, God called Fannie home. She would have had her seventh birthday if she had lived a few more months. Isaac said, "The Lord just lent her to us for a short time. Now she is safe in the arms of Jesus and will not have to face the trials of life we do."

Friends and neighbors came and helped out in any way they could. The next day was her funeral, and her body was taken to the cemetery and laid to rest beside her brother David.

Now they had two little angels in Heaven. Yes, life truly held many changes and trials.

Mattie did get some things out of the garden to eat and can, but it certainly did not compare to normal years. Isaac harvested very few crops that summer due to too much rain. He was most grateful for what they did get.

School would soon be starting, and Mattie knew the children would need some new shoes. They could go barefoot for a short time. Isaac suggested Mattie go along to take the eggs, cream, and butter to town to trade at the general store. "Why don't you mark around their feet on paper, and we will see how far the money reaches?"

"Really," Mattie responded, "Deemy and Levi will be the only ones going to school as Katie is now finished. Fannie would have been old enough if she were still with us. Andy needs shoes, too, but I think Mattie and Millie can wear some the older girls have outgrown."

By getting only what was most necessary, their produce money reached. When the children saw their new shoes, they were delighted. The next week Mattie and Sarah busied themselves with sewing clothes for the school children. They sighed with relief when that was done.

One day Shem had a chance to talk with his mother alone and said, "Mom, I have something to tell you. Anna and I have decided to get married January 29, 1893. I thought I should tell you in plenty of time so you can get me a new suit. I think I would like a gray serge."

"Well, I'm glad you gave me some time to get your things prepared," Mattie answered. "I will look for your suit material the next time I go along to town."

Winter soon arrived, and with it came butchering time. That was always quite a strenuous activity. They would also give some meat to

Enos and Sarah. Early in the morning, Enos and Sarah and some of the neighbors came. A fire had been built under a large metal trough that was filled with water in which to scald the hogs. When the people came about daylight, the water was hot. A few hogs were shot, then scalded in the big trough. Next they were laid out on a piece of tin where the men got busy scraping off the hair. Then they were hung on a scaffold and gutted. After that, they were ready to cut up the meat. The meat was trimmed off the bones, then the bony pieces and liver were cooked. The meat was then picked off the bones and ground up for liverwurst. Mattie made sure her daughter-in-law did not exert herself as she knew her time was drawing near. By evening, the hams had been cured and a nice amount of sausage made. Everyone who helped butcher was rewarded with enough sausage for a meal. Some meat was put in a salt brine for later use when it would be brought out and soaked in clear water overnight to remove some of the salt. Then it was fried for a meal. Their mouths watered at the thought.

Sometime later Enos came to get his mother as Sarah was soon to deliver. Mattie had been midwife for others and was glad to help with her first grandchild's birth. When the baby was born, it was a boy, and they named him Harry. Sarah's sister, Abbie, came and took over household duties for them. Enos and Sarah were thankful for the safe arrival of their strong, healthy baby.

By now Mattie had seen to it that Shem's gray serge suit was all done and ready for his wedding day. Mattie and daughter Sarah had made new clothes for the other members of the family. Again the grandparents came by train from Ohio to attend Shem and Anna's wedding. They remarked how each child had grown and how they missed little Fannie and her happy countenance. They also made mention how she was a step ahead of them in glory.

Shem and Anna's wedding day, January 29, 1893, was a cold winter day and folks dressed accordingly. Anna was Jacob Stutzman's daughter, and they hosted the wedding dinner. The ceremony, or wedding church, was held at a neighbor's place and was conducted much the same as Enos and Sarah's had been. Shem and Anna soon moved into a small home of their own. This left another empty place in the Chupp home.

Shem had such a jovial nature and always had a joke to tell which caught everyone's attention. He took much pride in his horse and kept it well curried. It held its head high and could usually outrace any one else's horse.

By this time daughter Sarah had a special interest in Eli S. Beachy. He was a frequent visitor at the Isaac Chupp home. The younger children observed the romance with interest. Sarah always tried to make sure the house was in order over weekends and that they were supplied with pies and cake and fresh bread. By now, Sarah had learned the art of baking bread just right. Her older brothers would sometimes jokingly remind her of how she had once baked bread when her parents had gone to town. "That's been a long time ago," Sarah would say.

Spring arrived, and it was time to get gardens planted. Isaac had not sown winter wheat like usual. The problem was just opposite from a year earlier; this year the ground was too dry to plow when it was time. However, the oats produced quite well. Mattie did get some garden planted, although it didn't do very well due to the drought.

Chapter 7
Drought - Depression - A Birth and Death

The drought was not the only problem they faced that summer and fall of 1893. Prices had dropped so low that farmers, as well as businesses, were in a real financial crisis. Wherever they went, people were discussing how they could struggle though this depression.

Isaac and Mattie thanked the Lord for what they did harvest. At least they had been blessed with a good oat crop to feed the animals. What a contrast it was from a year earlier when it had been so wet! They had something else to think about that fall: to get children supplied with shoes and clothes for school. Somehow they managed with what was the most necessary.

September 26, 1893, Mattie nudged Isaac out of his sleep to go for the midwife. Isaac was soon wide awake and dressed. He harnessed the horse, hitched it up, and was on his way. In a short time, he was back. Soon the baby was born, and they named her Lydia. She would help fill the vacancy they had felt when Shem married. Millie was past two years old and chattered constantly. She was quite excited when she awoke and saw the baby. She said, "Pretty baby."

Mattie soon noticed that this baby was not strong. Often Mattie sat, rocking and singing softly to her little one. The thought came to Mattie, "Will she grow up?" When baby Lydia was less then a month old, on October 22, she took her last breath when God called her home. Her little body was laid to rest close to her sister, Fannie, and brother, David. Isaac tried to comfort his sorrowing wife and children. He said it was not the Lord's will that she stay with us. Katie had her fourteenth birthday a week after the baby died, but it was not a happy time.

Deemy's father often desired to visit her, and at times, he did. If Deemy saw him coming, she would grab Millie or one of the younger ones and hide in a closet or anywhere she thought she would not be found until he was gone. When she was found and brought out, she trembled with fear. The candy he offered her didn't interest her as much as it did her siblings. He could hold the younger ones without any problem, but not Deemy. Once she told her sister Katie that she disliked his mustache. He finally agreed to stay out of her life. However, he asked one thing of Isaac and Mattie, "Be sure she always keeps the Warren name." They agreed to do this, but Deemy resented it. At school one year they had a new teacher. When she asked each child's name, Deemy decided to say "Chupp" so as to avoid having to make any explanation why her last name was different from the rest of her family. This worked until she brought home her report card. When Isaac noticed the Chupp name, he explained to her that they had promised her father to keep the Warren name. This made Deemy very sad so Isaac offered to come to school and explain the situation to the teacher which pleased Deemy.

December 7, 1893, Shem came after his mother in the early hours of the morning to assist with the delivery of their first child. It proved to be a slow process. After Anna finally gave birth to a little baby girl, she was pretty worn out. Mattie stayed all night to make sure she would get her rest. They decided to name her Deemy after Shem's foster sister. When Mattie got home and told the children about the new baby and the name, Deemy was very happy to have a namesake. Her blue eye sparkled. Mattie said, "Now, Deemy, you must give the baby a dress. What color would you like?" Mattie got out a few different pieces of material and let Deemy choose. Deemy chose a deep blue that was left over from her favorite dress. Mattie said Sarah should go to Shem's house and take over household duties until Anna regained her strength.

Isaac and Mattie felt the children would do alright alone while they took a short trip. Katie, as well as Deemy, was such a big help. They could help Sarah with the washing and cooking, and they could also help Levi do the chores.

A new Amish settlement was starting up in Fayette County, Illinois. On December 25, 1893, Isaac and Mattie and the two little girls boarded the train and went there to hold a church service for the small group as there was no minister there. This was the first Amish service to be held in that area.

When they returned, they were pleased to see how well the children had done the work in their absence. Shem had been by to help with anything major they could not handle.

When the weather was cold and Mattie kept more fire going in the big stove, she would cook a big iron kettle of mush. On cold mornings she sliced and fried it, and the aroma of the mush frying filled the whole house. She often made liverwurst and oatmeal to complete their breakfast. Often the iron kettle on top of the stove had beans cooking. They all liked bean soup for supper. While the beans cooked, she could heat the sad irons to do the ironing.

Chapter 8
Sarah's Wedding - Land Scouting in the South

Sarah had confided to her mother the plans that she and Eli Beachy were making to get married which didn't surprise Mattie from what she had observed of their friendship.

There was much unrest in the area of Newton County, Indiana. Isaac had gone with Benjamin Miller and his son Ananias to Texas and Oklahoma to look at land. With the adverse weather they had experienced the last few years, maybe they could find a more unchangeable place. They soon came back, unimpressed with what they saw.

About this time, John T. Yoder took his wife to Florida. She had such a cough and trouble with her lungs, and they hoped warmer weather would help that condition. When Enos Yoder and Eli Beachy heard of it, they decided to go along. They were curious about the South. When they returned, they, too, were unimpressed. Enos said he preferred Newton County so he bought a 160 acre farm for $6,000. Eli S. Beachy owned 320 acres in Newton County, and he got busy making repairs on it as Sarah and his wedding day was drawing near.

Everything was quite busy at the Isaac Chupp home as they prepared for the wedding of Sarah and Eli. There was a lot of sewing to do so each member in the family had suitable clothes for the big day. Next the house was cleaned from top to bottom including every nook and closet. Cookware was scoured with powdered brick until it looked like new. Next was preparing food. Neighbors and friends came to help butcher chickens and make noodles, bake pies, cakes, and plenty of fresh bread, then stew the prunes and cook the puddings. Enos and Shem came and helped Isaac make the wedding table. It was built around the corner of the room as was the custom for Amish weddings.

Mattie stressed to Sarah that they wanted to be careful not to do anything for pride. "Let us be sure we keep everything simple for the honor and glory of God."

The day before the wedding, the team was hitched to the wagon to go meet the train as the grandparents from Ohio and some of the uncles were coming. It was February and very cold so plenty of covers, as well as hot bricks, were sent along to keep the travelers warm on the way back from meeting the train.

The next day was February 25, 1894, and it dawned brisk and cold. The wedding church was at their closest neighbor's farmhouse. Isaac preached first, then Grandpa Shem who then joined them in holy matrimony. While the closing hymn was being sung, Eli and Sarah and their witnesses put on their wraps and went out to the waiting buggies where the chauffeurs were waiting for them. Sarah pulled her shawl snugly around her and tried to turn her face so her large bonnet would keep out the cold wind. When they got to her home where the bountiful meal was ready to be served, Mattie met them at the door and wished them a happy marriage. Mattie thought in her heart how nice Sarah looked in her navy wedding dress. She was so petite, and with her white cape and apron over the navy, she looked so pure and young. Sarah had removed her black head covering and replaced it with a white one as a sign that she was now a wife. She was twenty years old, and Mattie would surely miss her. But she must not dwell on such thoughts now as people were coming for dinner, and the bowls must be filled, and the people seated. Katie helped wait on tables or wherever she was most needed. Deemy was kept busy looking out for the younger children which pleased her. She was nearly twelve but still preferred to be in the background. She was so good with Millie and Mattie who were three and four. Levi was eleven and could show the men where to put their horses when they unhitched them. Andy, who had just had his sixth birthday, was busy trying to figure out what was going on. After a delicious supper and a good hymn sing, the day came to a close.

Since Eli had the house ready and also had some furniture, they moved the wedding gifts into their own home. Grandpas could see where they moved before they went home to Ohio. Mattie felt Eli would be a good provider and make a good home for Sarah.

Earlier Mattie had made a comforter and quilt for Sarah. She did want to make another quilt and decided it would be a good time while her mother was there to help. Then she invited some women from the church to come and help quilt. By the time her parents left, it was all done.

Sarah was so happy with her own home. Eli had gotten a cookstove and another for heating. He had also bought a bed. They went shopping for a cabinet and dry sink and a chest for their clothes. This pretty well furnished the house. It was so much fun to unpack her dishes and tin cookware. She even had an iron kettle which was a must if she wanted to cook mush just right. She knew Eli liked that as well as her family did. Sarah had made some dark navy curtains for most of the rooms except the bedroom, which had black curtains. Eli had a team of horses and a few cows and pigs. In the spring, Sarah would get some setting eggs from her mother and a hen. Then they could have chicken to eat when the chicks grew big enough.

Sarah did miss her younger brothers and sisters. The house seemed so quiet when Eli was out working. She was always glad when her family came to visit. Sometimes she enjoyed going home for a day and helping her mother. Soon it was spring, and Eli was busy doing field work and getting the garden ready for Sarah to plant.

Isaac and Mattie missed the older children, although they were busy teaching the younger ones to shoulder more responsibility. Mattie did not feel well and soon realized what her problem was. She was on the family way again. Since she was forty-four, it came as a surprise. She accepted the fact and felt the Lord had a purpose in it all. She was thankful for each child.

Isaac's father was also failing in health, and Isaac felt obligated to help there when needed. He was surely glad his brother Simon lived nearby to also assist with his care.

Chapter 9
Menno Born - Mississippi Move - Nathan's Death

During the year of 1895, more people were talking of moving south. Several people asked Isaac if he would consider moving with them. John T. Yoders had gone south different times for his wife's health and wished there would be an Amish church there. Gibson, Mississippi, was mentioned as a possibility to relocate. They felt the warmer climate would be beneficial to their health. Because of that, some of the men traveled to Gibson, Mississippi, by train to inspect the area. They soon found a realtor who was very helpful and showed them various tracts of land. The men were impressed. Here they could buy land anywhere from $10 to $20 per acre. They reasoned among themselves, "How could we go wrong? After all we can easily sell our Newton County land for $50 an acre." The realtor told them there was no way they could lose. They could buy larger tracts in Mississippi for less money, and this appealed to them. They returned home by train telling others what they had found. They asked Isaac, "Would you consider moving? We would need a minister." He talked it over with Mattie and the family. After much consideration, he consented to move.

On December 11, 1895, Mattie told Isaac to go for the midwife. Soon after the midwife came, Mattie delivered her last baby. They chose to name him Menno. This pleased Andy as he had a cousin by that name, and he loved to play with him. Because Menno was so little and weak, Mattie carried him around on a pillow. She didn't gain her strength back like she had other times, but her main concern was this tiny baby. As her thoughts sometimes drifted to the little ones who had not survived, she gave him the best of care. Katie and Deemy were sixteen and thirteen years old now and were a big help. That month eight or nine families had public auctions and were getting ready for the move to Mississippi. Because Isaac's family was also moving, they sold some things at other auctions. A special train had been chartered to take the belongings of those who would be making the move. Isaacs decided they would send their belongings and all the children on the train. They and baby Menno would go later as he was too small to make the move. Isaac also felt responsible to stay and help care for his father, Nathan, who was getting weaker all the time.

December 30, 1895, was the day when the belongings of John T. Yoder, Eli V. Yoders, Ananias Millers, Noah B. Mullets, Daniel J. Yoders, Emanuel N. Hochstetlers, Eli S. and Sarah Beachy, Enos D. Yoders, and Isaac Chupps were loaded on a special train. There was one passenger car with fifty-six people on board. They had two boxcars full of tools and household goods, and another car was loaded with seventy-five horses. It was a cold winter day, and the snow was deep. Many people stood watching this decorated train pull out of Mount Ayr, Indiana, bound for Mississippi. Yes, Isaac and Mattie had to shed a few tears to see their children and belongings leave while they stayed behind with their tiny baby.

They watched as the train rattled down the track. Nathan was quite ill, and Isaac and Mattie and baby Menno moved into the Doddy house with Nathan. Mattie cooked, and Isaac was kept busy caring for his father. The baby also took much of Mattie's time. He was so frail that she took special notice when he gained a little.

Mattie was also gradually gaining in strength while Nathan was losing out. Isaac would try with little success to feed his father the broth that Mattie prepared. He simply had no appetite. Some nights they lost a lot of sleep because Isaac kept turning him one way and then another to make him more comfortable. Some nights Simon would come help out so Isaac could sleep.

On the evening of January 1, 1896, the train pulled into Gibson, Mississippi. It was quite an adventure for all the children, as well as the adults. The sun was just going down, but it was still warm, and the little black children were barefoot. The next question was where to go now. Some went to John T. Yoders as they had been there since November in order to avoid the cold weather. They could accommodate some people for the night; however, most folks ended up sleeping in the train coach.

The next day the train was unloaded, and everyone had a makeshift shanty in which to live. The black people were very friendly and helped unload and transport each family's things to their new home. On this train were six single men who were good carpenters. They were soon put to work building houses and barns. With the warmer weather, they could shift in their small shanties. Everyone, as well as the children, was busy.

In a month or so, Grandpa Nathan passed on to his reward. Isaac and Mattie helped with funeral plans. Isaac's brothers and sisters from other parts of Indiana attended. After the funeral, the family divided what was left of their father's earthly belongings.

At this time, Shem and Anna were also ready to move to Mississippi. In February, Shems and little Deemy and Isaacs and baby Menno boarded the train for Gibson. It was a happy day when the train pulled in at the depot, and Isaacs were reunited with their children. Enos, Eli, Levi, Katie, Deemy, Andy, Mattie, and Millie were there to welcome them. Each one was eager to see the baby and their little niece, Deemy.

Chapter 10
Getting Established - Building

When they got home the two Sarahs had supper ready. The children were eagerly telling about their new friends among the black children. Isaac finally said, "Don't all talk at once."

He told about Grandpa's death and funeral and all the aunts and uncles that came. "Oh, yes, Andy, your cousin, Menno, carried your little brother, Menno, around the day Grandpa's things were divided."

When it was daylight the next morning, Isaac looked around and said, "Children, I think we have enough work to keep all of us busy for a long time." Levi was thirteen and Isaac's main help. Katie was seventeen and helped wherever she was most needed. Sometimes they helped in the house, and sometimes they stacked lumber that Isaac had sawed.

Isaac realized they needed a new house. Presently they were living in what had once been a sharecropper's hut with tar paper around it to keep out the wind and cold. With Mattie's approval, Isaac talked to the young carpenters to see when they would be available to help build. He knew they had been very busy building houses and barns for the settlers. One of them was Noah Yoder, formerly from Ohio. He promised to help as soon as he was done at his present job.

John T. Yoder had set up a sawmill so Isaac could use it to saw logs into boards. It took much hard work to cut down trees and make logs with his trusty crosscut saw. The children also helped.

Wells were needed so son-in-law Eli Beachy and Joseph C. Miller pooled money to buy a drilling rig. They were soon busy drilling wells for themselves. After they finished, they sold the machine to two others. These did likewise until nearly everyone had owned shares in it at one time or another, including Enos and Shem.

After Isaac was there to minister, they held church services every two weeks. On alternate Sundays, they had Sunday school which they had started before Isaac moved there. That was the beginning of Sunday school for Amish people. They enjoyed it so much that it was continued after Isaac's arrival.

Being the only minister, Isaac took his calling very seriously. Saturday afternoon often found him and the local black minister together to study and prepare their sermons for Sunday. Mattie tried to organize the children with work outside so they would not disturb them. Isaac was very much a man of peace and order. He and Mattie both stressed the importance of humility and love.

By the time the lumber was sawed and hauled home, Noah Yoder was ready to start building their house. It would be a modest-sized house but adequate for their needs with a big porch on the south side. It would be tight and not have cracks like the hut they lived in had, which was so far off the ground that the chickens could roam under it.

Noah was a quiet man who appeared to mind his own business. Isaac enjoyed working with him. Enos and Shem also helped at times on the house as well as Eli and Sarah.

They always enjoyed coming home to eat their mother's cooking. Noah stayed at Isaac's home during the building, and deep down he admired this active family. But that was not all he admired. He noticed the beauty of their daughter, Katie, who had such rosy cheeks and pretty dimples when she smiled. He went out of his way to do her favors by offering her rides with him to Sunday evening hymn sings. Since she had no older brother to take her, she accepted. Soon they developed a deeper relationship although he was much older than Katie.

One moonlight evening as they were driving home from the singing, Noah mustered up enough courage to propose to her. Katie's heart was thumping at the words. Quietly she replied, "I will discuss it with my parents." He said that was fine with him. In her heart she knew she loved him but felt her parents would have wise counsel and wanted to talk to them first. When they got home, she waited until he had unhitched the horse; then they went in together. After she set out a snack, they ate and chatted until they saw what time it was and wondered where the evening had gone. After bidding each other good night, she softly went to her room and knelt by her bed, asking God's direction for her life.

The next evening Katie lingered nearby until everyone was in bed but her parents. Shyly she approached them with the question uppermost on her mind, "Would you consent to Noah and me getting married? Last night he proposed, but I knew I needed your consent."

"We are happy you considered us in this matter. Truthfully we could think of no one better from what we have observed of Noah and his character," replied her father. Happily Katie went to her room knowing she had her parents' blessing. She was so excited she could hardly wait to tell Noah the good news.

The weeks flew by, and the house was progressing nicely. Katie and her mother were busy sewing and doing what they could beforehand. The married children came home and helped their parents move into the new house. By now, they had been told of the upcoming wedding. Deemy was so happy for her sister and admired her ability to say the right things in every situation. Deemy, with her shy nature, did not trust herself to make many comments but often depended on Katie to fill in for her.

Chapter 11
Katie's Wedding - Trials - Deemy Weds

On Katie's eighteenth birthday, Noah and Katie drove to the courthouse to get their marriage license. They bought a few items they still needed for their wedding. On November 2, 1897, was the day they had so long been anticipating. A few of Mattie's brothers came from Ohio, which was a highlight for the whole family. Mattie could not keep from shedding a few tears as her mind drifted back to the day of her first marriage and the many trials and triumphs she had experienced since then. God had always seen her through, and she knew He would guide them also. Katie's eyes sparkled as people wished them the best in their new life together. Noah glanced admiringly at his bride. He would do his best to provide a good home for them. Soon they moved into their own little home. It seemed Noah could make almost anything they needed to furnish their house.

As time went on, Katie realized that she was on the family way. They were both very happy at the prospects of being parents, and Noah was very protective of her. The next time Katie and Sarah went to spend a day with their parents, Katie broke the news to her mother and sisters that she was going to be a mother. They all rejoiced with her, and Sarah said, "What a blessing! Eli and I have not been that fortunate."

On November 13, 1898, Noah went for his mother-in-law with the news that Katie's time had come to deliver. She quickly got a few things she wanted to take along. Soon a baby boy made his arrival and was named Lonnie. Mattie decided she would stay and help a few days, then Deemy could come and take on the housework. However, Katie was in a weakened condition, and it was soon evident that she had acquired tuberculosis. Mattie spent much time at her bedside. Although she tried many different herb teas and every known home remedy, it was all to no avail. So many mothers and children were dying of tuberculosis and other lung ailments. People thought the wet swamps may have been the cause. Often Mattie was called upon to help by using her home remedies. Noah could hardly bear to see his young wife suffer. He helped in any way he could.

Katie continued to grow weaker and on February 6, 1899, with Noah, her parents, and other family members by her bedside, she took her last breath. She bade them good-bye and was gone. Noah was heartbroken. All his dreams were shattered! Mattie's thoughts went back to the time she gave up her first husband which was the first of her many trials. Her Heavenly Father always saw her through, and He would see Noah through, too. This young settlement had experienced so many deaths that it had made for a real intimacy in the church.

While he worked, Noah took his baby to the grandparents, and Mattie and the girls gave little Lonnie the best of care. Noah usually ate supper at Isaac's house then took his little baby home for the night, or sometimes he stayed at Isaac's. He offered his help with the baby whenever possible. Little Lonnie was not a strong baby. Mattie fixed *brie* (a formula replacement) made with milk, sugar, and a little flour, and tried to mix milk and syrup to feed the baby. They could not help noticing that the baby was growing weaker. Twenty-three days after Katie died, baby Lonnie also departed this life, which was another sorrow for Noah.

Levi and Deemy were grown and attended Sunday evening hymn sings. Deemy loved to sing; however, she tried to keep her distance from the boys.

One Sunday Isaac and Mattie invited the youth group to their house for dinner. Being a very capable worker, Deemy helped prepare food such as baking bread, pies, and cakes for dinner. When they had all gathered around the table to eat, there was one vacant place. Mattie said, "Deemy, you may sit there with the others, and the younger girls can help me in the kitchen." Obediently Deemy sat down, but she felt awkward in the presence of all those boys and girls. Oh, if she could only be as outgoing as her foster brothers and sisters! But that was not her nature. If any conversation was directed toward Deemy, she would blush. She used to depend on her sister Katie, but now she was gone. How she missed her!

Enos and his family moved to Arthur, Illinois, in November of 1898. On March 9, 1900, another son was added to their family, and they named him Eli as a namesake for her father. Soon Enos thought back to Mississippi and decided they probably should have stayed there. After discussing it with Sarah, they agreed to move back. Although Sarah dreaded the packing, she was excited because she would be closer to her parents. She hoped Enos would then be satisfied, and they would not need to move again. By December 5, 1900, they and their belongings were on the train traveling to Mississippi.

Because of the rainy climate and the swampy terrain, Isaac and Noah had tiled the ground shortly before this. They set up a kiln and began the business of Chupp and Yoder Tile and Brick company.

The Amish settlers tried raising cotton which provided plenty of work for all the children, both black and white. The cotton plants took a lot of hoeing. Cotton picking provided a way for the black children to make some extra money which they always appreciated. They became good friends with the white children. Sometimes they played tricks on each other which added spice to their work. One little black neighbor girl loved to come to Isaac's house to see Mattie and play with their children. She would knock lightly on the door, and Mattie would say, "Come in."

She would say, "I would like a piece of apple butter bread."

Mattie would say, "First, you must tell me your name."

She would answer, "My name is little Corrina, sweet double Lena, my Sally Mae, Lilly, Lilly Belle," then she would always add, "but they call me Nitchie." Then Mattie, with a smile, would give her the slice of apple butter bread. Each time she came, they went through the same ritual, and Mattie delighted in hearing her recite her little piece.

It was always a pleasure when Enos, Sarah, and their children, and Shem, Anna, their Deemy, Daniel, and their baby Enos who was born February 22, 1900, and Eli and Sarah Beachy and Noah came home for family gatherings. Deemy, Mattie, and Millie loved to play with the little ones. Sarah and Eli enjoyed taking one of the younger children like Millie or Menno home with them at times.

Once when Noah had gotten a new buggy and came to Isaac's place to show it off, he asked Deemy, "Would you like to have a ride?" She shyly accepted for she felt at ease with him, though his presence did bring back memories of her dear sister Katie who had been so close to her. Noah sensed this was a good time to express his love for her. Deemy blushed as he proposed to her, although she was delighted. She said she needed to talk to her parents about it first to which Noah did not object.

When she timidly asked her parents, they gave their approval. As they reminded her that there was quite an age gap, they added, "You never showed any interest in boys nearer your age. However, this is for you, and we have high respect for Noah and would not want to interfere."

When she saw Noah again, she said, "The answer is yes." Noah was more light-hearted then he had been for a long time.

On January 9, 1902, their wedding day, they joined hands and hearts. Noah truly cherished her and did all in his power to make her happy. Tears came to Mattie's eyes as she thought of the poor, helpless baby Deemy had been when they had taken her into their home and hearts. Isaac and Mattie wished them a long and happy married life. Mattie hoped in her heart their life together could be triumphs rather than trials. Noah took Deemy to his house which needed a woman's touch. She was a good cook and had been taught all the basics of homemaking.

By this time, the church had two more ministers, Ananias B. Miller and Andy J. Mast. They were a big help to Isaac.

Mrs. John T. Yoder still had many health problems, and Mississippi had not been the answer as they had hoped. She passed away in August, 1896. While Isaac was preaching the funeral sermon, he could not finish because he had chills and fever. An elderly Miller preacher finished the service. Many local blacks attended to give their last respects. They were very helpful to their Amish friends.

Mississippi proved to be an unhealthy climate. The many swamps were breeding spots for mosquitoes which, in turn, caused malaria, and many people also contracted tuberculosis and lung problems.

When a few of Mattie's brothers from Ohio came to visit, they were impressed with the harmony they sensed in the church there. One evening after the children were in bed, they had a intimate talk with Isaac and Mattie. They mentioned the warmth and love they perceived in their church. In their area of Ohio, they had not had Communion for a few years because of so much bickering and misunderstandings. Isaac had a deep feeling for them and said, "This is not pleasing to God for it is His will that we work together in love."

Some of these brothers were ministers, and they asked Isaac and Mattie to come visit and see if Isaac could help restore love in their congregation. Isaac replied, "Of myself, I can do nothing but only as the Lord directs and leads." Mattie agreed. Isaac promised to pray about the matter and let them know later. As Isaac prayed before going to bed, he felt the Lord directing him to give his answer the next morning. On their way to take the brothers to the depot to meet the train, he told them they would try to come and visit them after the cotton was picked if nothing interfered.

Cotton picking went well with the help of their neighbors. He felt fortunate to get eight cents per pound for his cotton, which he thought was a fair price.

"Well, I think we should get our train tickets to go to Ohio now that the cotton is all harvested and sold," Isaac told Mattie.

She replied, "I've been trying to get my work caught up to go." Mother talked with Sarah and Deemy, and they consented to come help Mattie and Millie if they needed it. Since Menno was young enough to go fare free, they decided to take him along.

Chapter 12
Isaac - Mattie - Menno to Ohio

The tickets were purchased, and the needed clothes were packed. Levi took them to the train with the spring wagon. Menno was elated that he could go along. He was sure to notice everything that happened on the train. It was exciting to see the conductor passing through the car and saying, "Tickets please," and to hear the train whistle blowing, and then the train rumbling down the tracks. He would have so much to tell when he got home. His mother had packed some lunch, and he was really hungry after riding so long. At times, he pressed his nose against the train window and watched the scenery pass by. Finally he went to sleep with his head on his father's lap. Occasionally, he awoke as the whistle blew indicating another stop in a small town to allow passengers to exit or enter the train. He asked, "When will we be there?" His father assured him they would go through many more towns before reaching their destination.

Finally, the conductor announced, "Next town, Millersburg."

Isaac smiled at Menno and said, "That's our stop." Menno pressed his nose against the window as the train came to a halt.

One of Menno's uncles was there with his two-seated buggy, and he helped carry their baggage. Then they all got into the buggy and were on their way to his house. Menno perceived this area was quite different from Mississippi as they went around curves and up and down hills. He had never seen such big houses and barns. He missed not seeing any black people. It was like another world.

Menno soon became acquainted with his uncle's children. They showed him around and played tag and many other games. These cousins had no little black friends. Menno wondered if Mississippi was the only place where children had black playmates.

Every day he went with his parents to visit more relatives. Menno never imagined they had so much kin. His mother was so happy to see people she had not seen for many years. Isaac was asked to preach in many different Amish churches often sharing an afternoon service. People drove quite a distance to hear Isaac humbly and meekly present the word of God. He preached on love, mentioning the greatest commandment to love the Lord thy God and thy neighbor as thyself. The manner in which he delivered his sermons touched the hearts of the audience to the extent that those who harbored spite or ill will were convicted. Ministers, and bishops as well, realized where they had failed. Many went to one another and confessed their wrong feelings.

Two weeks soon ended, and Isaac, Mattie, and little Menno were taken to meet the train for the long journey home. Many extended their thanks for their time and concern and bade them farewell with tear-filled eyes. Isaac invited the relatives and friends to come visit them in Mississippi. Then they boarded the train and, as the whistle blew, they found their seats, and the train soon rattled down the track.

"Well, we are now homeward bound. I'm eager to see how the family fared while we were gone," Isaac said to Mattie.

"I, too, hope we find all is well," exclaimed Mattie. Menno was soon fast asleep.

When they finally arrived home, the family gave them a hearty welcome, including children and grandchildren.

Everyone was eager to hear about their trip. Of course, Menno had a lot to tell. He exclaimed, "They don't have any black friends in Ohio."

A few weeks later they received a letter in the mail from one of Mattie's brothers. It read, "I hardly know how to express our gratitude for your kind visit. I cannot find words to express what has taken place here since you left. The bickering has stopped, and we plan to hold Communion soon." Isaac's eyes filled with tears as he said, "It's nothing I did. I was only preaching what the Lord laid on my heart."

One winter day, a black neighbor knocked at the door. As Mattie opened the door and invited him in, she thought he looked gaunt. He cried as he spoke, "Could you spare a little food? We have had nothing to eat for two days. I can go longer, if you could just spare some food for my wife and children."

Mattie said, "I will see what I can find." She went into the pantry and got some beans, cornmeal, a few sweet potatoes, a jar of apple butter, a jar of meat, plus a loaf of homemade bread, and a small bucket of milk. When she handed it to him, she said, "You shall eat, too." Through his tears, he thanked her heartily.

Mattie thought how sad it was that they didn't know how to budget for the winter. She also was aware there were times when white people took advantage of the blacks which wasn't right.

At the dinner table, Mattie told Isaac of her visitor. He said, "I'm glad you gave them food. In God's sight, their soul is worth as much as ours."

Sickness was very prevalent, and in all, fifteen people from the Amish church died thus far. Seven were mothers and left many little children behind. One was a father and seven were children. Among these was Isaac and Mattie's daughter Katie and baby Lonnie. One child was a son of Enos and Sarah, whose name was Harry. He died December 9, 1897, at the age of four years and eleven months. It was a common thing for Mattie to get called to the home of those who were sick. With her many home remedies, she sometimes got good results, and other times all efforts seemed to be in vain. She was always ready to help out where needed.

Chapter 13
Sickness - Deaths - Move to Kansas

With so much sickness and so many deaths, there was a great deal of talk that the climate did not agree with the white settlers. It was agreed that some men would go to Garnett, Kansas, to consider the land there. They brought back the report that there was plenty of land there for all those interested.

Isaac's health was failing, and Mattie and the children were quite concerned. Shem's son, Daniel, was also sick so they would not be able to move with the others.

Levi and Andy were good workers and managed what needed to be done, but Isaac also depended on his married children for many things.

It was decided that a move would be made to Garnett, Kansas, as soon as all the arrangements could be made. Isaac and Noah sold their tiling machine and other unneeded items. Isaac took care of necessary business. On January 18, 1904, eight families, with their belongings loaded on the train, left the warm Mississippi weather behind and rolled down the tracks for Kansas. Isaac's health was steadily declining, and the long trip tested his endurance.

An extra passenger car was chartered. Those going were Isaacs; Enos Yoders and four children: Tobias, Shem, Eli, and Mattie; Eli and Sarah Beachey; Noah and Deemy Yoder; Solomon Beachey and family; Joseph Bontrager and family; and Deacon Mose J. Hershberger and family. Shem's family did not go with the train because their son Daniel was too sick. They moved into Noah and Deemy's house in Mississippi.

Eventually they arrived in Garnett, and many willing people with teams and wagons helped unload their belongings from the train and hauled them to their new homes. The trip was very exhausting for Isaac, and he was thankful for the help of others. Levi, almost twenty-one, was very capable, and Andy, sixteen, was a big help as well. Mattie and Millie also assumed responsibility in helping their mother.

Isaac's place was located southwest of Garnett, and Noah and Deemy's farm was further west. Enoses and Eli Beacheys moved onto nearby farms. Noah's place hardly compared with the nice new house and barn they had left behind in Mississippi. Their house, made of stone, was sixteen feet square with one door and two windows.

On February 27, slightly over a month after the move, they received the telegram from Shems that seven-year-old Daniel had died. He would be buried in the Amish cemetery where so many others were buried in the eight short years that settlement had existed. Isaac and Mattie wished they could be near to comfort them, but this was not possible. With Isaac gradually becoming weaker, their own future looked uncertain. He had a bad cough and was diagnosed with tuberculosis. This, along with typhoid fever and malaria, had been the cause of many deaths in Mississippi.

With spring work coming, Isaac had to direct the work from his bed. They put the bed beside a window hoping the sun would help his condition. It was difficult for the family to see their loved one weaken steadily. After Daniel's death, Shems had also moved to Garnett. He exchanged work with Levi and Andy to help plant crops.

On April 14, 1904, Noah came for his mother-in-law with the news that Deemy needed her to come as it was time for her to deliver her firstborn. Isaac encouraged Mattie to go as he knew Deemy needed her. The baby boy arrived safely, and Deemy said she would like to name him Isaac in honor of the father she so highly respected. Deemy recovered quickly. Mattie said, "I will go home and send daughter Mattie over to help you. You get your rest so you will get your strength back sooner."

Chapter 14
Isaac's Farewell - Changes Take Place

The married children came often to visit their father. Each time he seemed to look a little more feeble. On July 16, 1904, word was sent to the children that Isaac was very ill and they should come home right away. With all the children around his bed, he extended his farewell, admonishing each one, "Live for Jesus. Take good care of your mother and help her when she needs you." He took little Menno's hand in his and said, "Obey your mother, and be a good boy." He expressed his desire to see them all in heaven some day. Mattie held his hand, and he gave it a light squeeze as he took his last breath.

Tears flowed freely as Mattie reflected on this latest trial she needed to face. Isaac was only forty-six years, six months, and seven days old. Menno was eight years old, and now she must raise him alone. After she got her composure, she said, "The Lord makes no mistakes. Blessed be the name of the Lord." She put her arms around little Menno to comfort him. The following days were a blur. Isaac was laid to rest in the nearby Amish cemetery with family and friends paying their last respects.

A short time later, Mattie asked her children to come home so the will could be read. It read as follows:

"I, Isaac Chupp, a married man of Garnett, Anderson County, Kansas, being of sound disposing mind and memory do make and publish this my last will and testament hereby revoking all former wills made by me.

First I direct that all my just debts (including the mortgage on my farm I now occupy, as a home) and funeral expenses be paid.

Second I direct that $600 dollars be expended in repair and fixing up the buildings on my farm that I now occupy, said repairing and fixing to be done by the executor as my wife Magdalena may direct.

Third I give, devise, and bequeath to my beloved wife all my personal property and the use of my farm as long as she lives.

Fourth I direct that all my children remain on the farm with my wife Magdalena and work for same as they work for me until they become of age or until they get married.

Fifth I direct that the executor sell my farm in Mississippi being the East half, (½), of section twenty-five, (25), of Township fourteen, (14), of Range five, (5), less forty (40), acres out of the north east corner, containing 304 acres all in Chickasaw County, Mississippi to the best advantage and comply with the specific bequests above stated.

Sixth After the payment of my funeral expenses, just debts and specific bequests above stated it is my will that all the remainder of the money left from the sale of the Mississippi farm shall be divided equally between my children.

Seventh I nominate and appoint Shem D. Yoder executor of this my will and testament on this 18th day of June 1904.

Isaac Chupp

We the undersigned witnesses to the above will say the testator signed said will in both our presence and he declared the same to be his last will and testament and he called us both to witness his signature to said will, and we in his presence and in the presence of each other at his request signed our names to said Will as Witnesses on this 18th day of June, 1904."

Noah J. Yoder Eli S. Beachey

(This was copied from original will and is basically unedited.)

With the efficient help of her sons, Levi and Andy, and the girls, Mattie and Millie, life went on. Mother told Millie and Menno that she expected them to keep the woodbox filled for her. When Millie complained to her mother that Menno didn't help, Mother said, "Oh, Menno came in and has a stomachache so you just fill it. Menno went to lie down, and I hope he soon feels better. You bring it in this time. Maybe he will feel better tomorrow evening." It seemed the next evening the same thing happened. Mattie felt so sorry for this poor fatherless child. She tried to doctor him up, and he thrived on all the extra attention. Menno seemed better after supper; however, the next evening the same ailment struck him again. He soon realized that he could manipulate his mother. His brothers and sisters, however, saw through his tricks.

As the church grew, they discerned a need for another minister. An ordination was held November 13, 1904, and Eli S. Beachy, son of Solomon Beachy, was chosen by lot. His wife, Sarah, Mattie's daughter, was well aware of their new responsibilities, and she would be a support to him.

For sometime, Levi had been keeping company with a young lady by the name of Anna Eash. He confided in his mother of their plans for a December wedding, and she did not object. They would rent a house or a farm, but he and Andy would still work together with the farming.

While Mattie had this on her mind, Millie informed her mother that she needed to get married to Ananias (A.D.) Borntrager. Millie was so young, and he was ten years older than her. Mattie didn't have the highest regards for Ananias.

Levi and Anna had a nice wedding on December 11, 1905, and Millie and A.D.'s wedding was set to be on December 21, 1905. With Millie being so young, it was hard for Mattie to put her heart into the preparation of the marriage. Oh! Where had she failed her? Millie, however, was very skillful, and she got busy sewing her wedding dress. Mattie noticed that she was preparing to arrange pleats in the skirt and press them down to the hem. "Oh, don't put those pleats in it," Mattie pleaded. "That is just for pride, and we don't want anything for fancy." That evening when Millie went to her room, she laid her dress skirt on the floor and pinned the pleats all the way to the hem. Then she placed the trunk on top of it to weight it down. By morning, the pleats were pressed so they lay flat.

When the wedding was over, the house seemed so empty with two leaving the nest so close together. Only Andy, daughter Mattie, and little Menno were left at home.

Early in the morning of February 20, 1906, Mattie was called to the home of daughter Millie and A.D. to assist in the delivery of their first child. It was a nice sized, healthy boy, and they named him Daniel or Dannie for short. Mattie thought of Millie as not being much more than a child herself, and now she had the responsibility of being a mother.

Enos, with his spirit for adventure, informed his mother they were moving to Montana. "Oh! But what do you want there?" she asked.

"Take a claim and develop the country," he replied.

"I wish you well, but it sounds like quite an undertaking with a family of five little children."

Enos purchased train tickets, and in March, 1906, Enos and Sarah and their children, Tobias, Shem, Eli, Mattie and one-year-old Malinda, boarded the train in Garnett with their belongings. Glendive, Montana, was their destination. The total train fare was $143.55. As the train jostled along, Enos' thoughts were of the success that lay ahead upon their arrival. He said, "Just think, Sarah, we can get 160 acres for $25 if we pay the recorder and then homestead it. You know we can't go wrong on a deal like that. They say the railroads own a lot of land they are willing to sell for $3.50 to $7 an acre." She did not share his enthusiasm, but, being a submissive wife, she didn't say much. It had not been easy for her to pack to make the move.

Their brother-in-law from North Dakota rode along on the train with them and helped keep the children together when they changed trains. They arrived in Glendive, Montana, the morning of March 23, 1906, but this was still thirty miles from where they would take their claim.

Two men, each with a spring wagon and team, were there to meet them. Both wagons were piled high when everything and everybody was loaded.

At this time, there were ten families, plus a few single boys who lived on their claims. One was Mose Mullet who let Enos' family live in his house until they filed their claim. Enos filed on 160 acres on April sixth. It was located across the ridge from the other Amish families. Enos erected a tent he borrowed from someone and moved his family onto their claim until he had built their own small ten by twelve foot house. With his clever ideas, he built a loft above their bed where the three boys slept and a trundle bed that was pulled out from under their bed where Mattie slept. This small bed could be pushed under their bed during the day. Baby Malinda slept in a cradle. A stove used for cooking and heating, a dry sink, a small table with a bench, a few chairs, and a clothes chest furnished the small room. Enos soon put up a shed where he could milk the cows and stable the horse. He dug a well and built a little pump house above the well. This provided shelter when pumping water for use in the house and for the animals.

When he finally completed their new, larger house by the side of a hill, the family rejoiced. It was quite comfortable and had a walk-in basement as well as walk-in on the main floor. Now they had room for company which happened frequently as people from other areas came to inspect this new area.

Because wolves were plentiful, they had to herd their sheep and cattle to protect them. They also had to constantly guard against rattlesnakes. One year Enos killed eighty of them. The children were warned and taught to recognize those snakes.

Once when they had company from a distance, and all were seated around the table eating dinner, there was a knock at the door. When Enos opened the door, there was a man asking for work. When he said he was hungry, Enos invited him in, and they offered him a place to sit at the table. After thanks was returned, they began to pass the food around the table. Shortly another knock was heard, and Enos again got up to answer the door. To his surprise, he recognized the sheriff. He said, "Have you seen a stranger on foot around here?"

Enos answered, "Yes, he's sitting at the table."

Upon hearing the sheriff's question, the stranger seated at the table lost no time escaping the house. He fled down some steps to the lower level and bolted toward the shed with the sheriff and his deputy in hot pursuit after him. They shouted, "Stop! Stop! or we will shoot!" By now, everyone had left the table and was peering out the windows. The children had never seen so much excitement, and their hearts beat rapidly as they witnessed the scene. Although the sheriff shouted again, "Stop! or we will shoot!" the man did not stop.

Bang! Bang! and the man dropped. Soon he was handcuffed and

loaded onto their car. The sheriff told Enos the man had escaped from jail.

When Enos wrote his mother about all the excitement, her heartbeat sped as she read it. "Oh, my!" she said to herself. When she shared the letter with the other children, they decided Montana must be a wild country.

July 24, 1906, Noah and Deemy had their second child, and they named him Jonas. Mattie took little Isaac, who was a busy little fellow, home with her for a few days so Deemy could rest better. Daughter Mattie went and assumed the household duties.

In 1906, Dodge City, Kansas, was booming. Advertisements in the Budget sounded so enticing. A.D.'s enthusiasm increased as he read these ads. He said, "Millie, listen to this, 'Great wheat belt land prices range from $10 to $15 per acre.' I've heard of others moving there and read their comments in the Budget. Maybe we ought to move there, too. I'm going to inspect that place and see for myself." He bought a train ticket, and he was off. He liked what he saw, and when he came home, he announced that he had rented a place. They would move in September.

When Millie told her mother, Mattie said, "Oh, my! Enoses moved, now you want to move, too. But you are your own boss. How we will miss you and little Dannie! He is such a sweet age. You are still so young, and soon you will have another addition. You will need help at times, but I guess others from there will help you. We will help with the packing. I guess I also moved away from my parents soon after I got married."

Soon it was September, and A.D. and Millie and little Dannie, along with their belongings, were boarding the train for their new home in Dodge City. Mattie's eyes filled with tears as she embraced Millie, and they bade each other good-bye. The other children had been at Mother's home the evening before as a farewell. Sarah and Deemy told her how much they would miss her when they came to spend the day with their mother and Mattie. Yes, Millie was her youngest daughter and had so much responsibility at such a young age. One thing she had to admit, although she was young, she was more mature than most girls that age. She was a good housekeeper and neat seamstress.

The train departed with the whistle blowing and the smoke rolling out of the stack. Mattie and the girls dried their tears and started home in the wagon.

June 2, 1907, a bishop was ordained in the church, and Eli S. Beachy was chosen by lot. Mattie wished them God's guidance in their new calling. Their home had not been blessed with children; however, in this new calling, the Lord had other responsibilities for them.

November 13, 1907, Levi fetched his mother to assist in the delivery of their first child. It was a girl named Polly, and they were very delighted with her.

Work on the farm went on with Levi and Andy helping each other as the need arose. Menno was old enough to help with the work if he would. When he wanted to work, he did a good job. Sometimes when there was an extra difficult task to perform, Menno would surprise them and do it to everyone's amazement. But if he didn't want to help, no amount of encouragement moved him. If he did not desire to labor, his mother always understood his reasoning. He had been such a frail baby, and she did not want him to overdo himself. His mother gave him a lot of praise. Sometimes Andy complained to his mother when Menno wouldn't help. If his mother approached him about it, he had a logical excuse.

The letters from Millie were few, and when Mattie got one, she would eagerly open it to see how they were faring. The last of June, 1907, she got one, and daughter Mattie, Andy, and Menno stood nearby to hear the news she had to share. Mother said, "Well, A.D. and Millie have another baby boy born the 14th of June. They named him Andy after you, Andy." This made Andy smile. "He was a good-sized baby and looks like his dad, Millie wrote. She says Dannie is a busy little fellow, and her strength is slowly coming back. A.D. helps her with laundry and garden."

Church was in session November 16, 1907. This was the day the church had agreed to have minister ordination. Mattie's prayer was that the Lord's will be done. It was a solemn occasion as each member cast their vote as the Lord led them. Mattie was not surprised when she heard the name of son-in-law Noah as one of those in the lot.

Those in the lot were asked to move to the front bench and sit side by side. The bishop in charge and assisting ministers took the same number of hymn books as there were men in the lot. In one book, a slip of paper was inserted with the passage from Acts 1:24 written on it. After this the books were shuffled, and no one knew which one contained the paper. Then those in the lot solemnly filed by, each one taking one hymn book and then taking their seat again. When each had a book and was seated again, the bishop opened the books one by one. When Noah's book was opened, it contained the paper. The bishop announced him to be the one, and he was then ordained. After church was dismissed, Deemy went to stand beside her husband in his holy calling. Nearly everyone filed by and wished Noah God's blessings in his new ministry.

When the next letter came from Enos from Montana, it contained the news that they had a new member in their family. "It is another girl, and we have named her Abby. She was born November 24, 1907. That makes three boys and three girls. We are doing fine," he wrote. "I've been busy digging coal for heat this winter. Trees are scarce in this area so fence posts are shipped in by train. Alfalfa, wheat, oats, barley, and flax are our main crops. Some yields of winter wheat were forty-two bushels per acre. I heard of rye that yielded forty bushels per acre. We only got ten acres of oats sowed but were pleased with the 158 bushels per acre it yielded. We seeded it by hand. We also raised a wagon load of potatoes and sold some of those. We milk two cows and churn our cream and sell the butter to ranchers in the area. That's pretty good for this cheap land, don't you think, Mom?"

"Well," Mattie said to the children, "maybe Enos has finally found the land of his dreams."

Mattie enjoyed cooking, and it always meant a lot to her when the children and grandchildren came home. Sarah and Deemy and their little boys enjoyed coming to spend the day with their mother and sister Mattie. Then there were times when Shem's wife Anna and their daughter Deemy and Levi's wife Anna and their baby Polly would also come, each bringing handwork along. At those times, they especially missed daughter Millie and Enos' wife Sarah.

Chapter 15
1908 Shem's Wife Dies - More Trials

It was indeed another sad day in Mattie's life when Shem's wife Anna died on May 30, 1908. Shem was heartbroken, and Mattie could well sympathize. She had needed to part with two companions. Shem's daughter Deemy was fourteen, and his son Enos was eight. This was a traumatic experience for these children to suddenly become motherless. Deemy had been taught to shoulder a lot of the housework since her mother was not well. Mattie and daughter Mattie helped young Deemy when there was canning or extra work that needed attention. Sarah was also very helpful and longed to take these children under her wing since she had no children. Enos was often with his dad when he was not in school.

When the girls came to spend the day, Sarah would bring Shem's Deemy along. Sometimes they helped her with sewing or patching.

The summer of 1908, they received a letter from Millie, and she had given birth to a baby girl June 19, 1908. The baby lived a very short time, and they named her Abby. A short funeral service had been conducted before her burial. Millie was not regaining her strength like she wished. The summer heat made her more uncomfortable. Mattie wished she were closer so they could help her. She thought how young Millie was and now she had to face losing a child.

Chapter 16
New Babies - Menno's Wisdom - Weddings

Early the morning of July 28, 1908, Noah sent word that Deemy needed her mother's presence. Mattie said to daughter Mattie, "You may go with me and bring the little boys, Isaac and Jonas, home with you." The boys were thrilled to go home with Aunt Mattie. Later that day another son was born to Noah and Deemy. They named him Levi as a namesake for her brother; however, in time, he went by the name Lee. Deemy got along well, and the next day Aunt Mattie took the little boys home. She stayed and assumed the housework so Deemy could get the rest she needed.

Andy was interested in a young girl by the name of Susanna Borntrager. The way their friendship was progressing, Mattie expected them to marry soon.

On November 21, 1908, Levi summoned his mother's help with a delivery. He brought two-year-old Polly along to stay with his sister Mattie. The delivery proved difficult, and they appreciated the aid of a doctor and Mattie's assistance. Finally twin boys were born, and Anson and Andy were chosen as names. Mattie decided to stay a few days to help get the babies started and also to see that Anna received proper care. After that, daughter Mattie could come and help.

The next thing demanding Mattie's attention was Andy's wedding which would be in April. He would need a new suit and white shirt, and Mattie would also want a new dress. She wanted to get the sewing done before gardening time arrived. The wedding would be at Susanna's parents' home, and they would take care of the wedding plans.

Andy would need to find a place to live. When they discussed the future, Andy said, "I will still help out on the farm." Menno was there to help if he felt like it.

He had shown so much knowledge about business matters that Mattie had turned that part of the operation over to him. She felt he was superior in head knowledge to other boys at age fourteen. The other children questioned their mother on the wisdom of her decision to let Menno do all the banking and business. She answered, "I feel very comfortable with it. Menno can do anything he wants to if he sets his heart to it." How well his brothers and sisters knew that! They had observed how he left the dirty work for Andy. Menno found many excuses to go to Garnett, and his mother had full confidence that it was necessary if he said so.

The day of Andy and Susanna's wedding, April 29, 1909, dawned bright and clear. The entire church was invited as it was not a large congregation. One highlight for the Chupp family was that A.D. and Millie, and their two small sons, Dannie and Andy, came by train. What a joy it was to see them again! Dannie was three years old, and Andy was almost two. They appeared to like their new home near Dodge City, Kansas. A.D. and Andy's wife were related which gave them more reasons to come. They stayed a few weeks and visited relatives and friends.

After the wedding, Andy and Susanna moved into a small house near his mother's home. It was a pleasure for Mattie to see her children start new homes. She regretted that Isaac could not be there to see their children as they ventured on their own. But she knew he was in a far better place and did not wish him back. He was spared many of the trials she had to face. Mattie helped Susanna plant a garden. It was a joy to see the gardens grow and produce, and that summer was exceptional. Susanna often came along with Andy when he came to work, and she and Mattie helped each other with canning and drying vegetables and fruit.

Mattie and daughter Mattie went to Shem's place to help young Deemy with more difficult jobs. It was a very busy summer. Hay was a good crop and needed to be mowed and put on stacks. Wheat produced well which meant they needed to cook for threshers. They also helped Sarah or Deemy or Shems or Levis cook for threshers when they were there. Anna was fully occupied with her two babies, and she also received help from her side of the family that lived nearby.

Once when they got a letter from Enos, it sounded like it was not quite as grand anymore. Enos had been told that sheep were profitable so in the fall he had bought one hundred lambs and eight rams and enough ewes that they numbered 244 head in all. When the weather was nice, the boys herded them. When it was too cold in the winter, they kept them penned up. Because the winter had been exceptionally cold, the sheep ate all the oats they had. By the end of the winter, he had lost 110 sheep. Enos sold the remaining sheep that summer. After selling the wool and the skins from those that died, he still lacked $38 from breaking even.

Shem shared with his mother about his loneliness since losing his wife. He said, "I feel the need for a companion again. I've been seeing a young lady, Betsy Yoder, and she has consented to marry me."

"Isn't she a little young for you? You must consider your children. After all, your Deemy is fifteen. Will Betsy be good to your children? These are some things one has to consider. How old is Betsy?"

"Betsy will have her nineteenth birthday July 30th. We have chosen August 19, 1909, for our wedding date."

"I wish you and your children whatever is best. I think Betsy is a nice girl and has been taught to work," Mother replied.

When the wedding day arrived, it was a warm summer day, and everything went as planned. Shem's brother-in-law Eli Beachy joined Shem and Betsy in marriage. Enos and Sarah and their children came from Montana for the wedding so the family heard firsthand of their experiences.

Betsy was from a large family and the first to get married. She had been well taught in the art of housekeeping. Shem felt fortunate to have captured Betsy's heart.

Millie and A.D. and the boys could not come for the wedding as it was not advisable for her to travel at this time.

The latter part of September, Mattie received a letter from Millie. She wrote that a baby boy named Hosea had been born on the 23rd day of September, 1909. He lived only a short time and was buried beside baby Abby who had died shortly after birth a little over a year earlier.

"Yes, we would have desired to have him, but we know God makes no mistakes. We want to submit to His will." Millie continued, "A.D.'s brother Phineas and family now live in the area and have been such a big help. Our thoughts were there the day of Shem and Betsy's wedding, but I knew for my own good we had better not try to come. We do wish them a happy life together. I'm sure he had many lonely days. Dannie and Andy are doing well and were sorry our baby didn't live long. Hope you can come see us soon."

As Ever, Millie, A.D., and boys

Time moved on, and soon it was October. Mattie still had tomatoes and squash in the garden, but otherwise it was over. They had a good garden that summer, and they and Susan had put up all they needed, plus they had shared their excess with Sarah and Deemy and the others.

Andy arrived to ask his mother to come as Susan was not feeling well, and he wanted someone close by. Before the day was over, she gave birth to their firstborn, a son, named Rudy in honor of Susan's father. The date was October 26, 1909. They were happy to welcome him into their family.

Chapter 17
Romance - Twin Dies - More Trials

Mattie noticed the love growing deeper between daughter Mattie and Jonas Beachy, a nephew of son-in-law Eli. They exchanged some nice gifts and many lovely greeting cards containing nice verses. When Sarah and Deemy came to spend the day with their mother, sister Mattie thrilled in showing the nice cards and gifts he had given her for various occasions. They delighted in seeing them and rejoiced with her. Her brothers also enjoyed seeing them and the excitement of their sister. As time went on, Jonas often joined the others for Sunday dinner. At Christmas, Jonas was also there with the family, and more lovely gifts were exchanged between him and Mattie.

On February 17, 1910, Levi and Anna's twin son Andy passed away. He was not a strong child and did not linger long when he became ill. This left Anson, his twin brother, more fussy probably because he missed him so much. It was, of course, also hard on Levi and Anna and little Polly. They knew the Lord made no mistakes, and they accepted it as His will. Memories of her own departed little ones flooded Mattie.

Twin to Anson Chupp buried in Garnett, Kansas, son of Levi and Anna Chupp.

About this time, they read in the Budget by the Dodge City, Kansas, scribe, that some men had gone to Limon, Colorado, to inspect some land, and A.D. had gone along. He bought 160 acres in view of Pikes Peak, but later they learned he became apprehensive, and never moved.

In the meantime, Enos seemed to be growing more disgruntled with Montana. Sometimes their crops were destroyed by hail. Other times they had such hot winds that their crops burned.

On May 4, 1910, another son was added to Enos and Sarah's family. They named him Enos as a namesake. Enos was a hard worker. He cut hay on the railroad property, then pitched it on the wagon with a fork and hauled it home for his cows and horses. His boys were old enough to help unload it from the wagon when he got home.

Mother and Mattie often went to help Deemy with canning or other work such as butchering chickens or gathering vegetables from the garden. One of those times was August 23, 1910. When they were about ready to go home that evening, Deemy said, "Oh, Mother! I wish you could stay longer. I think I will let sister Mattie take the boys home and have Noah go for the doctor." Of course, Mattie gladly stayed as she was often called upon to assist in deliveries. That night a little girl was born and was named Sarah in honor of Deemy's sister. They now had three boys and a little girl which was very welcome. Mattie rejoiced with them.

Daughter Mattie confided in her mother that she and Jonas were making plans to get married. If Mother agreed, they were considering early 1911. "Oh, I don't object," Mattie responded when her daughter sought her blessing. "I believe you have seen enough of each other to know what you want. I appreciate your telling me so we can start preparing. We must get your quilts and comforters made. I also want to get a set of china dishes for you. The next time I go to Garnett you may go along and see what you like. Maybe you will find some nice material for your wedding dress. We have ample time to prepare yet. I don't like to leave too much for the last minute."

The next time Mother saw Noah, she asked if he would make a chest of drawers for Mattie. Noah agreed to work it into his schedule. As Mother and Mattie worked, it seemed everything was coming along smoothly. The girls and daughters-in-law came home to help quilt. Each was excited for Mattie and wished her well.

Granddaughter Deemy adored her aunt Mattie and felt included in the planning. Menno also took an interest in the upcoming event. He was fond of Jonas and felt close to him.

By fall Mother had some other concerns as Mattie had such a persistent cough. One day she said, "Mattie, I have an uneasy feeling about your cough. You are starting much the same way your father did. I do hope it soon improves." Mother tried many remedies on Mattie; however, nothing seemed to help. Jonas often came to discuss plans with Mattie. They agreed to wait to announce their wedding date until her health improved. In the meantime, Noah finished the chest of drawers and delivered it. Mattie was happy to have it and expressed her appreciation.

When her condition continued to weaken, Mother said, "Menno, you go tell Dr. Harris to come. I'm afraid Mattie has tuberculosis or consumption" (as tuberculosis was often referred to in those days).

Dr. Harris came to their house, and after doing a few tests, he shook his head and said, "This seems to be a case of consumption. There is not much to do for it which I hate to tell you at your age." Mother, Mattie, and Menno felt like a hard blow had struck them. Oh! how would they break the news to Jonas? Dr. Harris had advised them to put her bed in front of the south window as sometimes with this illness, the sun had a healing effect.

When Jonas received the news, it was like a bolt of lightening had hit him. He came often to visit his lovely betrothed and attempted to make her final days as happy as possible. Mother stayed busy trying to prepare food that might tempt her, but Mattie had no appetite and ate very little. Gradually her health declined, and on January 28, 1911, Mother saw her end was nearing. She sent Menno to let Jonas and the children who lived nearby know. Shem and Betsy, Eli and Sarah, Noah and Deemy, Levi and Anna, Andy and Susan, Mother and Menno, and Jonas all gathered around her bed, and with Jonas holding one hand and Mother the other, she took her last breath. Mattie lacked only a few weeks from her twenty-first birthday.

This was one more trial for Mother Mattie, but she did as she had done so often before committing it all to the Lord. It was hard to see how crushed Jonas was. For Jonas, all his dreams and plans were now gone as a shadow. Mother said, "Life is but a vapor here on earth. But life goes on for us who are left behind." She tried to comfort Jonas as he had grown very close to the family.

The grandchildren would miss their aunt Mattie very much. Shem's daughter Deemy looked to her aunt Mattie as her role model, having lost her own mother a few years previously. Her aunt Mattie had helped her over many difficult times in life. She would always remember her for that.

Telegrams were sent to Enos' family in Montana and to A.D. and Millie near Dodge City, Kansas. Enos got train tickets for himself, Sarah, the little girls, and the baby, and they left as soon as possible for Garnett. A.D. and Millie could not come which didn't surprise Mother. She knew Millie was again on the family way. Mattie had kept those who lived away from Garnett informed of daughter Mattie's condition. She also had Millie on her mind a lot, but knew it was not possible to go visit her when daughter Mattie was so sick. She often prayed for her knowing she had lost the last two babies.

The whole family was glad to see Enoses again. This was the first time they saw their baby Enos. Everyone commented that the children had grown. Enos was so glad to be back with the family, he mentioned that sometimes he was tempted to move back.

Mattie, daughter of Isaac and Mattie Chupp.
Buried in Garnett, Kansas. Engaged to Jonas Beachy.

Soon Mattie got a letter from Millie, and she wrote, "Oh, Mother! I must write you the news that our home was truly blessed February 24, 1911, with a baby girl. We have named her Ida Mae. She is a little jewel and seems healthy. I prayed a great deal before she was born, and the Lord answered. A.D. and the boys are also rejoicing. How we desired to be there for sister Mattie's funeral, but knew we dared not risk the trip. I feel the Lord repaid us with a healthy baby. Dannie says the baby is his birthday present since he had his fifth birthday four days before the baby was born. Andy stands by her cradle and admires her, and A.D. really has an extra gleam in his eyes, too. Oh, I wish you could see her! Our thoughts were with you and especially Jonas during this great sorrow of sister Mattie's death. How his dreams must be shattered! But the Lord will see him through."

When mother shared the letter with daughters Sarah and Deemy and the others, they all rejoiced with Millie that she again had a healthy baby. Sarah said, "At times I have to wonder why the Lord hasn't blessed our home with children after all these years. Then I try to accept the fact that He has other plans for us that He will reveal in time."

It seemed there were constant changes in the family. On March 1, 1911, a son was born to Andy and Susan. They named him Levi as a namesake for Andy's brother. Almost every day, Mattie went there to help as little Rudy was sick and required a lot of care. Mattie fixed poultices and greased him with skunk oil which was a common remedy in those days. She spent considerable time rocking him which gave him some comfort. She tried sponging his little body to bring down the fever, but all efforts were in vain. When baby Levi was six days old, on March 7, 1911, little Rudy died. Susan's parents came and stayed a few weeks to help. A short service was held, and Susan sat on the rocking chair during the service. Mattie was well acquainted with the pangs that grip one's heart when a loved one is buried in the earth. She had experienced this with two life companions and five children. Yes, life has many trials.

March 8, 1911, Shem and Betsy had a baby girl with Dr. Harris in attendance. They named her Anna like Betsy's mother. Mattie did not go to see her the first few days because she realized Andy and Susan needed her worse. She knew Shem's daughter Deemy was seventeen and very capable with all the household duties, and Betsy's family would also help. Shem's son Enos, eleven, loved being with his dad and was quite dependable with the chores and other work outside.

Mattie and Menno put forth extra effort to go to Dodge City to visit A.D. and Millie before they were too busy with garden work. They took the train and enjoyed their visit immensely. Dannie and Andy enjoyed showing their uncle Menno around the farm. Of course, Mattie enjoyed getting acquainted with Baby Ida Mae. She was so glad they had a healthy baby. Millie and her mother had plenty of visiting to do on what had happened since they had moved away. Mattie enjoyed helping Millie with her work. They went to visit A.D.'s brother Phineas and attended church where they got acquainted with the people from the area. Soon the two weeks ended, and Mattie and Menno bade A.D., Millie, and the children farewell as they took them to meet the train for the return trip home.

When they got to Garnett, Andy was there to meet them. As they drove in at home, Mattie said, "It looks like the garden really grew while we were gone. We will need to get the hoeing done before the weeds overtake the vegetables."

It seemed rather lonely now that she and Menno were alone. She was glad Menno could read German well. He was also gifted in getting the right tunes on the slow hymns that were sung in the Amish church. He was able to get the right pitch to the *Lob Lied* which was difficult for many who were older than he. Sometimes after supper Menno and his mother would sing and read their testaments. She felt Isaac would be delighted if he was living and could observe the brilliance of their son.

Chapter 18
1911 - More Babies - Enos Move Back

Summer was drawing to a close. Crop yields had been fair, and gardens had done well. One day Menno brought in the mail, and there was a letter from Enos. Mattie quickly opened it and read, "Oh! They have another baby boy named Andrew. That will make Andy smile. The baby was born September 3, 1911. Enos says they plan to move back to Garnett this fall. My, 1911 has been a year of many occurrences for our family. First was daughter Mattie's death in January, then in February, the birth of A.D. and Millie's Ida Mae, in March, the birth of Andy's son Levi, and Shem's Anna, and the death of Andy and Susan's son Rudy, and Enos and Sarah have a new baby son Andrew. Now Enos writes they expect to move back this year. Life brings many changes."

Enos had dealt on a 200 acre farm in Garnett, and they would move as soon as possible after Andrew's birth. By this time, Enos had quite a few horses and was doing better in Montana. He decided it would be better to relocate before things went poorly again. They let someone rent their place in Montana. They had stayed there six years which was longer then they had stayed at some places. The entire family was excited to live closer to the relatives again. Because of the packing necessary for the move, Sarah had a hard time regaining her strength after Andrew's birth. The oldest daughter Mattie was nine years old and ran lots of errands for her. Sixteen-year-old Tobias was a big help. The next two boys were also busy wherever they were most needed to pack and load the railroad cars for the trip. After being on the train for days, the train finally arrived in Garnett. Mother Mattie was amazed at the size of the older boys. She helped unpack and arrange things, then she cooked a big kettle of mush for them. She was well aware that boys usually had hearty appetites. She also brought of her homemade cheese spread along for them to eat. After the long train ride, they were extra hungry. The relatives had a generous meal prepared for them the day they moved. By the time the weather turned cold, they were once again settled in Garnett.

Now the children all lived nearby except Millie. That winter Menno persuaded his mother that he was capable of taking care of the farm by himself. Andy's wife Susan had a desire to move to Reno County, Kansas, to be near her parents. The spring of 1912 found

Andy and Susan on the train with their belongings headed for Yoder, Kansas. Shem's daughter Deemy was eighteen and went along to help establish them in their new home. She also worked for others in the area and made many new friends.

Menno had great plans on how he would run the farm. Mattie, not wanting to deprive him of his dreams, said, "Menno, you will have a lot of responsibility. Are you sure you won't overdo yourself?"

He assured her that he was sixteen and could manage by himself. "I have a lot of confidence in you," she said.

One day Menno went to Garnett and met a young homeless boy named Tommy. After talking with him a bit, Menno said, "You can go home with me and help me for your keep."

Tommy said, "I will take you up on your offer." When Menno got home, he took Tommy in to meet his mother. Then Menno took him upstairs and showed him his room. Tommy had a small bundle of clothes with him which he left there. He then followed Menno to the barn where he was told what would be expected of him. Mattie prepared more for supper because she thought the poor child looked like he had not eaten much for quite a while. After consuming the delicious meal, he thanked her heartily as he left the table.

Tommy was a willing worker and very polite to Mattie. He did well to help Mattie in the garden that spring and summer gathering vegetables, digging potatoes, hoeing weeds, or anything else requiring attention. With all the business Menno needed to do, she could not expect much help from him.

As time went on, Menno demanded more work from Tommy and took it a little easier himself. There were times when Tommy did not know how he could accomplish some jobs that Menno gave him to do. His love for Mattie's cooking, however, was reason enough to try hard to please. He kept the stables clean in the barn which was one job Menno detested. Sometimes Menno told Tommy, "When you complete your work you can go fishing in the creek." This was an incentive to work even harder as he loved to fish.

May 13, 1912, Levi and Anna were blessed with a baby girl named Gertrude. It helped fill the vacancy little Andy had left. Mattie frequently offered her help. They also had a maid.

Before the summer was over, Mattie received a letter from daughter Millie. She wrote she gave birth to a baby girl on July 26, 1912. They named her Anna. "Her life was short, and she was buried in the same row with babies Abby and Hosea. Now we have three children in heaven. Although we don't understand everything, we want to submit to God's will."

Mattie enjoyed the children and grandchildren that were close by as they often helped each other with the work. In the fall, they cooked apple butter outside in a big copper kettle. The tempting aroma gave everyone an appetite for the finished product. The day before, Mattie had baked big golden loaves of bread. At times, the children stopped their play long enough to check if it was about done. Mattie assured them she would call when it was, and they could each have a slice of bread with homemade butter and fresh apple butter.

By mid afternoon, it was ready to dip into jars. Mattie ladled some into a bowl and called the children. It did not take long for them to come, and while the women were outside dipping in jars, Mattie was busy spreading bread with the fresh apple butter for the children. Oh, yum! Was it ever tasty! After the jars were filled, they divided them for each family. Daughter Sarah cherished these times with her nieces and nephews since they had none of their own. In turn, they adored her as she had a way of remembering their birthdays with a handkerchief or a card including a Bible verse as a gift. She had an indelible ink pen with which she wrote the name of the child on these little favors. Below that, she usually wrote, "From your loving Aunt Sarah."

Chapter 19
Visitors in Church - Mattie's Letter

That fall, a minister and his wife from Yoder, Kansas, and the deacon, a widower, from the same area were visiting the Amish church at Garnett. Mattie sat very attentively as the sermon was preached and realized she had many shortcomings. Then the visiting deacon stood and gave a very sincere testimony. He seemed humble as he further admonished from God's Holy Word.

Eli and Sarah invited the visitors to their home for supper, as well as a few more families. Sarah asked her mother to come. Sarah said, "Then you won't need to be alone when Menno goes to the youth singing." When Mattie mentioned it to Menno, he said he could easily come by Eli and Sarah's so she could ride with him. They went home early to chore. They milked only a few cows and had some other chores which were done quickly with Tommy's help. Soon Menno hitched his horse to the buggy and was on his way, leaving Mattie at Eli and Sarah's place. She learned that the minister was Jonas Borntrager, a bishop and his wife, and the deacon was Daniel E. Borntrager. They were both distant relatives to A.D. and son Andy's wife Susan. After supper, an enjoyable evening was spent visiting and getting acquainted. Mattie thought she detected Daniel occasionally glancing at her. Daniel saw a woman of deep faith and piety in Mattie. Later when Menno came to get his mother, he tied his horse to a post and went into the house and shook hands with the visitors. Daniel observed Menno's mannerly ways. His mother has taught him well, he thought. Soon Menno and his mother were on their way home. Mattie commented on the enjoyable evening she had.

One day Mattie received a letter from Haven, Kansas. Eagerly she tore it open wondering who would be writing her from that area. The hand writing was not Andy's or Susan's. She read,

"Dear Mattie,

Greetings in our blessed Savior's name. You are probably surprised to hear from me, but ever since that evening at Eli Beachy's home you have often come to my mind. I sensed God's presence in your life and an inner peace that I could not overlook. I have many lonely times since the Lord called my dear companion away last December. I never thought I would consider another life companion, but God in his wisdom knew the needs of a man when He said, "It is not good for man to be alone" (Genesis 2:18). My son Daniel and family live in the other house next to mine. They are good to me, and I enjoy their children. My other children also live in this area and are considerate of me, but they have their families and work. Since I am often very lonely, would you consider my friendship? I would appreciate hearing from you and your feelings toward me.

Yours in the Lord, Daniel

Mattie's heart fluttered as she contemplated an answer. She must give this some serious consideration. First she would seek the guidance of her Heavenly Father. After outliving two companions, would the Lord provide another for her? She also desired to discuss it with her children before she answered his letter. Would they give their blessing? And what about Menno?

Shortly after receiving this letter, Mattie was summoned to help Noah and Deemy with a delivery. A healthy, round-faced little girl arrived that day, December 9, 1912, and was named Katie for Deemy's deceased sister. She was their fifth child and second daughter. Little Sarah was two and quite active.

Before long, Noah and Deemy had a butchering day, and Mattie chose that time to ask the family about their opinions regarding the letter she had received from Daniel. She had previously discussed it with Menno, and he had encouraged her. As the day wore on, she found an opportunity to consult each of them at one time or another. They all seemed to think this would be appropriate for her, and some said, "You would be close to Andy and Susan and their children then." Shem mentioned they had considered moving to Reno County since Betsy's parents live there. She would attempt to send a reply by mail soon.

Mattie took her pen, ink, and tablet and began answering Daniel's letter.

Dear Daniel,

How does this find you? I am well and must say I was surprised to get a letter from you. You mentioned being lonely. I know what you mean as I am often alone when son Menno goes to the singings. My heart leaped when I read your letter. I have prayed about our friendship and also talked to my children. They encouraged me, even Menno. He is 17 and the only one at home. He seems so mature for his age. It is up to you and me if we keep up our friendship. So I can just say *Gott sie by dir.* (God be with you.)

Lovingly, Mattie

Noah and Deemy consented to go with Mattie to visit Andy's family. They would take little Sarah and baby Katie along. Since Noah was a minister, they would have a good excuse to visit in Daniel's home without arousing any suspicions. By this time Daniel had discussed his friendship with his children, and they were eager to get acquainted with these Garnett folks.

When they discussed plans for marriage, they agreed that March 27, 1913, would be an ideal day.

Soon after they returned home, Shem went to Reno County and rented a farm near Yoder. They planned to move as soon as possible.

On February 20, 1913, Shem asked Dr. Harris to come. Soon after his arrival, a son, named Joseph, like Betsy's father, was born. His name was shortened to Joe. He was born two days before his half brother Enos' thirteenth birthday. Shem's daughter Deemy was there to take care of the household duties and help pack for the move to Reno.

In the next letter Mattie had from son Andy, he informed her that they had a baby girl named Lizzie born February 12, 1913. Mattie was glad the babies had arrived in time for them to attend her and Daniel's upcoming wedding.

Chapter 20
Preparations for Wedding - More Moves

Mattie was busy sewing herself a navy cashmere dress for the special day. Nearly every week, daughter Sarah and Deemy came to spend a day. They wanted to be with her as much as possible before she moved to Reno County and also to help with wedding plans.

Sarah and Deemy wanted their mother to give them precise instructions on how to make her delicious *smear kase* or cheese spread. Try as they would, theirs did not equal their mother's. Another thing they had never mastered was the soft hand soap she made. Mattie was delighted to show them every secret she knew on these products.

Shem's family decided to move after the wedding at the same time Mother did. That way, all their belongings could be loaded on the same train.

About this time, Enos decided he was ready for another move. He had gone to Ford County to visit A.D., Millie, and their children who actually lived a few miles into Gray County at this time. Enos found out land was even cheaper in Finney County so he bought a farm there.

Much preparation was made for Mattie and Daniel's marriage. Levi and Anna agreed to move on the home place after the wedding. Many changes were taking place with Mattie and Shem's family preparing to move to Reno County and with Enos' family moving to western Kansas.

March 27, 1913, the day of the wedding, dawned bright and clear. Andy, Susan, and their two children had come by train a week earlier. A.D., Millie, and their children arrived about the same time, and Millie helped organize the final plans and prepare food. Mattie was pleased that they could come as Millie was a good hand in preparing for the wedding. The wedding guests consisted mostly of both sets of children and the church and neighbors. Daniel's children came only a few days before, and they welcomed Mattie into their family.

For the ceremony, Noah preached an inspiring sermon after which Eli Beachy joined them in marriage. The reception was well managed by Mattie's daughters and daughters-in-law preparing and serving the food and seating people at the tables. The afternoon was spent in singing. Supper was served to both sides of the family which provided an ideal opportunity for them to get acquainted. The next day most of them left for their homes by train.

Daniel and Mattie were busy finishing the packing the next week. The things she no longer needed was divided among her children. She wanted Menno to have the chest of drawers that Noah had made for daughter Mattie. Shem's family was also busy packing and seeing to last minute details. When all was completed, their belongings were hauled to Garnett and loaded on the train for Yoder. Shem, Betsy, and their children and Daniel and Mattie bade good-bye to those left behind. It was hard to leave the girls and their families and Levi's family behind. She would miss the girls' weekly visits. She was pleased Menno had consented to stay there to help Levi and Anna and their youngsters get settled into her house. Later he would join his mother.

Enos' family was ready to move to Cimarron, Kansas, located in Finney County, in a few weeks. Enos was eager to get established and had already moved some things. He had done some work on their farm when he had gone out before. Enos knew the nearest Amish church was located twenty-five miles away in the Dodge City area. However, he did not let that discourage him for he thought since land was so cheap other people would soon relocate to Finney County and help to establish a church there.

Mattie was glad that her sons, Andy and Shem, and their families would be near her in her new home. They would also be closer to A.D. and Millie, and Enos' family would not be much further. She was so glad A.D.'s had been able to spend some extra time with her before the wedding. Dannie was seven years old and Andy nearly six, and little Ida Mae was two and brought much joy to her family.

The summer of 1913 proved to be quite difficult for Enos' family. Due to a severe drought, crops did very poorly, and hungry grasshoppers devoured the little that did grow. Early one morning, A.D. and Millie and their children drove to Finney County to visit Enos' family. They found Enos was putting up Russian thistles for hay. By that time, Enos had decided that in order to survive they would need to move again and Centerville, Michigan, was being considered. He discussed the upcoming move with A.D. saying, "We can't go on like this." Since it was so far to go to church, they had attended only a few times in the year they lived there. In the early spring of 1914, Enos again loaded their belongings on the train bound for Centerville, Michigan.

A.D. and Millie were also hurt by the drought. They were impressed with Thomas, Oklahoma, and made plans to move there. Soon after their move, Millie felt so sorry for the motherless Mose Mast family in that area. The mother had been badly burned and had died as a result. She left behind her young husband and seven children who were being cared for in various homes. Millie wrote to her sister Sarah concerning them. One little girl, Barbara, was two years old, and the baby, Johnny, was less than a year old. The oldest was ten. Sarah and Eli discussed the situation, and Sarah said, "Eli, do you think the father would consider to let us have the two youngest?"

"Well, the only way to find out is to make a trip to Oklahoma and talk to their father about it," Eli answered. So they purchased train tickets and went to Oklahoma. They visited in A.D. and Millie's home and also in the motherless home of Mose Mast. After Mose sought advice from friends and relatives, he agreed to let them adopt Barbara and Johnny. Eli and Sarah were overjoyed to take these little ones home with them. Sarah said, "Perhaps God had this in mind for us when we were not blessed with children of our own." Barbara had blond hair and pretty blue eyes, and Johnny was learning to crawl. For Eli and Sarah, it was indeed a pleasure to watch these little ones grow as they filled an emptiness in their home.

By this time, Daniel and Mattie were getting adjusted in their life together. They often went to visit their children. Sometimes Menno came to visit them, then returned to Garnett again.

Daniel had two granddaughters who had married shortly before he and Mattie had married. One was Polly, daughter of Daniel's oldest son Jake. She married February 13, 1913, to Enos Mullett. The other granddaughter Mary, oldest daughter of his son Rudy, married March 13, 1913, to David K. Bontrager. These girls were seventeen and eighteen and were the same age as another granddaughter, Barbara, the oldest of his daughter Fannie and Andy Bontrager's children. These three girls were often together and had all been baptized at the same time. Mattie soon took a great interest in Barbara, and as she became better acquainted with her, she admired the qualities in her character.

Chapter 21
Meet Daniel's Daughter - Fannie's Family

Daniel and Mattie lived only a few miles from his daughter Fannie and Andy whose family will now be introduced. Andy's father had bought a 160 acre farm near Yoder, Kansas, with the intentions to move there from Indiana in time. However, this never came to pass, and instead, at the age of seventeen, Andy was sent to Kansas to care for the farm. As he batched and farmed alone on this place, he was often homesick for his parents and younger brothers and only sister Mary Ann. During this time, he had developed a deep friendship with Fannie, daughter of Daniel Bontrager's. They were both eighteen when they were married on September 20, 1894. After this, Andy found life less lonely as Fannie added a woman's touch to the home. They were happy as they worked together.

On July 12, 1895, their home was blessed with their first child whom they named Barbara as a namesake for Fannie's sister. It was a hard day for Fannie, but she felt well rewarded as she looked at the baby in her arms. The local granny and Fannie's mother were in attendance at the time.

Fannie's mother Mary whispered to Fannie that it was customary to pay these grannies a few dollars for their services. So Fannie softly conveyed the message to Andy, and he gave her a few dollars when he took her home.

That fall, Andy had a letter from his parents in Indiana to inform him that another son, Amos, was born to his parents. How Andy longed to go visit his family, but felt money was too scarce. Then on January 7, 1897, a son was born to Andy and Fannie which made Andy very happy. They named him Eddie in honor of Andy's oldest brother. Barbara grew so fast and was soon saying a few words like baby, da-da, and ma-ma.

When Barbara was two and a half years old, Andy told Fannie he felt they had a fair year, and he would buy train tickets to go to Indiana to visit his family. Fannie was busy preparing clothes for the children and themselves. Andy found someone who consented to chore for them while they were gone. Later, when Barbara was in her nineties, she commented to a granddaughter how she still remembered the red velvet seats on the train and thought, "We are riding in luxury."

Andy's parents met them at the train and took them to their house. Aunt Mary Ann immediately favored Barbara as she had no sisters, and this was as near as she would get to having one. They were close friends as long as they both lived. All too soon the time came to board the train to return to Kansas.

Andy and Fannie were kept busy when they came home. One day, Fannie told Andy, "Eddie is outgrowing the cradle, and we will soon need it for the next baby." Andy occupied himself making a box with twelve-inch sides with casters underneath. It was big enough for Barbara and Eddie both to sleep in. It could be rolled underneath the bed during the day and would save space. Fannie sewed a ticking bag, and it was filled with fresh straw for a mattress. It was then placed in the box and Barbara and Eddie were allowed to jump up and down on it until it evened out which they enjoyed.

One evening after the children were in their box bed, Mother and Father kneeled beside their bed to pray before they retired for the night. Barbara and Eddie started snickering, and soon their father came and pulled their ears a bit. That was the end of their misbehavior.

When Barbara was four years old, her parents decided to add a few rooms to their small house and put a basement under the new part. Grandmother came from Indiana to help with painting and other interior work. One day Grandma went to the basement to get something. The house was not entirely enclosed yet, and it was very windy. The wind caught her wide, wide skirt which embarrassed her terribly. Barbara laughed until she realized the embarrassment it caused her grandmother.

That fall on October 10, 1898, another son was born to Andy and Fannie. They named him William, as it was during the time William McKinley was President, and Andy thought he was such a good president.

In the fall of 1900, Barbara started to school and had a three-fourths mile walk. Her teacher wore a long dress with a full skirt, and when she walked, she lifted her dress slightly to appear more ladylike. The teacher wore her hair in a knot at the top of her head. At Christmas, she presented each child with an orange.

Barbara provided much assistance with the younger children. May 11, 1900, another baby girl was born to Andy and Fannie, much to Barbara's delight. They named her Mary as both Andy and Fannie had a sister by that name.

One cold winter day, Barbara and Eddie were awakened early as this was butcher day at *Doddy's* (grandpa's). They were told to hurry as they wanted to leave early. Before they left, they were to bring in cobs and carry in wood. Because it was still dark, they carried a kerosene lantern. As children sometimes do, they procrastinated. Finally their father came on the scene and punished both of them. From then on, they knew he meant what he said.

February 2, 1902, another son was born to Andy and Fannie, but they couldn't agree on a name. Fannie thought Dannie would be a good Amish name, but Andy wanted to name him Clarence in honor of his brother. Fannie thought Clarence was too fancy for an Amish name. As a result, he was nameless for a few months. When friends would inquire what his name was, they replied, "We haven't decided yet." Finally Andy got tired of giving the same answer every time, so he said, "Clarence." From then on, he went by that name.

That spring, Andy built a chicken house with different compartments for the setting hens. Barbara was sent to the neighbors to exchange eggs to put under the hens as her mother felt they would do better that way.

When Barbara was seven years old, a severe diphtheria epidemic swept through the community, and she was a victim. She became very ill and was in bed for quite sometime. She finally recovered, but some of their neighbor children died from it.

On the cold snowy night of January 2, 1904, Fannie needed the local granny. Andy went to their neighbors, Mose Shrocks, and asked him to go fetch her as he thought he should stay with Fannie. All went well, and the next morning when the children awoke, they discovered their mother in bed with a new baby girl. She was named Annie as a namesake for one of Fannie's sisters.

Chapter 22
Grain Hauled to Hutchinson - Move to Oklahoma

When Barbara was eight years old, her father asked her mother if she could spare Barbara for a day. "What do you have in mind?" she asked.

"Well, I have two loads of wheat that need to be hauled to Hutchinson. We have a safe team and if she would follow my team and wagon, I feel she would do fine."

Fannie said, "It may be good for her to go. I depend on her help so much. The younger ones can also help a bit."

The next morning, Father was in a hurry to get started, but Mother felt they needed a hearty breakfast before they go. She fried mush and made liverwurst and tomato gravy, then they had oatmeal for cereal to top it off. Just as the sun was starting to rise, Father had the horses hitched and helped Barbara up on the seat. Then he jumped onto the first wagon and headed out the lane with Barbara and the other wagon close behind. (No cars then to scare the horses.) It was an interesting ride for Barbara as she jostled along. At times, she saw jack rabbits run across the fields. When they passed other farmsteads, it was interesting to see those people going about their work. She wondered what those at home were doing by now. She thought maybe Eddie would have to do the dishes.

When they reached the elevator in Hutchinson, their loads were unloaded and Father collected the money. They drove the teams to the livery stables and unhitched them, then they watered and fed the horses. From there, they walked to a place where they could buy some dinner which tasted great as Barbara was really hungry after the long morning. Next they went to some stores and shopped. To Barbara's delight, Father said, "I think you need some new shoes." After trying on several pairs, they settled for some shiny black high tops. She felt really privileged and would have much to tell when they got home. Next they hitched up their horses and went to buy groceries. Father bought a barrel of crackers, one hundred pounds of sugar, one hundred pounds of flour, fifty pounds of cornmeal, a big bag of salt and last, but not least, a pound of peppermint candy. Now they were ready to head for home.

When they arrived home, it was imperative to chore immediately. Father unloaded, and Barbara ran to feed grain to the chickens and to gather the eggs. By this time, the cows were in the barn, and Barbara would need to milk at least one. After that, she went into the house and washed and set the table, then helped Mother put supper on the table. The younger children had missed her and crowded around her, eager to hear the details of her day.

When baby Annie was a month old, her parents decided to move to Custer County, Oklahoma, to be near her paternal grandmother and her four uncles and one aunt. Andy's parents had moved to Oklahoma from Indiana on August 21, 1902. His father died on January 8, 1904, only four days after the birth of Andy and Fannie's baby Annie. Now Andy felt he could be a help to his mother and her family if they were closer.

Andy and Fannie got busy preparing for a public auction. They decided to give a free sack lunch to all that attended the sale which Fannie's mother and sisters helped prepare the day before. The next day these lunches were handed out, and a big iron kettle in the yard was filled with hot coffee and was free for anyone. The relatives were served a delicious cooked meal inside.

When the day arrived to load their boxcar in Yoder, Fannie's parents and sisters and brothers came with wagons and teams to haul their belongings to the boxcar and help load. When all was loaded, Andy rode in the caboose, and Fannie and the children, Barbara, Eddie, Willie, Mary, Clarence, and baby Annie rode in the coach. They had packed some food to eat on the train. When the train finally arrived in Weatherford, the weary travelers were met by Andy's mother and brother Enos. Soon they were on the way to Grandmother's home for the night because it was too late to unload. That would take place in the morning with the help of more people.

Barbara observed how neat and clean Grandmother's house looked. With so many little ones, it was almost impossible to keep their own house tidy. Grandmother had supper prepared for them, and it was soon time to go to bed. Barbara would sleep with Aunt Mary Ann. Some of the younger children were bedded down on the floor and were soon fast asleep.

Oh, how Barbara adored her Aunt Mary Ann! Her uncle Amos was only a few months younger then Barbara and had a pretty easy life. He loved to tease. Andy's brothers, Enos and Clarence, were also still at home. Ed was married and lived nearby with their three children.

The Indians fascinated Barbara and Eddie. Many still lived in tepees at this time. Their men wore long braids, and the squaws wore colorful shawls and carried their babies on their backs.

One time Barbara's father and mother took Grandma to town with them and left Barbara and her younger siblings with Aunt Mary Ann. Mary Ann entertained them with Indian stories, then they went outside to play. They were having a good time when Mary Ann glanced down the road and saw a half dozen covered wagons coming their way. She said, "Children, come in the house quickly." Quickly, Mary Ann and Barbara ushered them inside, locked the doors, and pulled the curtains. "Now I want everyone to be really quiet," she said. Mary Ann lifted the corner of the curtain and peeked out the window. She whispered, "The wagons are driving into our lane. Sh! Sh!" Their hearts beat wildly as they wondered what would happen next.

To her relief, they watered all their horses at the well and then drove out the lane again. When they felt the Indians were far enough away, they went out to play again.

It was a hot, summer day when Father took the children to Grandma's house to spend the day. It was July 11, 1905. When he came to get them, he told them they had a new sister at home. They named her Fannie as a namesake for his mother and his wife. Barbara was really happy as the next day would be her tenth birthday. Grandma decided this would be a good experience for Mary Ann to help, and she was excited to have this opportunity. Barbara soon realized that Mary Ann was not accustomed to working so hard. Between the two of them, they somehow managed with Grandma's help until her mother could resume responsibility.

In the summer of 1906, Fannie had such a yearning to go to Reno County, Kansas, to visit her parents and siblings that Andy said she could go. He took her and little Annie and baby Fannie to meet the train. Andy had tied the horses close to the tracks as he helped them onto the train. When the train whistle blew, it scared the horses. They tore loose and ran away, demolishing the buggy. Someone helped Andy catch the horses and retie them. After that, Andy went to a hardware store and bought a brand new buggy. When he came driving into the lane, the children saw him coming and were excited about the new buggy. They could hardly wait until Mother came home so they could tell her.

Barbara was ten years old and pretty much in charge of the house and younger children. Grandma and Mary Ann came to help wash the clothes and do other major jobs.

Father raised a lot of large, sweet watermelons. One day some Indians came and wanted some. Because they had no money, they gave them two white dishes in exchange. These were always referred to as their Indian dishes.

In 1906, Barbara remembered seeing her first car. It belonged to Doctor Omar from Thomas. When the children heard its noise from a distance, they would run to see this amazing machine that needed no horse to pull it.

On March 1, 1907, another baby girl was added to their family and was named Mattie. Aunt Mary Ann helped them, but was more experienced than the previous time, and the work went better. Barbara was nearly twelve and also more capable. They helped Father plant potatoes and other vegetables.

They nearly always milked six or eight cows while sitting on a one legged stool. During the summer, the flies were often so pesky that one of the younger children would stand behind the cows waving a small branch to keep the flies away while the others milked.

Chapter 23
Move Back to Kansas - Getting Settled

In the fall of 1907, Andy said he was ready to move back to Kansas. He admitted he never liked Oklahoma very well. This thrilled Fannie at the thought of being near her family again. Andy boarded the train and went to Yoder. Word got around that he was looking for a farm. When he met Ananias Miller, he said they would like to move to Oklahoma. After some discussion, it was decided they would trade farms which proved to be a successful arrangement. Andy went home and told his family what the plans were. Fannie got busy packing dishes and other household items, and Andy sold what they no longer needed. By this time, Barbara was twelve, but with seven younger children, it took a lot of effort to get everything ready for the move. Grandma packed a big bag of food for them to eat on the train.

When the train arrived in Yoder, Fannie's dad and brothers and in-laws met them with teams and wagons to load their belongings to take to their farm.

With so much help, everything was soon in place. Dishes were unpacked, and stoves set up. The relatives all remarked how the children had grown. Barbara was glad to get reacquainted with her cousins who had grown so much since she last saw them. Father put the horses and cows in the pasture and got his tools arranged.

Soon it was time to cook apple butter in the big copper kettle over an open fire outside. Fannie liked to cook twelve to fifteen gallons every fall. The aroma was enough to stimulate anyone's taste buds. Fannie always baked eight or ten loaves of bread twice a week for their large family. That homemade bread and fresh apple butter would have been fit for a king.

Fannie was a calm person and was not easily flustered. Barbara remembered one time, however, that her mother was a bit upset. She had put cream in their barrel type churn and set it in the middle of the floor. She told the younger children they should take turns turning the crank. All went well until close to dinner time when they saw a buggy load of company driving into the lane. Quickly Fannie tried to think what to make for dinner. "Barbara, quickly wash the younger children's faces. Mary, you pick up so it doesn't look so *hudlich* (messy)." When the children became aware of the company coming, they ran pell-mell over each other trying to look out the window. In the process, they spilled the cream all over the floor. "Children! children! What shall I do?" Barbara and her mother worked as fast as they could to clean up the mess. They dipped most of it into a bucket, and the hogs had a rich diet that day.

By the time dinner was on the table, and the company seated around it, Fannie could chuckle again. By this time, the children were trying to use their company manners.

Fannie was a good cook and loved to cook for her large family. One thing that Fannie could not grasp was sewing. When she did try her hand at sewing, the finished product just did not fit properly. Her sister Annie came over and did most of the sewing for Fannie and her family. Barbara was very observant of every detail that her aunt did as she sewed. She noticed that her aunt pressed the seams flat with the sad irons that she kept on the cook stove. When she completed a garment, it looked professional and always fit neatly. Barbara dreamed of the day she would sew like that. If one of the children was in dire need of some new clothes, mother said, "Barbara, I will let you sew Eddie a new shirt. Here is the material, and here is a shirt that fits. You can make it this size." Barbara cut it out and sewed it the best she could. When she was done, Barbara could tell it was not as good as Aunt Annie's work. Her mother said, "It is fine. He needs it so badly." At times, it was a dress Mother wanted her to make for one of her younger sisters. Neatness was not a priority with her mother, but that it served its purpose.

Chapter 24
Barbara Sews - More Siblings Born

One day her mother said, "Barbara, Willie needs a new coat for church. I think you can make it." Her mother laid out the material and a pattern. "I think this is the one Annie would use. You can measure over his other coat a bit to see if it's the right size."

Barbara thought it looked like a big job, but she would try her best. She was thirteen and felt important that her mother had so much confidence in her. Barbara laid the fabric on the table then placed the pattern on top of it. She took a sliver of soap and marked around the pattern then cut it out. Now she was ready to sew. The pieces fit together surprisingly well. When Barbara had it all sewed, alas! something was wrong. One sleeve turned forward and one turned back. When she showed it to her mother, she said, "I don't know what you did wrong. We will just lay it aside until your aunt Annie comes again. Then we will ask her what is wrong." Barbara had this coat on her mind often and pondered where she had erred.

One day Aunt Annie came. Barbara shyly brought the little coat and showed it to her. Annie explained that she should have sewn the one sleeve the opposite way, and then they would both turn forward. Annie ripped out the sleeve that turned back and sewed it the opposite way, and everything was fine. Barbara never forgot that and later in life, she made many coats and men's Sunday suits.

The summer of 1909, was a busy one on their farm. While Eddie and Willie were busy helping their father, Mary helped her mother in the garden. Barbara had learned to bake bread and cook. Every spare minute, she was occupied with sewing for the large family. Annie, Fannie, and Mattie were usually playing or getting into things. Clarence was seven and could help care for his younger siblings and could carry vegetables from the garden. It took a lot of produce for the large family.

August 12, 1909, another son was born to Andy and Fannie. He was very welcome as the last three had been girls. When Fannie suggested they name him Andrew, Andy agreed. He was the ninth child for their family. At this time, Barbara was fourteen and never lacked for work.

One highlight in Barbara's life was the times they went to her grandparent's place, especially when the aunts and uncles and cousins were all there. She enjoyed her cousins, Polly oldest child of Uncle Jake's, and Mary, oldest child of Uncle Rudy's. They were almost the same age.

Her aunts, Barbara and Annie, had little children. Uncle Hans and Uncle Harrys and their children lived close by, and Aunt Mary, married to Joni Plank, lived close to Harrys. Uncle Dan and his wife Polly lived in the big house next to her grandparents. It was quite a group when they got together which happened about once a year. These were carefree years in Barbara's life.

One week, Barbara worked for Jake Yoder's wife. She cooked, cleaned, washed, and ironed. In exchange, his wife made a new overcoat for Barbara's father. There were times that Barbara helped butcher in some young mother's place. She was paid fifty cents a day for that.

When Barbara's parents butchered, they dressed a beef one day and five or six hogs the next. Neighbors and a few relatives helped. The meat was either canned or put into a salt brine in large crocks. When it was put into the brine, it would need to be soaked in clear water a day and a night before cooking it. This was done to rinse some of the salt from it. The hams and sides of pork were home cured and smoked in the smokehouse.

During the busiest time of the summer, June 28, 1911, another baby girl, Edna, was born in the home of Andy and Fannie. Barbara was nearly sixteen and could easily take over the household duties. The younger siblings ran errands and sometimes argued about whose turn it was to hold the baby. With canning, cooking, washing and all the other work, Barbara hardly found time to hold her.

When Barbara was sixteen, she started to attend the youth singings. She often rode with Mose Schrock's children, as their daughter Rosie was one of her best friends.

One Sunday, as Barbara sat meditating on the sermon, the Spirit moved in her heart, and she felt the need of a personal Savior. With tears in his eyes, her grandfather stood and gave his testimony. He warned the people of drifting from the straight and narrow way. He quoted 1 John 2:15-17, "Love not the world neither the things that are in the world. If any man love the world, the love of the Father is not in him. For all that is in the world, the lust of the flesh, and the lust of the eyes, and the pride of life, is not of the Father, but of the world. And the world passeth away, and the lust thereof: but he that doeth the will of God abideth forever." Barbara wanted the will of the Father in her life. After discussing her feelings with her cousins, Polly and Mary, and good friend, Rosie, they shared her desire to live for Jesus. These girls shared their feelings with their parents, and they encouraged them. Then the girls told the ministers of their desire to live for Jesus and started in the instruction class for baptism and church membership. Great joy came to their grandfather Daniel's heart to see his three oldest granddaughters decide to follow Jesus. In the fall of 1912, they were baptized on their confession of faith. Barbara had sewed herself a black dress for the occasion. Her white cape and apron and her black cap on her head was her attire for this very solemn day.

Barbara felt sorry for her grandpa as he was often lonely. On February 2, 1912, his wife, Mary, had become ill very suddenly. Daniel sent his son, Dan, to go to Hutchinson for the doctor. After examining her, he said, "Your wife is very sick, and operating is all I could recommend."

Andy and Fannie had been there earlier, but they needed to go home and take care of some things, then come back. Sadness crossed Daniel's face, as well as other family members, as he inquired what would be involved to operate. The doctor explained that if they had extra boards for the table, it could be done there. "We will get them," Daniel replied. Then his wife, Mary, was placed on the table, and was given chloroform and whiskey to put her to sleep. Then the doctor cut her open, performed the surgery, then sewed her shut, and she was carried back to her bed. It was soon evident that her condition was very serious. Someone was sent on horseback to notify Andy and Fannie of her critical condition. Quickly Andy hitched the horse to the buggy, and Fannie gave some last minute instructions to Barbara, and they were on their way. The ground was covered with pure, white snow with a nice moon shining. As they neared her parents' home, they suddenly saw a white figure rise above the ground and ascend upward. Andy said to Fannie, "Did you see that?"

"Yes," she said. "What do you think that could mean?"

When they arrived and entered the house, most of Fannie's sisters and brothers were already there. They said, "Mother just took her last breath a short time before you came."

Fannie had never seen her father so broken. Finally after regaining his composure, he said, "The Lord called her home, and we must carry on without her. The weather is cold, and we can keep her a few days if we keep her in a cool place before the funeral." She was fifty-nine years, five months, and ten days old. She left behind her sorrowful husband, Daniel, five sons, and four daughters and many grandchildren.

Grandfather Daniel had many lonely days. Sometimes he would hitch his faithful horse, Baldy, to the buggy and go visit his children. The grandchildren looked forward to these times as he would sit on a rocking chair and teach them the German alphabet. Sometimes he would tell stories of his boyhood days which fascinated the children as they tried to visualize their grandpa as a child.

Sometime later, the bishop and his wife wanted to go to Garnett to visit and thought it might be good for Daniel to go along for a diversion. They were aware that he had many lonely days. Daniel readily accepted their offer. He said, "It may do me good to get away." They attended church and were all invited to the Bishop Eli Beachy home for supper. Eli's mother-in-law was also there, and he learned that she was a widow. He especially noticed her sincerity. He learned that her husband, Isaac Chupp, had died in 1904. Daniel admired her faith and the way she rose above circumstances. She still had one son, Menno, at home, and he had been so kind to bring his mother there on his way to the singing. Later when he came to take her home, he had taken the time to tie his horse and to come in and shake hands with the Reno County folks. He thought that not all young men would be that considerate.

When Daniel returned home, widow Mattie Chupp's face would often come to his thoughts. He could not get her off his mind. As he visited his children one by one in their homes, he mentioned her to them to get their opinions about a friendship with her. They all agreed it might be good for him as they knew how alone he was.

As he sat down to write her, his heart was asking many questions. He thought if she would not be interested, he would feel foolish. He got down on his knees and prayed. When he arose, he felt at peace, and the writing was much easier.

But that was all behind him now, and they were married and enjoying each other's company. Since cooking was something she enjoyed, they often invited his children, one by one, with their families. Mattie enjoyed getting better acquainted with his children, and they were happy with the choice their father had made. They still missed their own mother, but they knew she was in a far better place.

His children invited them to visit in their homes anytime they desired. Mattie also enjoyed visiting sons Andy and Shem and playing with their little children. Their babies, Lizzie and Joe, were growing so fast.

On May 23, 1913, Andy and Fannie were blessed with another baby girl, Amelia. Now they had eleven children. One day Daniel and Mattie went to see the new baby, and Mattie was really impressed with their oldest daughter, Barbara. She went ahead with the work and assigned jobs suitable for the younger siblings. This gave Fannie a satisfaction knowing that the work continued even if she did not help. Andy was also a hard worker and provided well for their large family.

Chapter 25
Menno in Reno County - Singing - Barbara's Date

Mattie's son Menno had attended the Sunday evening singings a few times in Reno County, and Barbara learned to know him that way. One of her girl friends said to Barbara, "Did you notice the new boy tonight?"

"Yes," Barbara said, "I saw him." Her friend remarked she would like to get better acquainted with him. Barbara wished her well as she herself was not that impressed. But when it was time to go home, Menno asked Barbara if she would give him the pleasure of taking her home. She hesitated a little, then she answered that she would accept his offer. Since she had no other way home, she really had no good excuse to refuse.

As they drove home in his buggy, Menno spoke unrealistically. His conversation sounded so educated that she did not know what to say so that she would not appear ignorant. She did want to treat him politely as his mother was now her step-grandmother. Barbara shyly invited him into the house when they got to her home. After spending more time visiting, he prepared to leave. He asked her if he could stop by and take her to the singing on the next Sunday evening. After some hesitation, she accepted his offer.

The next morning her mother asked, "Who brought you home last night?"

When Barbara answered, "Menno Chupp," her parents seemed rather excited about it. After all, her two cousins, Polly and Mary, were already married. Seeing the reaction in her parents, she said, "He already asked to take me to the singing next Sunday evening."

"Oh, really! And what did you say?"

Barbara replied, "Because of his mother, I hated to say no, so I accepted."

"Well, we would think you wouldn't say no! After all you know your cousins your age are married. You are already seventeen and will soon be eighteen, so you must not be too picky. His mother says he is such an obedient boy, respectful of the church standards, and he never gets angry."

Although Barbara did not experience the excitement she expected would come with true love, their friendship continued. When she shared her feelings with her parents, they said, "Love grows as time goes on." They suggested she invite him over for Sunday dinner which would give them a chance to get better acquainted with him. When she invited him, he promised to come.

Her mother was very helpful to make sure they had a delicious meal. When Menno came, her father asked him to come to the living room to visit with him until dinner was ready. Father and Menno were absorbed in a lively conversation, and Barbara's father was impressed with his Bible knowledge. Before long, they were called to the table for dinner. Barbara's siblings were fascinated with their visitor and stared shyly at him. They wondered why he was their only guest and finally concluded he was attracted to Barbara.

Sometime later, Menno asked Barbara, "Would you consider me for a life companion?"

"I think I should discuss it with my parents before I give an answer."

Menno responded, "I respect that, and I will wait."

When Barbara told her parents, they gave her a hearty approval. When they asked her how she felt about Menno by that time, Barbara answered, "I hardly know what to say. I guess I feel somewhat apprehensive, and sometimes, I wonder if he really is the one for me?"

"We can understand your feelings, but if you let this chance go, you may end up with someone that won't nearly measure up to Menno. He knows the Bible so well and can sing the *Lob Lied* (a song sung at each Amish church service). He is in the church standards which many his age aren't."

The next time Menno came, he asked Barbara if she was ready to answer his question. Barbara stared at the floor as she replied slowly, "The answer is yes."

Menno held her hand and said, "Good girl. I am afraid you are so busy with your younger brothers and sisters that you don't consider yourself. Now let's discuss a date for our wedding." They decided February 26, 1914 would be an excellent time because that would be before spring work started, and her parents agreed.

When they heard the news, Menno's mother and Barbara's grandfather Daniel were pleased. Mattie commented to Menno, "From what I have observed of Barbara, she is very capable and will make you a good wife."

From then on, the work fairly flew in the Andy Bontrager home. Her parents took Barbara along to Hutchinson to buy supplies and material for her wedding dress. They found some serviceable Henrietta in dark blue that Barbara liked. Although it was priced at one dollar a yard, her parents said, "If that's your choice, we will get it for you." They informed Barbara they wanted the best for her. When they shopped for wedding shoes, they found a pair for two dollars. They also bought material for the younger girls, and Barbara was to sew their dresses, too.

Mother told Barbara she should make herself a new bonnet and white cape and apron and cap for her wedding. Barbara was kept busy sewing dresses and caps not only for herself, but also for her mother and younger sisters. Besides this, her father and brothers needed shirts and pants which she would sew. Mother (Fannie) and the younger girls were occupied with other things. Her sister Mary was thirteen, Annie, ten, Fannie, nine, and Mattie, seven. Sometimes the little girls became so silly they would forget to do their work. They would laugh and say, "Sister Barbara will be a *frau* (wife) then." Mother could not help but chuckle softly at the girls' childish talk.

As the day for the big event drew near, aunts and neighbors came to help prepare food. Besides chickens to butcher, it would take a lot of pies and cakes and other food.

While others were busy preparing the food, Barbara and Menno went to Hutchinson to get their marriage license. They were both eighteen and would not need anyone to sign for them. It was chilly, and as they rode along in the buggy with the robe tucked snugly around them, the cold wind blew in their faces. As they discussed what they still needed for their wedding, Menno suddenly stopped the horse, looked at Barbara, and said, "Should we really get married? Or shall we give it up?"

If Menno would have suggested canceling the wedding a few weeks earlier, Barbara would have consented. But now she said, "Oh, think of all the people at home preparing the last minute things. I would be embarrassed to give it up now."

"You have a point there," he said. He slapped the lines on the horse's back and called, "Giddy up!" as they proceeded to Hutchinson.

Chapter 26
Menno and Barbara Wed - Own Home

February 26, the day for which they had been so busily preparing, arrived. Menno and Barbara, along with the bridal party, went to the neighbors early where the ceremony was to be held. Those in the bridal party were her brother Eddie, and Menno's niece Deemy, and Jakie Petersheim and Lizzie Miller. Many friends and relatives attended while the cooks were busy at her home preparing the noon meal that would be served after the service.

All of Menno's brothers and sisters came, as well as her Oklahoma grandmother and Uncle Amos who was table waiter with her cousin Clara. First Eli Beachy preached, then Jonas Borntrager, who was the home bishop, joined them in matrimony and pronounced them husband and wife. Barbara was happy to see her cousin Polly and her husband Enos there and cousin Mary and her husband Dave Borntrager. They appeared to be so happy and came to extend their best wishes to Menno and Barbara.

The wedding dinner consisted of fried chicken, mashed potatoes, gravy, noodles, coleslaw, stewed prunes and raisins, mixed fruit, and cranberry and raisin pies. Layer cakes on footed stands decorated the tables. Of course, homemade bread and jam and pickles were also included.

Menno's family welcomed Barbara into their family circle which made her feel accepted. His nieces and nephews were excited that their Uncle Menno was married. His mother was glad for both of them and wished them the Lord's blessings, along with Barbara's grandpa and her parents and her uncles and aunts. Barbara's younger siblings could not comprehend what all this meant.

Barbara's father had rented a forty acre place for them southwest of Yoder. Since they could not move onto it for six weeks, Menno's brother Andy offered to let them move into three rooms of their house until their own place was ready. Her parents gave them a cow, and Menno bought two more. They milked them in his brother Andy's barn until they could move onto their rented place. Barbara's parents also gave them a team of horses. Barbara noticed that Menno's brother Andy cleaned his part of the barn every day, but Menno did not clean his part. In a few weeks, he suggested to Andy that they trade stalls as his part seemed to accumulate more manure.

But Andy only chuckled and said, "Mine would look just as bad if I didn't clean it every day."

Barbara's parents gave them a cook stove, a chest, a bed, a few chairs, and a table. For wedding gifts, they had received some aluminum cookware and dishes and many other useful things. Each was given a few quilts, along with other bedding, from their parents. Barbara got busy making curtains for the windows and hemming some feed bags her mother had given her for dish towels. Soon it was time to plant garden, and Barbara enjoyed planting seeds in the soft ground. Menno plowed some ground and sowed a few acres of oats.

Barbara enjoyed cooking for two, but she often made too much because she was accustomed to cooking for so many at home. Because everything was so much quieter than she was used to, she felt lonely at times. She especially missed her baby sister Amelia who was at such a cute stage. Sometimes when she and Menno went to visit her parents, she was allowed to bring three-year-old Edna home with them for a few days. She always added spice to their home because she was such a little chatter box.

One time when they visited Menno's brother Shem's family, Shem told them he bought a big threshing machine and steam engine to do custom work that summer. He offered to give both Andy and Menno work that summer. Shem knew Menno was mechanically inclined and would promptly detect any problem. After some consideration, both Andy and Menno accepted his offer. Shem's son Enos was fourteen and would be the water boy. It would be his responsibility to keep the water wagon available because the steamers used a lot of water.

One Sunday Menno and Barbara were invited to some friends' house for dinner. On the way home, he told Barbara to let him off close to Yoder, and he would get the train for Garnett. "What is the occasion?" Barbara inquired.

"It is really none of your business," he answered. "You go home and do the chores, then you can go to my brother Andy's for the night if you don't want to be alone."

Barbara did as she was told then drove to Andy's place, but no one was home. She felt so forsaken, she began to cry. What should she do now? Finally she decided to go to her doddy's home, Daniel and Mattie Bontrager. She sobbed as she drove along, many skeptical thoughts whirling through her mind. When she arrived, they asked where Menno was. Barbara replied that he had gotten the train for

Garnett. “Oh,” Mattie said. “He probably had some business to pursue.” Barbara stayed overnight at his mother’s house and cried herself to sleep. He never revealed what his mission was.

Soon Eli and Sarah Beachy decided to move to Reno County, too. By now, they had adopted Barbara and Johnny Mast. Their older brother, Joas, also stayed with them for some time.

Mattie enjoyed these children and readily accepted them as her grandchildren. The children loved to spend the day at doddy’s home while Eli and Sarah went to Hutchinson. Grandma Mattie would let little Barbara turn the handle of the butter churn and wash the dishes which made her feel important. Barbara would chatter to her heart’s content, and Grandma and Doddy listened. They were usually given some peppermint candy before they went home. Barbara liked to sit on the bench next to Doddy because he would spread her bread with a thick layer of Mommy’s delicious apple butter.

Chapter 27
Buying Mother's Farm – Move to Garnett

About this time, Mattie decided to sell her farm in Garnett. She discussed it with her children saying she wanted Menno to have the first chance since he was the youngest. Menno was pleased, and he bargained for a cheap price. His sisters and brothers said little because they knew it would do no good if Menno wanted it at that price. With some finances from his father-in-law, the deal was made.

In February, 1915, Menno and Barbara loaded their belongings on the train and bade good-bye to Barbara's family and Menno's mother and those of his family who lived in the area. Menno's brother Levi and Anna and children then moved into the big house beside Daniel and Mattie's house because Daniel's son Dan had bought a farm a few miles away and wanted to move on it. It was hard for Barbara to bid farewell to her family, but now that they owned their own farm, this was probably the best. She would work hard and help her husband in any way possible.

The church in Garnett was so small that everyone could sit in one room which was an adjustment for them. All of Menno's family had moved away except Deemy and Noah and their five children. Deemy and Barbara often helped each other with work and soon developed a sisterly friendship. Noah was always willing to assist Menno with his work. Before long, Barbara became good friends with another young couple, Jonas and Lizzie Beachy. They had married about the same time as Menno and Barbara. Jonas was the one who had been engaged to Menno's sister Mattie when she died. Menno and Jonas were already well acquainted at that time.

They were neighbors, and Lizzie and Barbara assisted each other with canning and various tasks. Menno was often gone during the day, and Lizzie's company kept Barbara from becoming so homesick. She always looked forward to letters from home. One day in May, as she went for the mail, she noticed a letter from home. Quickly she ran to the house and opened the envelope. She read, "This is to let you know you have another brother. He was born May 8, 1915. We named him David." Her heart tugged as she thought about the new baby. If I were closer, she thought, I could care for little Amelia who is nearly two. Baby David makes the twelfth child for my parents.

One day shortly after moving to the Garnett area, Menno came home from town, and Barbara noticed he had someone with him. When he had unhitched the horse and put it into the barn, she saw him walk toward the house with the boy. He said, "Barbara, this is Tommy. He used to live with Mamma and me before she married Daniel. I know he's hungry. Fix him something to eat." She poured a glass of milk and fried an egg for a sandwich. In short order, Tommy had downed all of it and thanked Barbara for the food. Then Menno said, "Come, let's go to the barn. Tommy, you may clean out the stables first. Then you can help chore, and we will eat supper after that."

When they came in for supper, Tommy came in, too. Barbara could not understand what was happening, so she whispered to Menno, "Is he staying here?" He assured her that was right. Barbara had a good garden, and it was easy to cook for Tommy. Menno was gone a lot of the time with Tommy faithfully doing the work.

Chapter 28
First Time Parents - Homesick - Train Ride

When Barbara got up to start the day on September 13, 1915, she told Menno she felt something would happen that day. Menno sent Tommy back to the pasture to fix fence, and Barbara sent his lunch with him. Before long, she asked Menno to get the doctor. Soon Dr. Harris came, and a baby boy was born to them, letting out a hearty cry. They named him William as a namesake for her brother. He would be called Willie for short. As she looked fondly at her newborn son, he seemed so tiny. She mused that her little brother David would probably be quite a bit bigger by now as he was four months old. It was a new experience for Barbara to be the mother instead of the big sister, and Menno was delighted to have a son.

Barbara had enjoyed sewing numerous clothes for this little one, and now she could use them. She had spent much time boiling and washing feed bags making sure all the print was removed so they would be softer for baby diapers. Deemy and Lizzie came frequently to see if she needed anything. Menno got a *maud* or maid to help while Barbara regained her strength.

When Mother Mattie and Doddy found out about the newborn, Mattie suggested they go to Garnett and help which was fine with Doddy. They boarded the train in Yoder and Menno met them at the Garnett depot. How Mattie rejoiced for this new grandson! She said, "My prayer is that you can bring him up in the fear of the Lord." It seemed wonderful to Mattie to be back on the place she had called home for so many years. They also spent a lot of time at Deemy and Noah's place and enjoyed being with those grandchildren again. She noticed how the children were growing and commented on it which made them feel important. Tommy was also glad to see Mattie again. Doddys spent a few weeks and also visited Jonas and Lizzie. Mattie was glad Jonas had found a good wife.

Barbara was young and soon regained her strength. Before long, she helped milk the cows, feed the chickens, and bring in the eggs. Often little Willie was crying when she came into the house. He was a fussy baby which disturbed Menno. When morning came, he would say he felt too tired to get up after having his sleep disrupted by a crying baby. He said he did not feel very well anyhow. Barbara thought she was strong, and she would go out to milk and chore so

Menno could get his rest. Because Menno liked to go to Garnett every day, he had little time for his work at home. Tommy was a good worker and able to do about anything that needed to be done. He had a home and food to eat, but at times he got discouraged. He wondered if there was any future in working for Menno. One day when Menno was gone, Tommy came in and went upstairs without saying a word. Soon Barbara thought she heard a thump but thought nothing of it. Quietly Tommy came downstairs and went outside. She saw him go around the house and pick up a bundle, then head out the lane. They never saw Tommy again.

That evening when Menno came home and put his horse away, he was upset that the work he had given Tommy to do was not completed. He questioned Barbara, and she told him what she knew. Menno said, "Here we give him a home and he acts like that. He will learn a lot in life yet."

As time went on, Barbara never knew what to expect when Menno came home from town. Often he brought some tramp along and said, "Barbara, fix this man something to eat." During the winter, the chickens laid fewer eggs, and she hardly had anything to prepare. Somehow she managed to find something to feed them. Menno would often get these fellows to chop or split wood for their food.

Barbara was so homesick that winter that she could hardly eat. How she longed to see her family, especially her little sisters, Edna and Amelia. She also desired to see her baby brother David and to compare him with their little Willie.

One evening Menno said, "If you are so homesick, I will put you and Willie on the train, and you go visit your family and stay as long as you want." Barbara was quite thrilled, and she could hardly believe what she heard. She thought how good it would be to see her parents and all of her siblings again.

She lost no time writing her parents telling them when to meet the train. She packed her suitcase, and Menno took her and baby Willie to board the train. Although it started to snow lightly on the way to the train, Barbara was not discouraged for she was eager to see her family again.

When the train pulled into Yoder, it was snowing and blowing hard. Her brother Clarence was there to meet her with the big two seated buggy. For some reason, they could not find her suitcase when she got off the train. All she had was her diaper satchel containing only one change of clothes for Willie and some diapers.

When they arrived at the home of her parents, she cried for joy to see all of them. Her mother met them at the door and gave Barbara a hug and kissed her, then took little Willie, their first grandchild, into her arms. Barbara noticed Edna's dress was rather short and how she had grown since she had last seen her. Amelia acted shyly at first. She rejoiced to see her baby brother David for the first time, and, yes, he was bigger then her little Willie. Her sisters were quite capable with the work, and Mother was busy with the baby. Before long, her father and the boys returned from the chores in the barn, and she greeted each of them. Barbara enjoyed the bountiful supper they had prepared. She had not eaten much on the train.

While they were eating, she told them that her suitcase did not get to Yoder with her. She mentioned she did not know how she would dress for church the next day as she had only one change of clothes for her baby and none for herself.

"By the way, Aunt Mary Ann from Oklahoma sent you a package, and it came today," her mother commented. "She wrote that she heard you and your baby were coming here for a visit." Barbara took the package and opened it quickly.

"Well, look here, she sent a new light blue dress and apron for Willie. How nice of her! He can wear it to church tomorrow." Barbara tried on a few of her sisters' dresses until she found one that fit her that she could wear to church. Her sisters took turns holding Willie until he wanted nobody but his mother.

It was pleasant for Barbara to once again sit in the church she had attended while growing up and to see her old friends and cousins. Her cousin Polly and Enos, had a little boy nearly two years old, and cousin Mary and Dave, had two children, a boy and a girl. To Barbara, hearing the familiar voices of the ministers she heard in her younger years was very comforting. She also enjoyed hearing her grandfather Daniel give a testimony and admonish against the evils of the world. Menno's mother lovingly held Willie in her arms and remarked how he looked so much stronger than Menno had when he was a baby. She said, "I wish Menno could have come, too, but I suppose he was too busy." Barbara hardly knew what to say.

Barbara stayed busy sewing for her mother while she was there. She cut some things to take along home to sew later. Barbara and Willie went to visit Doddy and Mattie, and they gladly took her to visit Menno's brothers, Shems and Andys, and Eli and Sarah and their new family. Since Levi and Anna lived in the other house by Doddys, she visited them and also some of her aunts and uncles.

Before long, the time came when she knew she needed to go home. She wrote Menno when she would come, and he was there to meet them at the train. On the way home, he informed her that Jonas and Lizzie had a baby girl a few days earlier and had named her Barbara. "Oh! I had hoped to be home when that took place," Barbara exclaimed. Soon she busied herself making a little dress for the baby. When they went over to see the baby, Barbara tried to return some of the help Lizzie had given her when Willie was born. She thought of Lizzie as more like a sister than a friend.

Barbara had many things to tell Menno about her trip. She said, "Menno, your mother said they went to Custer County, Oklahoma, to visit Millie and A.D. recently. Their boys, Dannie and Andy, are ten and nine, and little Ida Mae is nearly four and adds a lot of sunshine to their home. She says Millie's health isn't good. Your mother says they plan to go to Centerville, Michigan, when the weather gets warmer to visit Enos' family. Enos was ordained to the ministry since they live there. Their three oldest boys are grown, and that gives Enos more time to study and prepare his sermons. She said Sarah and Eli are enjoying their adopted children. Their children like to stay with Doddys when Elis need to leave them for a day. When Doddys took me there, Sarah loved holding Willie, and little Barbara enjoyed it, too. Doddy is still driving his faithful old horse Baldy. They still have their wiener dog for a pet. Now I want to hear how it went for you while I was gone," Barbara finished.

"Well, you know Deemy told me to come eat there any time I want, and others also invited me for meals. I managed, but I am ready to have a cook again," he said with a twinkle in his eyes.

"I appreciate that you let me go, but I am also glad to be at home again."

Chapter 29
Three New Matties Born All Cousins

On February 18, 1916, Noah and Deemy's children drove into Menno's lane and said they could spend the day. Isaac was thirteen and was old enough to drive. Of course, Barbara surmised what was happening. Before the day was over, Noah stopped by and said they had a baby girl named Mattie. "Oh, I know that will please Mother," Menno said. Now Noah and Deemy had three boys and three girls. Barbara said, "I want to come and help a day."

The following week, Menno's mother wrote that Shems had a new baby girl born February 20, only two days after Noah and Deemy's baby arrived, and they named her Mattie. She was the third of Menno's nieces named in honor of his mother. Enos' Mattie was several years older since she was born in 1902.

It seemed 1916 was the year for babies as October 30, Andy and Susan also had a baby girl named Mattie. Then on November 16, that same year, Levi and Anna had a baby girl, and they named her Fannie.

As Willie became a little older, he did not cry as much. Instead he got into all kinds of mischief. Barbara had to watch him constantly and was glad the yard was fenced. Every day, she wired the gate securely so he couldn't get out. One day, when Barbara went outside to check on him, she could not find him. She called, but got no answer. Oh, she wondered, where could he be? The gate was still wired. As she walked around the yard looking for a clue, she found a place where he might have crawled under the fence. Suddenly she thought of the barn where Menno had a big stallion and quickly ran to check. There she saw him, right in the pen with the stallion holding a stick in his hand. Barbara was exasperated. She went out and called the hired man as Menno was gone as usual. The man came quickly and rescued little Willie. Barbara held him close and breathed a prayer of thanksgiving for his protection.

On June 19, 1917, Barbara informed Menno that he should call for Dr. Harris. Soon after the doctor came, another son was added to their home. They named him Daniel for Barbara's doddy, although they always called him Dannie.

Menno fetched Lydia Shrock to work for them. She had also helped them when Willie was born. She had a sense of humor and was usually capable of anything asked of her. During the time she worked there, an old stray blind dog came to their place. Although Menno tried to run him off, he was unsuccessful. One evening, Menno asked Lydia if she would like to make fifty cents. "Sure," she said, "what's the catch?"

"Well, if you kill that stray dog, I will give you fifty cents."

She thought that would be pretty good pay and agreed to his offer. After supper, she got a string of twine and tied it around the dog's neck. Then she led him back through the fields and woods until she came to some neighbors who had boys. She asked their boys to kill the old dog for her, which they did.

When she got back it was about bedtime, and she informed Menno that the dog was dead. Menno gave her the money she bargained for. Later Menno, who had a sense of humor, found out what really happened and got a good laugh out of it.

Barbara had a busy summer with a baby and a two-year-old. Although Dannie was a contented baby, Willie kept her on the run most of the time.

That fall, Barbara had a letter from her mother to let them know she had given birth to a baby girl. She was born October 28, 1917, only four months younger then their little Dannie. This was their thirteenth child, and they named her Ida. Her sister, Mary, was seventeen and the younger ones also helped a lot. Her brother Eddie was twenty and had a friendship with a young lady, Elizabeth Miller.

Chapter 30
New Buildings on New Farm - The New Car

One day in 1918, Menno told Barbara, "I have decided to buy that eighty acres that joins our place on the west."

Barbara asked, "Do we have the money for that? You know it's pretty risky if we don't have the money."

He replied, "A person never makes anything unless he sticks his neck out. We will build a new house and barn and also a chicken house."

"Remember, everything costs now days," Barbara remarked.

"You look on the dark side too much," he answered. Barbara sensed she had said enough. After all he had to make the living.

Deemy and Noah were blessed with a baby boy, Eli, on February 13, 1918. One evening Barbara fixed an early supper, then they went to Noah's place to see the new baby. Menno knew his brother-in-law always had money, so he told Noah, "I plan to buy the eighty to the west of where we live. I will need $10,000 as I plan to put a set of buildings on it. Could you loan me that amount?"

Noah said, "I will need some time to think about it. You know that's a lot of money for a young man to go in debt." Noah talked it over with Deemy, and she felt they should loan it to Menno. Noah knew Menno was a good carpenter and could do the work himself if he felt like it.

This gave Menno new courage, and he got busy putting up the buildings. First he built the house, then the barn, and last the chicken house. Everything cost more than he had planned. They moved there, and like usual, the money was scarce. They had some cows and hogs but no money for feed. The hogs became awfully skinny, and if a chicken came close to them, they devoured it. Menno loved horses and owned thirty-five head, but without feed, they did not do well either.

Shem's daughter, Deemy, worked in Thomas, Oklahoma, the fall and winter of 1917, and had her home with A.D. and Millie. A young widower, Benj Yoder, from that area became attracted to her and came often to visit her at A.D.'s. By and by, he proposed and they set their wedding date for April 11, 1918. Deemy was twenty-four, and her grandma was happy for her. The wedding was held in that area of Oklahoma. Her parents and Grandma Mattie and Doddy made a trip to attend the special event. Noah and Deemy also attended, but Menno and Barbara were too busy getting established in their new home.

One day in 1918, Barbara went to get the mail and noticed there was a letter from her mother. She tore it open as she ran for the house, then she sat down to read it. As she read, her mind went in a whirl. Was this real or was it a bad dream? Yes, she was awake, and tears filled her eyes as she continued reading. How could her father do such a terrible thing? Her mother wrote that her own father had gone to Hutchinson one day and had come home with a car. Barbara had seen some of those contraptions, and they made so much noise that it scared the horses something dreadfully. Oh, yes, Dr. Harris had one, and she did not like to meet him on the road with his machine. Her mother wrote that he had given all the younger children rides out in the pasture that very evening. She wrote that it had broken her heart, and while she was crying, innocent little seven-year-old Edna came bouncing in, laughing, and said, "Mom, why do you cry? You should come out, and Dad would give you a ride, too."

"Supper was waiting when Father and the children came in and washed up to eat. I had no hunger left by then," her mother wrote. "The children ate heartily. After supper was finished, and the family was sitting in the living room, except for the younger ones who were already in bed, your father got awful sick. He had so much pain in his side, and finally Clarence rode the horse to the neighbors that had a phone and called for the doctor. Just before the doctor came, his pain left him. When the doctor examined him, he said he must go to the hospital in Hutchinson and have an operation. On the way to the hospital, we stopped at Joni Planks, my sister Mary, and asked her to come over for the night in case baby Ida got hungry since her baby is only a month younger. Then she could also nurse our baby. Your father's appendix was ruptured, and he is a very sick man. Pray that through all this, he could see his mistake and decide to sell that machine."

Barbara was also grieved for her father and hoped he would realize his error and repent.

Her brother Eddie and Elizabeth Miller got married June 2, 1918. Barbara knew they, too, were grieved that her father had a car.

A Mennonite church was getting started in the area, and Father and some other Amish families left the Amish church and helped to establish it.

Mother Mattie wrote that Shem's family was blessed with a baby girl born December 12, 1918. She was named Edna and was not as strong as some babies. She lived only until January 4, then she passed away.

Menno built this house near Garnett, Kansas. It's still standing.

Chapter 31
Three Orphans - Menno's Move - Baby Girl

On January 13, 1919, Menno received a telegram from Reno County informing him that his brother Andy's wife, Susan, died after a battle with the flu. This virus had already claimed many lives. Andy was left with three little children: Levi, seven, Lizzie, five, and Mattie, two. Menno went by train for the funeral. Barbara did not want to take the children, therefore, she did the chores.

Early in 1919, Menno sold what had been his mother's farm and bought the Halstead place. Although Barbara was not eager to move again, she packed their things as she saw no way out of it.

Menno's niece, Deemy and Benj, had their first baby, a daughter, April 24, 1919. They named her Anna in honor of Deemy's mother who had died when Deemy was in her early teens.

Later in the summer of 1919, on July 23, Menno went to call Dr. Harris to ask him to deliver a baby for them. This time they were blessed with a girl, and they named her Mary. Willie and Dannie were happy with a baby sister. Barbara's sister Mary from Reno County came to work for them while Barbara regained her strength. It was a pleasure to have her sister there, and the boys enjoyed being with their aunt Mary. All too soon, it was time for her to leave again, and Barbara was alone to do her work.

One time Barbara fixed a bed on the hickory rocker for baby Mary while she went to the garden to gather some vegetables. She told Willie, "If the baby cries while I am outside rock the chair a bit, very slowly." Soon the baby cried, and Willie quickly ran over and rocked the chair, but a bit too hard, and she fell off the chair. When he ran outside to tell his mother, she said, "Oh, did you pick her up?"

Willie said, "No, I didn't know where to get hold of her." Quickly Barbara ran into the house and picked up the crying child. Fortunately she did not seem to be hurt, for the pillow and blanket had slid down with her.

Another time, when they lived on the Halstead place, baby Mary was sleeping contentedly, and both boys were outside playing. Barbara decided this would be a good time to mop the kitchen floor. Suddenly, while she was busy mopping, she heard a loud shot, like a gun, outside. Instantly she dropped the mop and ran outside to look.

Seeing a cloud of dust, she ran in that direction calling, "Willie, Willie," then "Dannie, Dannie." She received no answer. When the dust finally settled, she found Dannie contentedly playing beside the shed. Eventually she found Willie and learned that he was the guilty one. He had run and hidden when the gun fired because it scared him so badly. Willie had climbed to where some hunters had their guns stored. Menno had given them permission to store them there, thinking they were out of the children's reach. When Willie handled one, it was loaded and went off. It shot in the dirt floor of the shed and caused a quite a cloud of dust. Again Barbara breathed a prayer of thanksgiving that her little boys were not hurt.

To earn a little income, Barbara sewed for others. When Willie was four, she taught him to make cornbread. Then she would cook beans and bacon to go along with it, and that made a good supper. They often ate cornbread with milk for supper.

Many times when Menno was gone for the day, Barbara hitched up the horse and, with her three little children, she went to spend the day at Noah and Deemy's house. Deemy was as close to her as any of her own sisters.

On September 6, 1919, Deemy gave birth to a baby girl named Millie in honor of Deemy's sister. They now had eight children, four boys and four girls. Their Sarah was nine, and Barbara marveled at the many things she could do to help her mother.

Early that fall, Menno told Barbara he was going to Reno County on business. He said, "I know you are scared to stay alone at night, so I made arrangements for someone to come spend the night with you and the children. She is a black lady, Mrs. Spotsville, and I have high regards for her."

Sure enough, about nine o'clock that evening a carriage drove into the lane. It was driven by the black lady's husband, and he was bringing his wife to spend the night. Barbara stepped outside to invite her into the house, and her husband hollered, "Did you cry yet?" Barbara had cried, but she was not going to tell him.

When Mrs. Spotsville came into the house, she said, "I don't know why Menno asked me to stay with you. If someone would come, I'd run." She proved to be really nice, and all went well.

Menno was always friends with the blacks, probably due to his memories of Mississippi as a young boy. One evening he invited eight or ten of them to come to their house to sing. They sang wholeheartedly, and everyone had an enjoyable evening. Barbara served them blackberry pie afterward, which they enjoyed immensely.

Halstead Farm House

Chapter 32
Storm Hits - Runaway Boys

Later in the fall of 1919, Menno, Barbara, and children went to Noah and Deemy's farm to spend the day. Barbara did some sewing, and Menno helped Noah with some task. After eating an early supper, they noticed dark storm clouds gathering. "The way those clouds look, I think we had better go home," Menno announced. When they got home, Barbara, with baby Mary in her arms and the little boys hanging onto her dress, ran for the house while Menno quickly headed for the barn to unhitch. Before he reached the barn, a severe hailstorm struck. Barbara and the children, however, got inside safely just in time. Windows were crashing, and Barbara ushered the boys ahead of her and the baby into the pantry. Menno dashed for the house as soon as he thought he safely could. By the time the storm ended, the pantry window was the only one that was unbroken. Everything in the house was drenched with water. Outside they found hail as large as hen eggs. The cabbage, corn, and other vegetables were shredded; however, they were able to salvage a few ears of corn. The corn crop was ruined. All the young fryers were killed, and Barbara skinned and butchered them that night, soaking them in a strong salt brine overnight. The next morning, hail was still piled around the house. Weeks later, they still found tiny pieces of glass in the house.

Many times when it was time to get up in the morning, Menno would say, "I just don't feel very well." Barbara would milk the cows, slop the hogs, and feed the chickens. Then she would return to the house to prepare breakfast and dress the children. Then Barbara announced, "Breakfast is ready."

Menno would respond by saying, "If you would give me a good back rub, I think I would feel better and could get up." Obediently she would rub his back, and he would get up. How thankful Barbara was for her good health and that she didn't have so many ailments.

Later when Barbara heard from her mother, she wrote, "Your father is gaining from his operation. So far he hasn't repented from buying that machine. Father has people praying that I and the children would also join the Mennonite church. But the more he talks like that, the harder I pray that I can remain steadfast to the Amish faith. Otherwise he is good to me and makes sure I have a horse and buggy ready to go to church on Sundays. I just pray the children will stay Amish. They don't understand what it's all about. He doesn't mind wearing Amish clothes, but he has always liked anything with a motor."

Because she lived away from her family, Barbara often felt lonely. Menno's frequent absences also contributed to her feelings of loneliness. Deemy had often told her to come and spend the day with them at those times. Barbara often went to Jonas Beachy's home, too. Lizzie and Barbara enjoyed working together. Lizzie also lived away from her family, and this seemed to make the bond between them stronger. They seemed almost like sisters. Their children were close in age and enjoyed playing together.

One day when she was very lonely, Barbara decided she would bring the horse in from the pasture and go to visit Noah and Deemy. It had rained, so she put on her overshoes to go fetch him. She noticed the horse was in a plowed field. It was so muddy, she got stuck with her overshoes. As she pulled and yanked to get out of the mud, her overshoes remained firmly in the ground. Right then, she gave it up to go. As she waded mud halfway to her knees, she prayed she would be able to return to the children. Finally she made it home to her little ones who gladly welcomed her. Later when the ground was dry, she went back to retrieve her overshoes.

One day, Barbara got a letter from her mother, and she wrote, "We are sad because Clarence and a neighbor boy, Enos Knepp, ran away. They plotted with each other, doing some things of which we parents disapproved. Now we don't know where they are. Clarence had wanted a motorcycle, but we felt that would be no good for him."

When Barbara told Menno, he said, "I heard those two boys are in this area. I will see if I can find them." He did find them and persuaded them to come stay at their place. They told Barbara not to write their parents of their whereabouts. Barbara did not promise, and she did write to tell them so they would not worry.

One evening, Barbara packed a picnic lunch, and they went to the creek to fish and to eat their supper there. While they were wading in the water and fishing, they heard a car coming. In those days, a car made enough noise to be heard from quite a distance. Clarence suspected it might be his dad. The boys were ready to flee, but Barbara pleaded with them and persuaded them to stay. When the car arrived, they saw it was Barbara's father and Levi Knepp, Enos's father, and her sister Fannie. They came down to the creek and joined them, but said little.

After spending the night, both fathers spoke privately with their erring sons. They asked what it would take for the boys to go back with them. "Well," Clarence said, "if I could have a motorcycle, I would come home."

Enos told his dad, "If you get me a buggy, I will come home." The fathers promised to fulfill their wishes, and two happy boys went home with their fathers.

A year and a half later, Barbara's mother wrote that Clarence became a Christian. He made restitution with those he had wronged and was baptized in the Mennonite church. One day, his father asked him to plow the orchard which was a job that tried anyone's patience, plowing around all those trees. Since Clarence did it willingly and without complaining, they knew his conversion was real.

Menno had a convincing way to get people to lend him money and was getting deeper and deeper into debt. Once, as a last resort, a certain person came and took his livestock and sold it in order to get the money Menno owed. Menno then went to a neighbor, crying and saying how badly he was treated, so the neighbor loaned him $300 with the promise that Menno would pay it back soon. Some years later, when these folks were old and unable to work, they wrote to Menno pleading to be paid, but to no avail.

One evening when Barbara came into the house from doing the chores, Dannie was chasing Willie with a stick that was burning on one end. He had opened the stove door and held the stick inside until it caught fire. Quickly Barbara grabbed it from him! As she noticed the corner of the quilt on the couch had a corner burned off it, she let out a sigh. "Oh! what next?" she said out loud. Little Mary was still sound asleep and unaware of any danger.

Chapter 33
Siblings Go Mennonite - Number Fourteen Born

The letters from home kept Barbara informed of what was happening. At times, some of her siblings went to church with her father, and others went to the Amish church with her mother. Now her brother, Will, had a girlfriend and had joined the Mennonite church. Her sister Fannie, fourteen, had also joined before her mother realized what was transpiring. Her brother, Will, and Martha Yoder married March 25, 1920.

Barbara received a letter from her mother in May, 1920, informing them that Barbara had a baby brother. He was born May 16, 1920, and was named Enos. He was the fourteenth child of Andy and Fannie, and Barbara was the oldest. She hardly knew her younger siblings.

On Christmas eve when Mary was one and a half years old, Barbara was in the kitchen popping popcorn. A person dressed like a Santa Claus knocked on the door. When Menno opened it, he stepped inside and set down a basket with fruit, candy, and lots of goodies inside. It scared Mary so badly to see a person dressed like that, she ran to the kitchen crying and screaming. This Santa Claus quickly left, and, though they were not certain, they suspected it was a neighbor who knew they were desperately poor.

Menno's mother Mattie wrote regularly and, after hearing some of the daring things little Willie attempted, was always concerned about him. "Do take good care of him," she instructed.

She had heard about Menno's business dealings and also warned him to be careful or he might lose everything. "Menno, will you be able to come for your brother, Andy, and Katie Borntrager's wedding? They have their wedding date set for November 4, 1920. She is a cousin to his first wife. I will be glad for his children. Lizzie has stayed here with Doddy and me much of the time. I enjoy having her but know it is best if the children can all be together again. Little Mattie stays at Shem's a lot, and Levi has been with his dad most of the time."

From your loving mother

Menno heard of a new settlement starting in Missouri. He spoke to Leff Yoder about it, and Leff and his wife went with him to see how they liked it. They left on February 22, 1921. Jacob Beachys invited Barbara and her little children to their home on Sunday so she wouldn't get so lonesome. She appreciated people's thoughtfulness.

Once when they had a letter from Menno's sister Millie, she wrote that their home was blessed with a baby girl by adoption. She was born March 5, 1921. She was only ten days old when they got her, and her name was Alma. She wrote, "Ida Mae is a very happy girl to finally have a sister. The rest of us are happy, too. Ida Mae often begged and prayed that she would have a sister. Her wishes are finally fulfilled. She is a good baby, and we all enjoy her."

On September 21, 1921, another daughter was added to Menno and Barbara's home. They named her Anna as a namesake for one of Barbara's sisters. Barbara had unpacked her baby clothes beforehand and patched them as they were getting threadbare after three older children had worn them. Barbara knew they had no money for any new clothes, so they must somehow make do. How happy Barbara was for a girl so little Mary would soon have a playmate! Their *maud* was a girl named Susie, and she confided in Barbara concerning a certain boy she was dating. For some reason, she did not feel right about him. What would Barbara advise? "If you are not sure, quit him now." Susie took her advice and later met someone about whom she had no doubts, and had a happy marriage.

On June 18, 1922, Noah and Deemy were blessed with another son. He was named Andrew in honor of Deemy's brother. Their children were growing, and the oldest, Isaac, was eighteen and able to do a man's work.

One day, Menno asked Barbara to cook a good dinner as several oil men would be coming. Barbara busied herself slicing some home cured ham, mashing potatoes, and preparing a full course meal. She also baked pies for dessert. Menno got paid well for the meal. At this time, Barbara had a hen with twenty-six fluffy little chicks that she lovingly cared for. Before the men left, they bought the pretty little chicks and the mother hen from Menno for six dollars. When Barbara heard about the transaction, it brought tears to her eyes. Of course, Barbara never saw the money.

They were so desperately poor, but still Menno smoked his pipe, and also chewed tobacco. Barbara pleaded with Menno to give up the pipe. She rejoiced when he threw it into the stove. Her joy, however, was short-lived. He promptly reached into his coat pocket and produced a brand new pipe. He laughed at the trick he had played on her and sat, smoking to his heart's content. He had a spittoon next to his chair, and Barbara made the little boys scrub it well every week. She prayed they would never use the stuff, and they never did as they hated the job so much.

Andy and Katie were blessed with a baby girl on November 26, 1922. They named her Millie like Andy's sister. Katie had a difficult time and never regained her strength. She died December 8, 1922, leaving her tiny baby motherless. This brought great sorrow to Andy as the children again needed to be placed in various homes.

On June 26, 1923, Menno received a telegram that his sister Sarah's husband, Eli Beachey, died in the hospital in Hutchinson. He died as a result of a hernia operation at the age of fifty-one. His death was hard on Sarah and her adopted children, Barbara and Johnny. Life had so many trials. Mattie could well empathize with Sarah, having lost two companions herself.

Chapter 34
Seafer's Farm - Son Born - Flood - Bootleggers

In September of 1923, Menno and Barbara and their children moved onto the Seafers' farm beside Cedar Creek. Since there was only one house, Seafers let them move into one part while they lived in the other part. Barbara hated to move again, but she knew, with finances as they were, they had no other choice.

A month later Barbara informed Menno she needed the doctor. He called Dr. Harris, but he refused to come. He said, "You must pay me to deliver your other four children first." Menno knew he was unable to do that, so he called young Dr. Hood. He consented and, with Mrs. Seafers' assistance, he delivered a baby boy. They named him Leroy. The boys were thrilled to have a baby brother. Leff Yoders were kind enough to let their daughter Katie help with the work while Barbara recuperated.

One day some Gypsies came driving down their lane with their covered wagon and a team of horses. When Barbara answered the door, they related such a sad story to her that she gave them some things. They kept asking for more things until Leff's Katie, the *maud*, was afraid they would also get the baby. She finally took the baby and the other children into the bedroom so they would not get them. Barbara was stunned and did what they said until they asked for a horse, then she came to her senses and said, "No." At last they left.

Menno had big dreams of making a fortune with chickens on the Seafers' place. He built two large chicken houses, and they lived in one. It had a partition in it, and one part was used for a kitchen and the other part for a bedroom and living room. Willie and Dannie slept in the kitchen area, and the others slept in the other room.

One day while they lived there, it rained so much that they were flooded. The creek overflowed, and water came gushing through the chicken house where they were living. Menno was not at home, and Barbara put the children and things she did not want wet on top of the table. Oh! Where could they go? Barbara saw the water rise over the fences, and the hogs floated away! The garden was covered, and all of it washed away. She was reminded of Noah and the ark, only they had no ark. She prayed the Lord would protect them, and her prayers were answered. When the water finally went down, they had a mess to clean up, but no one was harmed.

One morning, they discovered one of the horses had somehow broken its neck and died. They experienced so many hardships while they lived there that Barbara sensed the Lord must be trying to show them something.

It was during this time that Menno refused to go to church which was hard on Barbara. One Saturday, she pleaded with Menno to go the next day. He finally said, "If the road isn't frozen we can go. You know the horse isn't shod and can't go on frozen ground." Barbara prayed that the ground would not freeze. At midnight, she went outside to check and was pleased to see that it was not frozen. She knew the Lord had answered her prayers as she returned to bed for more sleep. But the next morning Menno had another excuse not to go. Sunday after Sunday they were just at home.

One Sunday, Noah Yoder's boys came with team and wagon and took the family to their home to spend the day. Barbara and the children were very happy to go somewhere for a change. The meal was such a treat for Barbara as Deemy and the girls had cooked such a good dinner for them. So often Barbara had very little food on hand to prepare. They often ate cornbread and beans or cooked mush, fried squash, tomato gravy, or wild berries if they were in season.

One day when Menno came home from town, he brought two guys in an old car with him and told Barbara they would eat dinner with them. Barbara was immediately wary of the strangers. Somehow she managed to scrounge up enough food for them to eat. After dinner, Menno took those fellows back to the woods and showed them around. Later when she questioned Menno about what those men were doing, he said, "They will cut down some timber for us." One day when Barbara knew they had quit for the day, she walked back to the woods and saw the big pile of trees they had cut. In her mind, she wondered what was going on because she often had to hunt for enough wood for her cookstove. She dared not ask.

Menno went to town every day, always tying the egg case to the back of the buggy. Barbara could not figure that out. She knew the chickens were not laying very well, but she knew better than to ask any questions.

The sugar bin was completely empty, and she had scraped the bottom to get every tiny granule. One evening, Menno came home from town with a hundred pounds of sugar. She was delighted as she envisioned the good things she could bake and cook with it.

But alas, the next day when she went to get sugar, it was all gone. What had become of it? When she asked Menno, he said, “You ask too many questions.” She also noticed that her empty jars were disappearing. This also mystified her, but she knew her questions would remain unanswered.

One day when Menno was gone and the guys in the woods had also left, some hunters came and asked if they could hunt. Barbara gave her permission as she knew Menno had usually allowed hunters to hunt at other places where they had lived. The hunters had a dog with them, and soon it chased a rabbit into the big brush pile. The hunters went over and discovered a slight opening at one end of it. Upon further investigation, they found a still and all the necessary equipment to make booze. In fact, they had fixed makeshift living quarters in there. The hunters soon left and went back to town, reporting their find to the authorities.

In a few days, the law came out to the farm and searched the house. They investigated under the beds and in every nook and corner. The hired man, Ernie Van Vee, saw who was there and quickly covered the booze in the haymow with hay. The law officers, seeing Barbara’s innocence, left for that day. They returned the evening of January 31, 1924, when Menno and his helpers were at home. This time they found what they were seeking and arrested Menno and the men and hauled them to jail. Menno assured Barbara, “Don’t worry. It’s a big mistake, and I will come home again.”

On February 9, Menno came home, a humble man. He stayed home and got busy on some work and hired Mose Beachy to help him. On the 27th of February, the law came and got Menno again because the other two men broke out of jail and skipped country, never to be heard from again. However, he was soon released on parole until after the trial.

Chapter 35
Menno to Prison - Family Moves to Reno County

The trial came up in April, and Menno told Barbara to be there with all the children except Willie. "Be sure to leave him at home because he might say something that would convict me. If they see the other children they will see how much I'm needed at home." So, with a heavy heart, Barbara did as she was told. She sat in the courtroom holding her baby Leroy, and Dannie and the girls, Mary and Annie, on either side of her.

Menno hoped to be proven innocent. The lawyer who defended him would hit the side of the still and say, "A still like this can only come from the moonshine state of South Carolina." The noise of his fist on the still echoed through the courtroom.

Then the prosecuting attorney took the stand and asked Barbara, "Is it true that your jars and sugar were disappearing?" Barbara answered that it was true, for she could not lie.

The trial lasted two days, and Barbara and the children were there both days. After the trial, Menno was sentenced to three years in prison at Ottawa, Kansas. Barbara went home with a heavy heart. She must put her whole trust in her Heavenly Father. She spent much time in prayer.

Folks were so kind to Barbara. A couple boys from Reno County came and cut wood and piled it close to the house so Barbara could easily get it for her cookstove. Church people brought food and clothes for Barbara and the children.

Barbara sewed dress suits for men and boys for a little income. She was a neat seamstress and had plenty of orders to keep her busy. Sometimes she was given old suits. She ripped them up, turned out the wrong side, and made suits for her little boys out of them. After they were sewed and neatly pressed, they had a new look again.

Every two weeks, Barbara and the children would go to see Menno in the Ottawa jail. A neighbor, Lincoln Holmes, was really helpful to take them. They had orders to bring the mail and his tobacco along each time.

Through these heart rending trials, she wrote,

Rules For Our Family

"Lord, help us to do our tasks more faithfully every day.

Get on our knees and pray every morning and evening.

Read a chapter from the Bible every day.

Do not talk and visit while eating but praise the Lord before and after each meal.

Do not tell things that are hard to believe as some might think you are not telling the truth and will never be any good to anyone.

Be quiet, and don't talk so much about other's failures, but think of your own.

O, Lord, help us to truly raise our children to be obedient and truthful in all things."

When Willie was six, he carried water from the creek in a little lard bucket for his mother to do the laundry. Then Barbara heated the water and scrubbed the laundry with a washboard until it was clean. After Menno was in jail, Willie sometimes helped someone with work in order to bring in a little money. He was only eight, but he knew his mother was desperate and was willing to help in any way he could.

Tears often flooded Barbara's eyes as friends and neighbors were so thoughtful and brought food and clothes their own children had outgrown and gave them to Barbara. Sometimes a sister from the church would come to spend the day and night with Barbara and the children. She felt so unworthy of all the kindness shown to the children and her during this time.

Barbara's parents came and stayed with them a week. On May 24, 1924, the bank foreclosed and sold all Menno's stock for the money he owed them. Then there was very little left. That was the second time the bank had foreclosed. The first time was in 1920 after living in the new house Menno had built a year earlier. That time they lost both farms.

That fall, her parents came again and took Barbara and her five children home to Reno County with them. They packed everything possible in her father's Model T Ford. Barbara said she would certainly need her sewing machine. Since the inside of the car was full of people, other necessities, the sewing machine was tied onto the running board of the car. Jonas Beachey took the rest of their belongings home on his wagon and stored them. In a few months, Perry Yoders planned to move to Reno County from Garnett and promised to bring the rest of their things along.

When they came to a slight hill on their way to Reno County, the Model T groaned and could not make it as it only had two gears. Everyone except her father would bail out of the car and push until they reached the top of the hill, then they got on board again. This procedure was repeated until they finally arrived at her parents' home.

Things had changed so much at home. Barbara's brothers, Eddie and Willie, were married and lived in their own homes. Her sister, Mary, was also married and lived in Sumner County, Kansas, and her sister Anna and Fred Yoder had just married in February and lived in the area. Those still at home were Fannie, Mattie, Clarence, Andrew, Edna, Amelia, David, Ida and Enos. The three youngest had been born since Barbara was married, and she had children about the same ages. The children thought it was quite special to be close to their aunts and uncles and to play together.

One time when Aunt Mary and John came to visit from Sumner County, they took little Mary and Amelia along home so the house would not be quite as crowded at her parents.

Barbara was very busy sewing men's suits, and her sisters and mother helped take care of her children. Her parents were so kind to her. Menno's mother Mattie and Doddy came over frequently to be near her grandchildren. Mattie was very sad that Menno was in jail. She said, "He should have been more careful who he let on his place. Now those bootleggers are gone, and Menno has to take the punishment." Menno received frequent letters from his mother to encourage him to strive harder for spiritual things, to read God's Word regularly, and to pray, for God would answer.

One day Barbara's maternal uncle Hans and wife Fannie came to see Barbara at her parents' place, and Hans said, "Barbara, we have an empty farmhouse across the road from your uncle Harry's. If you and your children would like, you may move there."

Barbara said, "I appreciate your offer very much, but I really have no money for rent."

"We won't worry about that," Hans replied. "You can pay some when you have money, and if you have none that is fine, too." So Barbara and her children moved to that house.

Before long, Perry Yoders moved their belongings by train and brought the rest of Menno and Barbara's things. She had a few incubators on the load, and soon she was busy hatching chicks for other people. Every evening she filled the burners with oil and turned each egg. During the day, she was busy at her sewing machine. That spring Willie worked for Ervin Yoders picking strawberries. Every day, he recorded his work in a little book. He grew so tired of picking strawberries that he would write, "Picked those crazy strawberries again."

Dannie would sometimes help pull weeds and do other odd jobs at Jakie Petersheims. They were so good to him, and he adored their son Sammie. They also had an older Amish man there to mow hay with the horses. Every time the man made a round with his mowing, he would swing his whip at Dannie and say, "Get to work, you little Chupp," while Dannie was pulling weeds or hoeing nearby.

One time, Barbara had such a catch in her back that it was a real effort for her to get around and do her work. Uncle Hans and his good wife had a real concern for Barbara's well being, and when they realized how bad her back was, they offered to take her to the chiropractor. Barbara said, "I don't have the money for a treatment." They took her and paid for the treatment, and Barbara felt much better after that.

That winter, little Mary got very sick with pneumonia, and Uncle Hans' wife Fannie came and stayed all night. She brought some herbs and brewed a tea with them and added some vinegar. She persuaded Mary to drink some. She also made poultices with fried onions to put on her chest, and she soon improved.

Chapter 36
Andy's Third Wife - Levi's Move to Illinois

Menno's brother, Andy, had spent some time in Illinois where he got acquainted with an older single girl by the name of Anna Yoder. They became close friends, and on January 4, 1925, they got married in Illinois. He moved to Illinois with his children, Levi, Lizzie, and Mattie, born from his first wife, and Millie, born from his second wife. Lizzie often stayed at Doddy Bontragers, and Grandma Mattie missed her very much although she rejoiced for Andy that he could have his children together again.

Mattie enjoyed son Levi and their family in the other house close by. Their girls came over to help her when she had company for a meal. They brought things from the basement and set the table and saved her many steps. Then she would say, "Now, girls, you eat dinner with us," which was a treat for the girls. They thought they had the best grandma anyone could have.

Levi's girls were good friends of Levi Knepp's girls who lived across the river from them. One day, they begged their mother to go to Levi Knepp's house to play with their girls. Their mother said, "If the river is low so that we can drive across it, we will go. It is too far out around." Levi rode a horse to check the river and came back with the news that the river should be easy to cross.

They asked Grandma if she would like to go along. She replied, "I'm not that busy. I will go with you." This delighted the girls. So the girls, Polly, Gertie and Fannie, with their mother and grandma, started out.

When they were halfway across the river, the horse stopped. No amount of coaxing would budge him. "Oh, my, what do we do now?" they wondered. After awhile, Levi happened to glance in their direction and saw them stranded in the middle of the river. He rode his horse down to them and unsuccessfully tried to coax the horse and buggy across the river.

Finally, he gave up and said, "I will have to take each one of you back to the bank on the horse." The girls thought it was funny when he got Grandma on the horse. She would let out a grunt with every step the horse took. When they were back on the bank, he rode back into the river, then the horse and buggy were easy to lead back to the bank where the others were waiting. They all climbed onto the buggy and went home.

Levi and his family had gone to Arthur, Illinois, when his brother Andy got married to Anna Yoder, and Levi could not forget that place. They decided to move there in January of 1925, and they had an auction to sell their unneeded items. Friends and neighbors came to Yoder to help to load the boxcar that would take their belongings to Illinois on January 28. Besides household goods and tools, they took seven horses. Levi fought back the tears as he said farewell to all their good friends and especially his mother, who took it so hard that they were moving so far away. In order to feed the horses along the way when the train made stops, Levi rode in the caboose. He was about four days on the train before he arrived in Arthur. He was delayed seventeen hours in St. Louis because he had to change from the Missouri Pacific to the C. & E. lines to finish his destination. His brother-in-law was at Arthur to meet him and took him home for the night. He was glad to sleep in a bed again. His wife and children had arrived two days earlier.

Sarah Beachy and her children had also been to Illinois for her brother Andy's wedding, and a widower by the name of Gid Kauffman took special notice of her and her two children. Soon they started corresponding with each other, and they were married May 26, 1924. So Sarah, Barbara and Johnny also moved to Illinois with their belongings.

Chapter 37
Shem Goes to Menno's Bail - Menno Works For Shem

Menno spent nine months in jail, and his family was all very concerned for him. Finally Shem, Menno's half brother, paid his bail and Menno was out on parole. Every month, Shem had to report what Menno was doing, what he worked, if he went to church, and so forth. Menno worked in Shem's blacksmith shop to work out his bail. Menno easily adapted to this type of work and had a knack to fix about anything he desired. The important thing was that he was out of jail and free again.

Shem had a few steam engines and threshing machines that Menno kept in running order. Little Mose, a neighbor, also had a threshing outfit and had an Amish man to run it for him. He had so much trouble with it and observed how Shem had his in running order all the time. Mose knew that Menno deserved the credit because of his mechanical ability. One day, Mose got up enough courage to ask Menno, "How much does Shem pay you to work here?" Menno told him, and Mose said, "I will pay you double that for running my threshing outfit." Menno talked it over with Shem, and he gave his permission for Menno to work for Mose. When the day came, Menno went early and looked the machine over thoroughly. Soon he noticed where a cotter key was missing, and he replaced it. That day to Little Mose's amazement, threshing went smoothly. He was unaware of what Menno had done.

Threshing machine like Menno operated for Shem.
Later owned by Shem's son Joe.

That evening Mose said, "I don't think we will need you after all as it seemed to run quite smoothly today." When Menno reminded him of his offer, he said, "That is plenty much to pay, and I think we will make out fine now."

"It's up to you," Menno replied. Slyly Menno took one walk around the machine, removed the cotter key, and went home.

After a few days, Mose came back to Menno and said, "I will stay by my offer after all, as we have had nothing but trouble since you left." Again Menno went back, replaced the cotter key, and ran the machine the rest of the season without any problems. He never told Mose what he did.

During the time Menno was on parole, he quit smoking but continued to chew. Barbara was thankful for the big change she saw in Menno. With Barbara's help, he butchered hogs and ground them into sausage. Then he took the meat and sold it door to door in Hutchinson. The lard was often sold, too, but Barbara still had very little lard and meat to use. Menno had cards made that said, "When you think of sausage think of M. I. Chupp." Mary was eight, and when her parents were busy butchering to sell, she would stand on a chair and prepare dinner. The children learned to work and take responsibility at a young age.

With Barbara hatching chicks and sewing men's dress suits, things were looking better. She had two incubators which held 1,500 eggs each and a few smaller ones. In all she could set 5,000 eggs at one time. It was a task to turn each egg every evening and also to keep the wicks trimmed and the burners filled with kerosene. People liked for Barbara to hatch their eggs for them because it was more efficient than putting eggs under a cluck. Because Menno usually collected the money for her before the eggs hatched and kept it, she rarely saw anything of it.

The children liked their new home and soon had many friends, and being close to their grandparents was also a real pleasure.

Grandma Mattie was glad when she received a letter from Levi's family with the news that they were blessed with a baby girl on May 26, 1925. They named her Sarah in honor of his sister. Her sisters were overjoyed to have a baby in their home again. Fannie, the youngest, would be nine on her next birthday.

Menno, Barbara, and their children often went to Doddys which was always a treat for them. The children thought Grandma Mattie's cooking was the best. They had been used to being with Levi's girls when they went there, and they missed them since they had moved to Illinois.

That summer and early fall, Doddy and Mommy went on an extended trip and visited each of the children that lived elsewhere. Mattie was thankful to see all the grandchildren and see how each one had grown.

Menno bought an old threshing machine and did some custom work with it. One time, as he was checking the gas tank to see if it was empty, it exploded in his face. It burned most of his beard off. When he went into the house, Barbara's sister, Anna and her husband Fred were there. Quickly Anna spread apple butter on his facial burns. He looked so funny that they had to laugh. When they took him to the doctor, he shaved off the rest of his beard and gave him some salve for it.

On Sunday, November 23, Grandma invited Menno, Barbara, and their family to come for dinner. As usual, she had a delicious dinner. How they all enjoyed the full course meal! During the meal, she mentioned that she was so hungry for coleslaw, but she dared not eat much of it because it always made her sick. She did eat a little anyway. She was her normal jolly self and told of the quilting she had attended at her son Shem's place on Friday.

Aultman Taylor Tractor used to power Shem's threshing machine.
Shem's son Joe owned it later.

Chapter 38
Mattie's Final Farewell - Doddy's Death

Soon after the dishes were done and the leftovers put away, she got sick with terrible pain. She lay down and moaned with pain. Finally the doctor was called, and he said, "It's a case of locked bowels." Menno spent the night at his mother's bedside, but Barbara and the children went home to chore. By morning, she was worse. Shem, Betsy, and their family and Barbara and their children joined Doddy and Menno, keeping a close vigil on her condition. Betsy and Barbara prepared dinner, and, when it was ready, Grandma Mattie peacefully passed away. Her trials and triumphs in life were concluded. Her greatest triumph had arrived as she went to be with the Lord. Doddy found much comfort in the words of Psalm 116:15, "Precious in the sight of the Lord is the death of his saints." They had shared eleven happy years.

The obituary was dated December 9, 1924. It stated:

"This community was greatly shocked November 24, at the loss of a kind neighbor and mother and faithful church member Mattie, married to Daniel Bontrager. She took ill suddenly the previous afternoon.

Her mind was clear to the last hour of her life. They had yet visited all her children that lived a distance, but one, this fall. She assisted a daughter-in-law with quilting yet on Friday.

She was the only daughter of Bishop Shem S. and Anna Miller of Holmes Co. Millersburg, Ohio. She was born May 16, 1851. Died Nov. 24, 1924 age 73 years, 6 months and 8 days. She joined the Amish church in her early youth and was a steadfast, faithful member to the end. It would be well for us to follow her truthful example of life. Always anxious to look on the Lord's side before giving advice.

She was first married to David J. Yoder of Lagrange, Indiana. To this union were born 4 children. Pre. Enos D. Yoder of Hazelton, Iowa, Shem D. Yoder of Yoder, Kansas, Sarah, wife of Pre. Gideon Kauffman of Arthur, Illinois, Annie, died at the age of 2 years.

Her first husband, D. J. Yoder, died at the age of 29 years and she was left a widow 2 years.

She was then married to Pre. Isaac N. Chupp of Rensueleer, Indiana. To this union 10 children were born: Katie who died at 20 years of age, David died at 3 months of age, Levi now living at Arthur, Ill., Fannie died at 7 years of age Andy at Arthur, Ill., Mattie died a few days before her 21st birthday. Millie wife of A. D.

Borntrager of Thomas, Okla. Lydia died at Newton Co. Ind. 1893 Menno I. Chupp of Haven, Kansas.

She was a faithful mother of 14 children and raised one daughter, Deemy, wife of Pre. Noah J. Yoder of Garnett, Kansas, as their own child who lost her own mother at three weeks of age. Isaac Chupp died at Garnett, Kansas, and she then married Deacon Daniel E. Bontrager, her last husband, who yet resides here at Haven, Kansas.

She leaves to mourn her departure a lonely husband, eight children now living and two brothers, Deacon Joseph S. Miller and Samuel S. Miller of Stark County, Middlebranch, Ohio and many grand- and great-grandchildren.

She was always ready to help one in need. Her granddaughter Lizzie A. Chupp, 11 years old, stayed with her in her home and assisted them the last 2 years of her grandmother's life.

The funeral was held on Thanksgiving Day, and many friends, neighbors, and relatives gathered to pay their last respects to the departed one from the earth.

Bishop Jonas Bontrager from home area and Bishop Samuel D. Hostetler of Goshen, Indiana, preached from II Corinthians 5. The children were all present but one."

(This was taken from the original and is basically unedited.)

Doddy Daniel was very lonely and would drive his faithful horse, Baldy, to visit his children. Sometimes he came to visit Barbara and Menno and their family. Although they missed Mommy, they were glad for his visits. He was glad to have the company of his little wiener dog, Penny. The grandchildren were also fond of the little dog.

A year after Mattie died, on November 30, 1925, Daniel passed on to his reward. His age was seventy-seven years, two months, and ten days. He was preceded in death by two wives. He filled his calling as deacon well, and it made him sad that not all of his children stayed with the Amish faith like they had been taught. His son Rudy was ordained a deacon in the Mennonite church in 1923. His youngest son Dan had joined the Mennonites soon after the church in Reno County was organized. Not long after that, Dan's wife died, twelve days after giving birth to a baby that died the day it was born. She left seven motherless children.

On December 5, 1925, Menno and Barbara were blessed with another son. They chose the name Andy in honor of his maternal grandfather and two uncles. He was their sixth child and fourth son. Barbara was thankful for a husky baby. Soon after that, they received a letter from Brother Andy in Illinois, who wrote, "We have a baby girl born on December 3. We named her Drucilla."

Menno held baby Andy and said, "Did you hear that? You have a little cousin that was born two days before you."

That summer, Barbara and the children would walk back to the pasture and pick sand plums. They sold them for three dollars a bushel. Barbara also had a hotbed and sold plants she raised, as well as garden produce. For the a complete men's suit, which consisted of coat, trousers, and vest, she received a total of three dollars and fifty cents. Willie and Dannie were hired out, and contributed their earnings to the family budget. Willie worked for a man whose wife made sure he ate sparingly. When he hoed her potatoes, he would sometimes intentionally hoe one out which he soon devoured. At the place where Dannie worked, they were so kind to him, even offering him a cookie between meals.

Barbara raised peas to sell, and one day, she picked fifteen bushels and sent them with Menno when he went to Hutchinson to peddle sausage. One man bought all of them, but he gave a check that was no good. Barbara thought of all the hard work she had put into raising and picking them, and now there was no money to show for it. The man never did make it right.

Because Menno's family was scattered, the family circle letter was always interesting and kept everyone informed on the happenings in the various families. A.D. and Millie and their family lived in Garnett, Kansas, but they were making plans to move to Wiggins, Mississippi. They hoped to move yet in 1928 to help start a new Amish community. They would take care of a large pecan grove. Enos' family lived near Hazelton, Iowa, and were planning to move to Arthur, Illinois, in a short time to be near Sister Sarah and Brother Levi and family, also Brother Andy's family. Andy and Anna had another baby girl born January 24, 1928. They named her Demma. A.D. and Millie's sons, Dannie and Andy, were both married by this time. Dans had two boys and Andys a baby boy, so Millie was a grandma already. Benj and granddaughter Deemy had another girl named Susie born October 15, 1920. At this time, they lived in Sumner County, Kansas. Shem's and Menno's families were the only ones left in Reno County.

Chapter 39
Special Son Born - Move to Chouteau, Oklahoma

That summer on August 9, 1928, another son, Levi, was born to Barbara and Menno. He was a special child and several of his fingers were grown together at birth. Barbara had worked very hard before he was born, and she thought that might have contributed to his infirmities. He was a contented baby. Because he was not demanding like the other children had been when they were babies, Barbara fed him when she felt he needed it.

It seemed the harder Barbara and the children worked the more Menno spent. Soon she realized he had made many debts in the area. Because his parole time was over, he was no longer accountable to anyone and was going into debt deeper then he could repay. He started talking about moving out of state. Barbara and the children liked it so well in Kansas that they hated the thought of leaving.

Barbara's mother and younger children often came to spend the day which was something the children really enjoyed. Mary and Anna were especially delighted when their Aunt Ida, who was not much older than they were, came along. Often she brought her rag doll and they played house in their playhouse. Ida was creative and frequently came up with new ideas.

One time Ida heard her mother making plans to go spend a day with Barbara later that week. A brilliant idea popped into Ida's mind. Somehow she managed to catch a sparrow and butcher it and cut it into pieces. She thought, when they go, she would take it along, and they would pretend to have fried chicken in Mary and Annie's playhouse. A few days elapsed, and Ida's mother started detecting a foul odor coming from the living room. When she investigated further, she found the dead sparrow wrapped in paper hiding in the woodbox. Of course, Ida had some explaining to do. Needless to say, the sparrow immediately disappeared, but the odor remained for a while.

By February, 1929, Menno had made arrangements to move to Mayes County, Oklahoma, much as the rest of the family detested the idea. Some people predicted he would be unable to move due to his numerous debts, but Menno found a way. He put the boxcar with their belongings under a fictitious name. Menno was eager to move. He had a ten year lease on a farm owned by a rich Tulsa couple named Sanders.

When the time came to move, Barbara and the children were very sad. Menno went with the train boxcar and their belongings, and Grandpa Andy and Grandma Fannie took the family in his car. The farm was located a few miles west of Chouteau, Oklahoma, along what was then known as the 33 highway. However, it was just a dirt road at that time, and when it rained, cars often got stuck in it.

As they drove along, the children looked over the countryside. They did not find it appealing. There were not many fences or trees, just open prairie. When they finally got there, the house was small as most of them were in that area. It had three main rooms with a wash house attached to the west end. A small room on the north side of the wash house served as the sleeping quarters for Willie and Dannie. Menno and Barbara set up their bed in the living room, and the girls and little boys slept in the bedroom. Off the kitchen, there was a small pantry and little entrance room that came in handy. An old building southwest of the house was used for the incubators. When word got around that she had incubators, she was soon busy hatching chicks for others.

West of the house there was a barn, an old chicken house, an outhouse, and another small building which was used for the wood and cobs. South of the house there was a well where they drew water. A rope was tied to the bucket and attached to a frame with a pulley.

The children missed their friends a great deal. One time when Mary and Anna went out to the well to draw some water, Mary looked at Anna and said, "Do you think we will ever be happy enough to sing again?"

Hatching chicks for people and sewing men's suits kept Barbara busy. Willie and Dannie milked some cows and fed the hogs. Dannie would find small scraps of wood or tin and make toy tractors and trucks for Leroy and Andy. Mary loved to cook which was good because Barbara was busy with other work. Anna enjoyed working in the garden and feeding the chickens and gathering the eggs. She was also often in charge of the younger children. Little Levi did not sit alone or move around much like other children his age.

Menno found it interesting to sit in Chouteau most of the day. When he came home in the evening, he would holler, "Yuep! Yuep!" Dannie knew it meant he was to come and unhitch the horse and put it away. How he dreaded that job! After Menno was through eating supper, he would sit in the living room on his rocker and say, "Dannie, come take my shoes off for me." Dannie didn't like that job either.

When Menno's family circle letter came, Enos wrote their new address was Ohio as they moved in November, 1929. "We only lived in Illinois three months this time. I think we will like it better here."

Noah, Deemy, and their family were making arrangements to move to Thomas, Oklahoma. "Plans are to move by April 26, 1930. So note our address after that date. With Isaac and Jonas both married to girls from that area, we thought we would like it there, too," Deemy wrote.

A.D. and Millie were still in Wiggins, Mississippi, and they raised many sweet potatoes and cucumbers to sell.

Chapter 40
A Daughter Born - The Rich's - Menno Bales Hay

Early on the morning of March 5, 1930, Mary was suddenly awakened by a crying baby. Although it was too early to get up, she felt sure that was what she had heard. She could not sleep much the rest of the night. When they got up the next morning, their mother was still in bed. She said, "Girls, you have a baby sister." Mary and Anna were delighted with their new sister as there were already five boys in the family.

Barbara wished to name her Fannie as a namesake for her mother, and Menno consented. However, he reminded her that the landlady, Mrs. Sanders, had given orders that when this baby came, she wanted to name it. A short time later, she came from Tulsa with her chauffeur. She said, "I want to name this baby because I never had any children of my own. I want her name to be Ada like mine." Since the baby was already named Fannie, they decided to call her Fannie Ada. Grandpa and Grandma came from Kansas and assisted the girls with the extra work since Levi was still as helpless as a baby. Because he was more sickly, it took more effort to feed and care for him.

When Barbara's sister Mattie got married to Eli Gingerich on April 20, 1930, Barbara and baby Fannie went to Iowa near Hazelton with Barbara's parents to attend the wedding. Little Levi stayed at Joe Mast's home while she was gone. Barbara was impressed with the area and wished they had moved there instead of to Oklahoma. The weather was so nice, and the horses had lots of pep. She had much to tell when she got home, but Menno was unimpressed. Barbara's brother Ed and his family also lived there, and it looked like they were prosperous. By this time, they had six children.

The oldest was a boy named Willie, born in 1920; next was Fannie, born in 1922; then Enos, born in the fall of 1923; Perry, born in the summer of 1925; Sarah, born in January, 1928; Harry, born in August of 1929. She had enjoyed her visit in their home very much.

Menno's sister Sarah regularly wrote letters to Menno and Barbara and informed them that brother Andy's had another daughter born May 11, 1930. They named her Anna, and she was the third daughter they had together. Lizzie and Mattie, from his first wife, helped well with the little ones.

A family named Rich, who had a couple children, stopped at Menno's house and asked to camp there. They were very poor and came from Colorado. "Sure!" Menno said. He would not think of turning anyone away. So they set up their tent across the lane and lived there. They cooked their meals over an open fire. Their older children walked to school with the Chupp children. Sometimes Mr. Rich helped a little with the work, and he was often Menno's chauffeur. In time, the Rich's moved west up the hill from them. Their oldest girl would put a barrel onto a sled and hitch it to an old mule to haul water.

Menno bought a baler for prairie hay and hired a crew of boys to help. He often met fellows in Chouteau he would hire. They were given fair wages, plus three meals a day. Menno shipped the hay by rail to other places. He had cards printed that said, "When you think of hay, think of M. I. Chupp." Every spring, Barbara raised a lot of fryers. She and the children raised a big garden, but by the time summer ended, they had very little left to feed their own family.

Although Barbara was very busy with two babies, she still hatched chicks for others. Fannie grew so fast, and before she was a year old, she was walking. Little Levi appeared to watch her, and soon he sat alone. In time he learned to walk. Before long, Fannie was saying words and talking, but Levi never learned to talk.

During this time Menno's niece, Deemy and Benj Yoder, moved into the area along with their children, Mary Ann (a dwarf) from his first wife, and Ray who was adopted by Benj and his first wife, and from his marriage to Deemy, Anna, Susie, Ezra, and Benjie, who was also born in 1930. Their family and Menno's had many happy times together.

One time, Menno had a car with a rumble seat, and the whole family piled into it and went to Benj and Deemy's for supper. This was a real treat as they seldom went places as a family. When Deemy's parents, Shem and Betsy, or any of their family from Kansas came, the two families got together.

One time Deemy's brother, Enos', and family from Kansas were visiting. They brought Benj's family along to Menno's for Sunday dinner and the afternoon. That year Menno's raised a lot of watermelon and had almost a wagon load sitting in the yard. That afternoon, everyone ate watermelon until they could hold no more. Their children played games with Menno's children and had lots of fun. The grown people sat on the porch and visited, discussing various happenings.

"By the way," said Menno, "from what we hear A.D. and Millie moved to a new place in Arkansas close to the town of Nettleton. They moved in November, 1932. The way it sounds it's been rough to make a living there also. They can raise good gardens because of the long growing season. A.D. says there's plenty of wood. When they need cash, he cuts a load of wood and takes it to town and sells it. Well, one time it didn't go too well for him. He collected the money for the wood, and some fellow came along and knocked A.D. in the head, taking his money. When he revived, he was lying close to his wagon and had no money to buy what they needed. Only a few other families live there. They feel the crunch of this depression same as we do here."

Menno and Barbara got an invitation from her sister Fannie for her wedding January 18, 1933, to a widower, Ammon Troyer. He still had four children at home. Lloyd, the baby when his first wife died, was being cared for by Fred and Anna who never had children. Barbara thought Fannie would need to make many adjustments being a new bride and caring for four children. She was in her late twenties and had much experience working for others. She had often worked for her uncle Dan after his wife died, and he also had children. Being from a large family, she was used to children.

When Willie was old enough to join the activities of the other youth, he didn't have a buggy to drive, so he would ride a horse. One winter, he did quite a bit of trapping for skunks, opossums, and other small game and accumulated the huge sum of fifteen dollars. With it, he bought a buggy which he felt was quite an accomplishment. He felt less inferior to the other youth his age.

Dannie was more concerned about his clothes. He would not attend church if his clothes did not measure up to those of the other boys his age. Often Menno was at home on Sunday, so he didn't encourage the children to go either. Eventually Dannie also earned fifteen dollars trapping furs and gave it to his mother, saying, "Buy material and make me a new suit. Then I will go to church." Barbara was very glad to do that. When the suit was completed, he felt almost equal to the other boys his age. Dannie gave the best of care to his new suit.

Menno still brought any kind of men home and gave them work.

He let them sleep in the barn, and Barbara was to cook for them. Since they had no room in the house for them to sleep, he would give them Barbara's good covers to take to the hayloft.

On August 10, 1933, Barbara and little Fannie attended the wedding in Reno County of her sister Edna and Orie Yoder. They married in the Mennonite church near Yoder. It hardly seemed possible to Barbara that she was getting married because she had been a little chatterbox when Barbara got married.

Menno's sister Sarah continued to keep Menno and Barbara posted on the news from Illinois which they appreciated. Brother Andy's Lizzie got married January 17, 1933, to Neil Jones. "To think Levi and Anna's Polly and Anson were married a few years already, and their Gertrude got married December 28, 1933, to Abe Gingerich. She had a nice wedding. Just wish youns could have been here. Now Andy and Anna have another baby girl born February 16, 1934. They named her Katie. Would love to come visit you all and suppose your children are growing up, too.

Lovingly Sarah, and children."

Menno had gone to Garnett to visit A.D. and his sister Millie before they moved away from there. They only lived there about a year. As their son Dan and his family lived in Kalona, Iowa, plans were that his parents would move there by March 5, 1934. The Great Depression continued.

Chapter 41
Haying - Sad Accident - Baby Girl Born 1934

The summer of 1934 was an exceptionably hot summer, and the girls and Barbara were busy cooking for the hay crew. For breakfast, the usual menu was biscuits, gravy, and syrup, as well as coffee. For dinner, they often had rice, salmon patties, tomato gravy, and sometimes green beans with a bit of bacon. For dessert, they usually had sand plums on bread with milk. With so many mouths to feed, the potatoes and meat supply were soon depleted. The common supper menu was cornbread, beans, and milk. Dannie had made a big table that was set up in the yard. They ate there because it was cooler than in the house.

On July 16, a man came to the door and handed Barbara a telegram. Quickly she opened it and read, "Clarence broke neck - is serious." Tears filled her eyes. "Oh! Can it be?" she said. "My own dear brother. I wonder what happened. I know he was attending college at Weatherford, Oklahoma. It must have been an accident." She watched the mail anxiously because she knew her mother or sisters would write the details as soon as possible.

The next day, July 17, 1934, before dinner was served, Barbara said, "Girls, let's give the younger children an early dinner because I'm sick. Then they can go to Joe Masts." Barbara went to the bedroom, and the girls, Mary and Anna, finished up the dinner for the hay help and got the children fed. Soon Menno brought the men in to eat. Then he went to Chouteau with his pickup and asked Dr. Bryant to come. The doctor grabbed his black satchel, and they were on the way.

Anna, Leroy, and Andy put Fannie and little Levi on the little wagon and started across the meadow for Joe Mast's place. Anna and Leroy suspected what was about to happen at home and stopped halfway across the meadow. They stood on the little wagon and strained their necks to look back. Anna said, "There's a car in our lane at home, and it doesn't look like Grandpa's car either. It's a man carrying a satchel. Maybe its the doctor."

Later that afternoon, Menno came in his pickup and said, "We have a baby girl at home." The children piled into the pickup to go home and get acquainted with this little newcomer.

That evening, a name for the baby was discussed. Four-year-old

Fannie thought she knew the best name of all. She piped up, "Let's name her Nora." Her maternal uncle Andy had a girl friend by that name, and she was sure nobody could be any nicer looking than she was. Andy said, "Let's not give her that name. Benj Yoders have a horse by that name." He suggested Salina as the hired girl Salina Detweiler seemed to be about as good as any girl he ever knew. So that is what she was named. Because of the hot summer, they dressed the baby only in a diaper and a thin little white apron.

Before long, Barbara received a letter from home with the details of Clarence's accident. It stated, "Clarence was doing hand springs at college near Weatherford, Oklahoma, with some other students. Somehow he broke his neck and was paralyzed from the arms down. He was brought home by ambulance. He has a real testimony and lies here praising God. His favorite saying is, 'Only one life will soon be past, Only what's done for Christ will last.' He was ordained to the ministry in October of 1927, and when this happened, he was getting education to teach school in the fall. His sisters spend much time here helping to care for him," her mother wrote. "Fannie and Ammon had their first child together March 17, 1934. When Fannie comes to care for Clarence, she brings her baby Charles and stepdaughter Irene along."

Barbara just prayed he would live, for, with a new baby, she knew she would not be able to go to see him for sometime.

On August 9, they received another telegram stating that Clarence passed away. Menno made arrangements with Mr. and Mrs. Kroecker to take Barbara and tiny baby Salina to Kansas for the funeral. They bought a baby basket with a large soft pillow to set on the back seat of the car for the baby. It was decided that little Fannie stay at home with Menno and the other children.

The funeral was conducted in the home of his parents. Leander Keim spoke in German and Alva Swartzentruber from Weatherford, Oklahoma, spoke in English. At the Mennonite church Milo Kauffman from Hesston, Kansas, spoke and also Harry Diener from the home congregation. The texts used were Ecclesiastes 8:8 and Revelation 21:4. Clarence had made his own funeral arrangements, and during his illness often sang, "Must Jesus Bear The Cross Alone." He had requested his Uncle Ed make his casket.

Clarence was the first of Barbara's family to pass away. His age was thirty-two years, six months, and seven days. He was still unmarried and believed he, like the Apostle Paul, could serve the Lord single. He was survived by his parents, eight sisters, five brothers, and many nieces and nephews and cousins.

They received an invitation to Barbara's brother Andy and Nora Yutzy's wedding which was to be November 4, 1934. Since Barbara had been to her brother Clarence's funeral in August, she decided not to go to the wedding. When she told the children, Fannie said, "Oh, I'm glad cause I like her. She is so pretty and I love her name."

By this time, Menno seldom went to church. The only transportation they had was Willie's single seated buggy, and Barbara often went with him. The younger children would get dressed for church and waited beside the road. If someone from church came along that had room for them in their buggy, they would get a ride. If nobody came, they stayed home.

Barbara had received some of her brother Clarence's books when his possessions were divided. Among them was a book "Hulbert's Story of the Bible," which the children enjoyed. When they could not go to church, Barbara read stories from it to the younger children. The older ones read it for themselves. One Sunday when they were at home, Leroy came to his mother and said, "I finished reading that book, and now I know better what the preachers preach."

Chapter 42
Surgery - Death - Loneliness - A Pony

The following week as the children were walking home from school with some neighbor children, Leroy lagged behind. When they passed the cemetery, he went in and lay down because he was sick. Finally he made it home, and his mother asked, "Where have you been?"

He said, "I have a terrible stomachache, worse than I ever had." He lay on the bed in the living room, and Mother rubbed turpentine and kerosene on his stomach. For supper, he ate only a few bites as his stomach hurt too badly. Soon he went to his bed. The next morning, Barbara asked him how he had slept. He answered, "Not very well. My stomach still hurts so badly, and I feel nauseated and also have diarrhea."

Mother said, "Then you better stay at home today." She tried more home remedies and let him lay on their bed in the living room. When Menno came home around four o'clock that evening, he was quite concerned about Leroy's condition. They immediately took him to the hospital.

The doctors performed surgery that same night and removed his appendix. The two doctors that did the surgery argued. One said, "It is ruptured, and we will need to insert a tube."

The other said, "It isn't." So they sewed him shut and did not insert a tube.

Leroy suffered much pain within the next five days. Barbara stayed by his bedside all the time. Every day someone brought little Salina, who was nine months old, into the hospital, and Barbara nursed her. The rest of the time the girls tried their best to feed her and keep her content at home. Leroy loved his baby sister dearly, but with all the pain he endured, he couldn't play with her when she came into his room.

Menno came often to see him. One time, Leroy said, "Oh, Dad, if I ever get well again, I wish we could all go to church on Sundays like other families do." A serious look crossed Menno's face.

On Saturday night, Barbara sat on a chair in front of his bed so he would not throw himself out of the bed as he tossed and turned from the tremendous pain.

The next morning, she tried to cheer him a little. She remarked as she pulled the curtain back a bit, "The night wasn't too long."

Leroy said, "Oh, yes, it was long! Tonight I'm going home." His mother knew it would not be his earthly home as sick as he was.

Once he smiled and said, "Do you see these white angels floating over my bed?" His mother could not see them.

That evening Leroy suddenly said, "Mom, something is coming over me. I'm getting as stiff as a board." With that, he passed away. It was April 14, 1935.

Barbara said, "We had nine children for nine months. Now we have a family started in Heaven."

Funeral plans were made, and Barbara's parents and some of her sisters and brothers came for it. Because Menno wanted a Mennonite minister to preach, a minister by the name of Hartzler from the Pryor Mennonite Church preached. Leroy was eleven years old and had almost completed the seventh grade in school.

Andy and Leroy were not only brothers, but also close friends and always played together. Now that Leroy was gone, Andy often sat on a chair close to his mother as she sewed. He was so sad and did not feel like playing alone. He had always depended on Leroy to suggest what they would play. Sometimes Mother would tell Fannie to go out and play with him under the shade trees. There the boys' homemade farm toys and make-believe farm that Dannie had helped them make were set up. She would go, but she could not take Leroy's place. She would rather have played with her rag doll and had never really paid much attention to her brother's way of playing.

Barbara prayed that, with Leroy's death, Menno would see the need to change his life and go to church again. One day a visiting minister came to call on them. Menno was impressed and took a liking to him. That afternoon he preached at the Amish church at Orie Troyer's place, and Menno decided to go with Barbara and the little girls. Fannie was so happy that her dad went to church with her mother.

Jerry Troyers from the Mennonite church often came to visit on Sunday afternoons. Knowing that Menno did not attend church, they invited them to come to their church. Sure enough, one Sunday morning Menno said, "We will go to the Mennonite church today, Barbara, if you don't mind." She got Fannie and Salina ready, and they attended that church, going in his pickup. Then they went to Jerry Troyer's place for dinner. Fannie was only five, but she thought it quite a treat that her daddy went to church again. She tried to imagine how it would be if her mother and father always went from that time on. Barbara prayed that Menno would get interested in going regularly again.

Menno also sensed Andy's loneliness. In an effort to cheer him up, he bought a spotted pony and small saddle for Andy. Andy was pretty happy with his pony, and it did help to ease his loneliness. He named her Nellie and rode her every day.

Chapter 43
Outdated Shoes - Weddings - Cows Starving

That fall Barbara's parents came to visit which was always a special occasion for the children. Her father had been to a sale where a store was selling out and sold a lot of outdated shoes. He knew that Barbara was always glad for shoes for the children and that she did not mind if they were outdated. She was more concerned that their feet stayed warm. Most were shoes that came up over the ankles. Some had buttons up the side and heels. That evening the box was emptied on the floor, and the children tried them on. If they found a pair they could wear, it was theirs. Little did it matter if they were women's shoes, if they fit the boys they would rather wear them than go barefoot. How little Fannie wished they would not be so big so she could wear them! The older children were not that impressed, considering how outdated they were.

Since little Levi learned to walk, it was often quite a task to keep track of him. He loved the big collie dog, and he was usually with him. When Levi wanted some favor, he always hunted up his sister Mary. She had such a warm spot in her heart for him, and he seemed to sense that. Although he was unable to talk, she could usually surmise what he wanted. One day when Mary was gone, Levi got a slice of bread and a knife and went to hunt for Mary. Not finding her around the house, he walked up the hill to the neighbors carrying the bread and knife. When the neighbor lady saw him, she figured he wanted apple butter on his bread and spread it for him, much to his delight. He went home, happily eating his bread.

Sometimes he walked away, and when the family missed him the search began. At times when they called, the dog would bark from a distance, giving a clue of his whereabouts. When the search was prolonged, the neighbors came on horseback to help hunt. One evening as people were helping to look for him, he suddenly came walking in the lane riding a stick horse with the faithful dog by his side.

Menno's sister Deemy lived in Thomas, Oklahoma, and her dear companion Noah Yoder died February 18, 1931. This left Deemy alone with her children. At times she came to Mayes County to visit her brother Menno and his family and her niece Deemy and her family. While there, she got acquainted with Rudy Detwieler who had been a widower for a number of years. They became friends and were married September 5, 1935. After her wedding she moved to the Chouteau, Oklahoma, area and lived across the section from Menno's. Barbara and Deemy had been close friends when they lived near Garnett, Kansas, and their friendship continued. Barbara enjoyed having more relatives living nearby.

Menno and Barbara received an invitation to her youngest sister Ida, and Enos Schrock's wedding planned for December 5, 1935. To Barbara, it hardly seemed possible that Ida was getting married. Barbara and three of her daughters, Mary, Fannie, and Salina attended, and Mary had part in the wedding. Grandma was glad to prepare a nice Amish wedding, because by this time most of Barbara's siblings were Mennonite. Amelia was the only sister still single.

Willie had been dating Amanda Troyer for some time, and they got married on September 24, 1936, a few days after his twenty-first birthday. John Troyers were moving to Michigan, and Willie rented their farm where he and Amanda set up housekeeping. Willie found some old chairs on a junk pile and wired them together so they would be usable. Orange crates were arranged to hold their dishes and cookware. Amanda made curtains to hang over these makeshift cabinets to conceal their true identity.

Menno gave Willie a cow or two, and Willie went to some auctions and bought a lame mule and a walking plow to till the ground. Although he worked hard, he was unable to get credit at the bank or anywhere else. When potential lenders learned his name was Chupp, they turned him away. His grandpa, however, took heart for him and loaned him three hundred dollars. With this, he went to auctions and bought another mule, a few more milk cows, and some tools at sales.

Menno was getting deeper and deeper into debt all the time and, being in the midst of the Great Depression, he perceived no way out of it. His hay money was pledged even before he received it. While he was gone with his pickup every day, Dannie tried to do the work at home. Menno generally came home later and later every evening, and the children were often in bed. Dannie, who was trying his best would say, "Dad, we have no feed for the cows and they are dying. What shall we do?"

Menno would reply, "I will try to bring some home tomorrow."

Because he was afraid the law would be watching for him at his home, he would park his pickup out of sight in Rudy Detwieler's meadow and walk home. He would tell Barbara to inform Dannie that he had left a few bags of feed in a certain draw in the meadow, and Dannie was to go get it for the cows. A few bags of feed were consumed in short order, and then the incident was repeated.

Menno had borrowed money from the rich landlady until she had no more and was forced to move into a small apartment, pawning her expensive furniture and paintings. She had to release most of her servants for lack of money to pay them. She and Menno were in partnership with the sheep, but they were not profitable either. Many of those also died for lack of feed. She had thought so highly of Menno, but now she was in question about his honesty.

Chapter 44
Warrants - Menno's Escape - Foreclosure

One cold day in January of 1937, the sheriff came to the door and handed Barbara three different warrants to arrest Menno. These were from people who had loaned him money in good faith. They had mortgages on his things and on some things Menno had never owned. Barbara had not been aware of these dealings although, when she was shown the papers, she saw her name was also forged on them. (Menno had faked her signature.) Menno had not been at home for four or five nights, and she did not know what to tell the sheriff.

That night Menno came home at one o'clock. Barbara had left the kerosene lamp lit dimly in the front room. She was still awake and had spent much time in prayer because sleep refused to come. When Menno came in the back door, she jumped to her feet and met him. "Oh, Menno," she said, "I know times are hard, but today the sheriff was here with three warrants for you. Please submit yourself. Perhaps someday the economy will get better, and we will get established."

Menno replied, "If that's the case, I will make my get-away immediately. They won't catch me and put me behind those bars again." Barbara pleaded with him to face the consequences, but to no avail. He went to Dannie's room, awoke him, and borrowed what little money he had left from his trapping. He warned Barbara never to let the boys hunt him because they would be sorry if they would. With that he left, and Barbara lay in bed crying most of the night.

The next day Barbara and nineteen-year-old Dannie discussed the happenings of the previous night. They searched through some of Menno's papers and found a mortgage to a certain bank in Muskogee. Dannie reasoned, "If they have a mortgage, then surely they will bring feed out for the cows so they don't die of starvation." That bitterly cold day, Dannie dressed in his warmest clothes and started to hitchhike to that bank thirty-five miles away. When he finally got there, he explained their situation to the banker. When the bank heard what was happening, they immediately sent a man back with Dannie. He brought feed and made arrangements to sell them out in ten days. However, the bank proved not to be the only mortgage holder because most things were mortgaged two or three times. Even the landlady's sheep, which they cared for, were mortgaged. Later Mrs. Sanders filed a lawsuit to prove they belonged to her, and Barbara had to witness in court that it was true.

The entire family suffered through the ordeal. The cows Menno had given to Willie were also mortgaged and needed to be brought back for the sale. The spotted pony and the small saddle Andy cherished so much were also mortgaged and would need to be sold. Andy was eleven, and to be forced to part with his dear pony was indeed another trial for him. But there was no other way because the bank would take the pony, too. Dannie helped Andy bring the saddle in the house and hide it so it wouldn't get sold.

Barbara wrote to her parents, informing them of their hardships and of their upcoming sale. Since it was so cold her father, being crippled, could not make the trip to Oklahoma for the sale. He wrote a letter to Noah Yoder who lived in the area, telling him to buy four cows and a horse and buggy for Barbara and the children, and he would pay him. He wrote he would come and see what could be done when the weather warmed up.

It was a very cold day in January, 1937, when the dressed-up bankers came to hold the auction. It had been only ten days earlier that Dannie had made their situation known.

Barbara was sick in bed that day having a miscarriage. But the bankers came right into the bedroom where she lay and wanted to know where the rest of the things were because more was mortgaged than they had. She looked at them pleadingly and said, "Are you even taking the hog we planned to butcher? How do you expect me to feed my children?" With that they were touched, and left the hog for them to butcher.

Fannie was six and was sent to bring some coal inside, and her friend Edna went outside with her. Because the coal bin was nearly empty, they scraped with their hands to get what little they could scrape together. Mary tried to fix some dinner for the hungry children who came with their parents, and Fannie followed her to the basement. Mary said, "What shall I make? We have only one jar of green beans left and one jar of peaches." Fannie noticed that Mary looked very sad. Mary cooked some rice and managed to get some food together for the children. It gave Fannie a sense of security to stay close to Mary's side.

When the sale was over Noah told Barbara he bought four cows for a total of approximately one hundred dollars, plus the hack buggy and the horse Alice that was trained to hitch to the buggy. The family was glad to have four cows left to milk.

Kind neighbors brought feed for the cows and chickens. They had a hundred pullets left that they moved to the big chicken house, and with feed, they were soon laying eggs. The sheep were still there since the landlady had ownership of those, and the children took care of them.

A few weeks after the sale, Barbara received a letter from Menno. He wrote he was in the South and was ready to go north. He also wanted to write to his brother Levi in Illinois because he realized he left her in a bad way. Since he planned to stay away for good, maybe Barbara could let his brother Levi take Andy and one of the girls so she would have less responsibility. Barbara could not see in what town the letter was postmarked. But of one thing she was sure, although she had the highest regards for his brother Levi, she would not think of giving up any of the children.

Later Levi came to visit and mentioned the letter he had received. He was not surprised that Barbara did not want to part with any of the children. She felt they would manage somehow. He brought a big box of chocolate candy for the children. By this time the children were at the point of really missing their father, therefore Uncle Levi's visit meant much to them. Aunt Sarah sent some things along for the children and wrote a nice letter saying they would remember the family and her dear brother Menno in their prayers.

Dannie was extremely discouraged, and Barbara had written to her folks about it. Dannie wondered, "Why do we children have to be responsible for the family, when really it should be Dad's problem?" When Grandpa heard this he had compassion and wrote he would hire Dannie. Dannie was pleased for he had always admired his grandparents. Before long, Grandpa and Grandma came from Kansas to get Dannie, bringing along a quarter of a beef for the family. Barbara could not keep the tears back when she saw it. They got busy cutting it up and putting it into jars to can.

Chapter 45
Dannie to Kansas - Girls' Jobs - Man Behind Tree

After staying with the family a week or more, Grandpa and Grandma left, taking Dannie along to Kansas. Dannie was glad for the chance to work for Grandpa. Grandpa bought a car for Dannie and let him pay for it by working for him. Grandpa sent most of Dannie's wages to Barbara which helped out immensely. Dannie attended the Mennonite church with Grandpa and met some of his old friends he had known before the family moved to Oklahoma. Eventually he joined that congregation.

A big load was on eleven-year-old Andy's shoulders since he was the oldest boy at home after Dannie left. He seldom got a chance to go to school anymore.

Mary and Anna took turns doing housework for some people in Chouteau who owned a store. They were paid two dollars and fifty cents to three dollars a week which contributed to the family's needs. How they dreaded to work there! They had an eleven-year-old boy who owned a BB gun, and he would shoot at them.

Andy and Anna took care of the sheep. Before going to bed each evening, they would light the kerosene lantern and go out to check the sheep and see if there were any new lambs. One moonlight evening, as they were coming toward the house after checking the sheep, Andy pointed to a tree and said, "Look at that tree. How wide it looks! It must be sprouting out the side." They walked over to investigate. Suddenly a man, who had been hiding behind the tree, jumped out. He leaped hurriedly over the fence, and they lost no time in getting to the house. They were out of breath as they told their mother what they saw. Needless to say, Barbara did not feel very comfortable in going to bed. All the doors were locked, and the curtains were pulled down. Barbara told the children to be very quiet. She went to the bedroom where it was dark and listened by the window for any unusual sound. Finally she heard a buggy coming. She waited until it was close, then they called to it from the porch. It was their good neighbors, Ray Chupp and family. They came in, and when he heard about their fears, he took a flashlight and searched through the buildings and the basement. He found no evidence of the man. After that Barbara and the children went to bed, surmising it might have been a detective.

When the law found out that Menno had skipped the country, some lawsuits followed. Mrs. Sanders and Barbara had to go to court to testify of their innocence in all the dealings Menno made. Barbara and the children continued to take care of the sheep. Because Menno had a ten year contract that was not yet expired, they stayed on the farm for a time.

One day, a poor black man came to the door and with tear-filled eyes, showed Barbara a mortgage he held on the team of white mules. Barbara felt so sorry for him, but by that time they had been sold by the bank. There were more people who showed mortgages they held who came after everything was sold. Some things that were mortgaged Menno and Barbara had never owned.

Chapter 46
First Grandchild - Mary and John Marry - Big Fire

Willie and Amanda were blessed with a baby girl on February 23, 1937. They named her Barbara in honor of her grandmother. This was Menno and Barbara's first grandchild, and they had no clue of Menno's whereabouts to let him know.

Barbara's sister Amelia wrote a letter saying she would like to go to Oregon in June. She wanted Mary to come and help at Doddy's during her absence. Although Mary was keeping company with John Henry Yoder, she knew she would need to have a job of some kind to earn some money. Going to Kansas to work would be better then working for those town people with their mean little boy. She liked the idea of working for her grandparents. They came to get her, and she worked there until October.

Mary and John continued their friendship by mail while she worked in Kansas. John Henry and Mary had plans to get married on December 3, 1937. John would have his twenty-sixth birthday the day before. Although Mary was only eighteen, Barbara gave her consent. John owned a farm close to the small town of Mazie where they would move after the wedding. When Mary came home from Kansas in October, it was essential to start preparing for their wedding.

As plans for the wedding meal were being made, Barbara knew they would need to be as thrifty as possible. They decided that celery would cost too much, and they would eliminate that from the menu. However, when Aunt Sarah from Illinois, who was a widow at this time, came, she said they would have celery, and she would pay for it.

They had a small wedding, and that evening after they had eaten supper and were singing, someone noticed a big fire close to Mazie. The next day, it was discovered that the barn on John Henry's farm had burned. They figured someone had set the fire for revenge because he married Menno Chupp's daughter. Because money was scarce, John and his father set up some poles and put a straw roof on it. John could milk there and put the horses into it until they could afford to build a real barn.

Chapter 47
Repairing House etc. - Move to Mazie

Since the contract on the farm where Barbara lived was about to expire, Grandpa felt obligated to find another place for Barbara and the children. The Depression was almost over and land was cheap. When Grandpa and Grandma came, he found an eighty acre farm on the west end of Mazie that he bought for them for $1,700. He made a down payment of $500 and made the loan so Barbara would have twenty years' time to pay for it.

All the windows were boarded shut, the plaster was down, and everything needed repair. Nobody had lived there for some time. Although Grandpa was crippled and got around with crutches, he could drive. He bought glass for the windows. Andy would follow Grandpa's orders to get the frames out and bring them to Grandpa who would then carefully putty them on the kitchen table. Andy was shown how to put them in again. It was a happy day when all the windows had glass again. The next job was to patch plaster, and one by one the rooms were papered. The woodwork was varnished, and some floors painted. They cleaned the well and put a tight cover on it. The water, which was very hard, tasted like iron. The well behind the barn had a new platform and a hand pump put on it. Eaves troughs were put on the barn and channeled to that well in order to provide more water. Fannie and Salina would take turns pumping water by hand for the cows. Anna worked for others most of the time to bring in a little money. When she had a few days at home, she helped Andy repair fences and clean up on the outside. Together they dismantled some old, rundown, dilapidated buildings. With the lumber that was worth salvaging, they built an outhouse and an open shed for the few sheep they owned. Anna and Andy hitched the horse to a walking plow, and one led the horse while the other tried to guide the plow to work the garden.

The family moved to Mazie during the winter of 1938. By then, Mary and John Henry had a little son named David. He was born on September 30. The day the family moved, they placed him in the doll bed behind the stove to keep him warm.

Alice, the horse they bought at the sale, was a bit hard to control. They knew they needed a more trustworthy horse. Enos Mullett's family, who was moving to Indiana, had a small buggy horse to sell.

They assured Barbara of her safety, so Barbara bought Bessie. Although she was slow, she was safe which was Barbara's main concern. She was broken for the buggy and got them to their destination if they allowed enough time.

To Andy's delight she had a colt, which he named Nubbin, soon after they bought her. He made a halter and led it around the barnyard. Fannie and Salina were confident that Andy was capable of anything. One day he was boasting about the well-trained colt to his little sisters. He said, "If you girls would like, I will hitch him to your little wagon and give you the lines and you can drive him." Fannie considered the offer but decided not to try it. When he explained to Salina how safe Nubbin was, she thought it was a brilliant idea. Andy hitched him to the little wagon and handed the lines to Salina. When she said, "Gitty up," Nubbin refused to move. But when Andy gave him a slap, Nubbin bolted, galloping around the house. Salina flew off, landing in the flower bed beside the house. Barbara heard a commotion and came out onto the porch to see what was happening. Salina was more frightened than hurt. Andy's tame little colt kept running until the little wagon was broken to pieces, and he was loose. Andy never tried another adventure like that.

Barbara sold little Mystery washing machines. They had a handle on the one end to move the agitator that was moved back and forth manually until the laundry was washed clean. Then one cranked the wash through the wringer into a tub of clean water to rinse it. After it was rinsed, it was put through the wringer again, and it was ready to hang on the line. It was much more efficient than using a washboard. Every young married couple in the community bought one for around twenty-five dollars from her. Barbara got enough commission from those she sold to pay for her own washer.

By this time, it was not profitable to hatch eggs for others because big hatcheries could hatch and sell them very reasonably. Barbara had sold her incubators before they moved to Mazie. She still sewed men's dress suits and did ironing for others. Andy helped others with odd jobs and the money he earned was used to buy groceries and other essential needs. Anna was in great demand to help others who had newborn babies. She was strong and helped Andy with any major project around home that needed to be done.

Fannie attended school in Mazie. She was in the third grade, and Andy enrolled in the seventh although he seldom had a chance to go.

Since he was the only boy at home, he was needed to do the work. Because he was absent so much, he lost interest and never finished school.

Their neighbors, the Parkers', had two girls and they and Fannie became fast friends. Wilma was a little older than Fannie, and Norma was a bit younger. Norma was in Fannie's grade. They walked to and from school together every day and went with each other to get the cows to the barn for the evening milking.

At Christmas, the children drew names at school, and the Parker girls asked Fannie what she wanted for Christmas. She could think of nothing that would make her happier than a real doll, for she had never had a real doll although her mother had once made her a rag doll. The limit to spend on a gift was twenty-five cents. As the time for the gift exchange drew near, Fannie became a little suspicious of who might have her name. When the time came to have the program and gift exchange, Fannie and the Parker girls sat close to the front. A big tree was set up in the gym and was decorated with popcorn and tinsel with a star at the very top. Fannie's eyes wandered over the tree, and on one of the branches was a doll. Fannie dared not think that it could be hers, for that would be too good to be true. She noticed the sparkle in the eyes of the Parker girls. Sure enough, when the gifts were handed out, the doll was handed to Fannie. She could hardly believe it was really hers. Wilma whispered to Fannie, "It cost exactly twenty-five cents." Fannie knew nobody was happier than she was that evening.

There was a demand for Barbara to do laundry for others in Mazie. Many people had washing machines with motors, but Barbara thought they would be too expensive for her and did not consider buying one. One day, a smooth talking salesman came to the door and had a brand new Maytag washing machine to demonstrate to Barbara. He showed Barbara how easy it was to operate. Fannie was at home and thought it was the biggest marvel she had seen in her twelve years. Barbara was tempted, but she explained to the man that she did not enough money. He offered to sell it to her on payments. After all, he reasoned that it was quite a job to do laundry for others with her little Mystery hand washer. The salesman kept pressuring her, and finally Barbara consented. The shiny new Maytag was unloaded onto the back porch. When Andy came into the house that evening, he found his mother sick with a headache. She said, "Did you see what is sitting on the back porch?"

Andy said, "Yes, it's very nice."

"But why did I let that man talk me into something like that? I'm afraid we can never pay for it. Just think, it cost one hundred dollars."

"Oh, Mom, don't take it so hard," Andy said. "With the washing you do for others, it will pay for itself." She didn't sleep too well that night. However, she soon had it paid.

Levi, the special son, caused a lot of apprehension when they lived near Mazie. He would walk away, and the first thing Barbara thought about was the railroad because it was only about a quarter of a mile away. Sometimes he opened an upstairs window and climbed onto the roof. Finally a neighbor would come and tell them he was on the roof. Because he could fall off and get hurt, this caused great concern.

Barbara was having health problems, and the county nurse would come to check on her. She advised her to place Levi in a state home in Enid, Oklahoma, where they had many children like him. She explained that they could often teach them to make things and to take limited care of themselves. With Barbara's health problems, she finally gave her consent. The home would keep them informed of his progress or of any needs. The family went to visit him at various times, and he seemed to recognize them even though he could not speak. His health was failing, and he was usually in bed.

Chapter 48
Births and Deaths 1939-1940

On February 4, 1939, Barbara received a telegram from Thomas, Oklahoma, stating her paternal grandmother Fannie died. Barbara's uncles, Enos and Clarence, from Indiana stopped at Barbara's home to take her along to the funeral. Grandma had lived with her only daughter Maryann and husband Benedict and family. Her age was eighty-seven years, seven months, and four days. That fall, her grandmother's things were divided, and Barbara, being the oldest grandchild, received her large china cabinet. This was really special to her because she had none. This china cabinet is now owned by a granddaughter, Karen, daughter of Salina and Joe.

Willie and Amanda were blessed with a son named Levi on July 5, 1939. He was a chubby little fellow and a happy, contented baby. The spring of 1940, Willie was busy shearing sheep for some extra cash and was often a distance away from the farm. Dannie was working at Willie's farm doing the spring work for Willie. It was time to do the evening milking, and little Levi had just awakened from his nap. Amanda placed him on the high chair, making sure the safety strap was fastened, and put some puffed wheat on the tray for him to eat. She set the high chair in front of the west screen door where she could easily see him when she finished milking each cow. She milked one cow and took a look toward the house, and, not seeing the baby, she ran for the house. He was hanging by his chin on the tray of the high chair. She released him and called for help. Dannie came running, and they got into his car and drove to the nearest neighbors. They left the car windows open, hoping it would revive him, but he was gone. This happened on April 27, 1940, and was indeed a great shock for the whole family.

The funeral was held May 1, and Grandpa and Grandma brought Preacher Levi Helmuth and his wife and Sadie Mast from Kansas to attend the funeral. Barbara thought, "Oh, where could Menno be? We can't even let him know when something like this happens." It meant so much to the family that Uncle Levi Chupp from Illinois came. His brother, Andy, and family had moved to Indiana by this time, and, with little children, it was hard for them to get away. They had a special daughter, Emma, born Dec. 30, 1935, and a son, Benjamin, born August 11, 1938.

On May 6, 1940, Mary and John were blessed with a daughter named Fannie. She was such a fussy baby and preferred only her parents to take care of her. Barbara surmised it was due to the sad time the family was experiencing when she was born.

The reports Barbara was receiving from the home where son Levi resided were not encouraging. They diagnosed his illness as tuberculosis. Barbara had someone take her to Enid to be with him and was by his bedside on June 4, 1940, when he passed away. The body was brought home, and the funeral was held a few days later. Barbara had the assurance that he had a perfect body in heaven as he joined his brother Leroy and nephew Levi. Again Barbara's parents and some of the relatives from Kansas came to extend their sympathy to the family.

Barbara received a letter from her sister Amelia who wrote that they were busy processing sweet corn. She continued, "Father was helping husk and clean corn to can and was his usual self. At noon we had corn on the cob, and Father ate some although he knew it wouldn't agree too well with his ulcers. In the afternoon he got very sick, so he was taken to the hospital in Hutchinson. Dr. Foltz says he's tough and will get well although he seems like a very sick man."

The next day, August 3, 1940, Barbara received a telegram. It stated, "Father died, bleeding ulcers." Barbara was stunned. He had been a strong man except for his leg problems. Dannie was at home and took the message to Willie's and John Henry's. Plans were made to attend the funeral. Dannie said he could take his mother, Annie, Andy, Fannie, Salina, and Willie, Amanda, and little Barbara in his 1934 Chevy. By putting a little stool between the two seats, they all managed to pile in.

When they got to Grandpa's home, it was dark, and many people were there. Andy had never been so far away from home and refused to leave the car. His cousin Howard soon joined him, and they stayed in the car together.

The day of the funeral arrived, and Grandpa was buried in the Amish cemetery a half mile south and a half mile west from their home. His obituary read as follows:

Andrew F. Bontrager was born near Middlebury, Ind., Dec. 14, 1874, and passed away Aug. 2, 1940. His age was 65 years, 7 months, and 19 days. The cause of his death was hemorrhage from his bleeding ulcers. He was very sick a year ago, but seemed fairly well again except his legs bothered him so much that he was in bed or on his wheelchair trying to heal his legs. He suffered much from his legs at times down through the years.

On Sept. 20, 1894, he was married to Fannie Bontrager. They lived in matrimony almost 46 years. To this union were born 14 children, all living except Clarence who passed away Aug. 9, 1934, at the age of 32 years, 6 months, and 7 days. He leaves to mourn his departure his sorrowing wife, 13 children, 41 grandchildren, 3 great-grandchildren. Four grandchildren and 1 great-grandchild preceded him in death. He leaves 4 brothers, 1 sister, and many friends.

(This was taken from the original and is basically unedited.)

David was twenty-five and engaged to Mary Weaver from Iowa. They had plans for a November wedding. He was in charge of the farming operation with the help of Enos, who was twenty. They would miss their father and his good advice, but being crippled and on crutches or a wheelchair, they had been used to doing most of the actual work themselves. Now that he was gone, they had to operate on their own.

Amelia was also single and was at home when she was not working away. Ida and Enos Schrock lived only about a mile and a half away. They had two little boys, William and Eli Jay. Ida often came home to spend the day with her parents.

Andrew and Nora were blessed with another son on August 2, the day before Grandpa died. They named him Wesley James, and he was their fourth child. The older children were named Maynard, Kenneth, and Dorothy.

Two of the children lived in the South Hutchinson area: Anna and Fred Yoder and son, Lloyd; Fannie and Ammon Troyer and their children, Charles and Marlin, and the four children from Ammon's previous marriage. The children who farmed in Reno County were Will, Martha, and their children, Morris, Laura, Howard, Linford, Billy, and Fannie Alice; Edna and Orie Yoder and their children, Delbert, Freda, and Baby Wayne; and Andrew and Nora and their children.

Barbara and her family lived in Oklahoma. Ed, Elizabeth, and their family and John Y. and Mary and their three children, Ezra, Fannie, and Susie; and Mattie and Eli Gingerich and their children, all lived near Hazelton, Iowa.

Chapter 49
Big Auction - War - Enos Drafted

David and Mary got married November 10, 1940, near South English, Iowa. They moved onto the home farm and lived in the east end of the house where the summer kitchen had been which was remodeled for them. His mother lived in the west end. The house had two stairways, therefore it was easy to divide the upstairs as well.

Before long, they had a large sale and sold most of Andy and Fannie's tools, farm equipment, and many, many miscellaneous items that had accumulated through the years. The sale lasted two days. Fred and Anna and Ammon and Fannie served lunch and could hardly keep enough food handy to meet the demand for the huge crowd.

Barbara and little Salina were there and bought a few keepsakes. One thing they bought was a small camelback trunk that Grandpa had gotten from his parents when he married. That trunk is now in the home of Barbara's daughter, Fannie, who resides near Leon, Iowa.

On December 7, 1941, Pearl Harbor was bombed by the Japanese. This involved the United States in World War Two and was a sad time for the entire country because young single boys were the first to be drafted to serve. The country respected those who had convictions against carrying arms. These men were called to serve as firefighters and various other jobs and received very little pay except for what their church sent them.

Shortly thereafter Enos was called. All efforts to get a farm deferment failed. His mother would miss him very much. He had sowed eighty acres of wheat, but before harvest he had to leave. His brothers harvested his crop. First he was sent to a camp in Fort Collins, Colorado, where he served six months. From there he was transferred to Lapine, Oregon, for one year where he helped build a large dam. Next he was moved to Hill City, South Dakota, where he spent fourteen months and again helped build a dam. With that project completed, he was sent to Gulfport, Mississippi, where he spent eleven months in construction which included building sanitary outhouses. After being in civilian service three years and nine months, Enos was discharged in February, 1946. He felt the calling to go to Holland to help rebuild this peaceful country that had received a great deal of damage during the war. By May, 1946, he was traveling to Holland and was rebuilding houses and doing general clean-up there until May, 1948. He spent the first eighteen months on Wolphin Island and was near Amsterdam for the last six months.

Barbara and her children continued to work hard, and things looked better. Anna continued to work out, and her wages went to her mother until she was twenty-one. John and Mary had their third child, Lloyd, a bright-eyed little boy on August 12, 1941. Anna was there to help with the work. Their little Fannie was only a year old and was a busy little girl. David was nearly three and loved adventure. There was never a dull moment!

When the war started, Andy was sixteen. He had established a dairy herd of ten cows which were all milked by hand by Andy and his mother. Andy prided himself in his cows' production. Sometimes Fannie would help milk if there was an easy milking cow. She was so skinny and had little strength in her hands. Every evening it was her job to bring the cows home from the pasture and to feed them. She also gathered the eggs and did some other chores. Fannie and Salina took turns filling the stock tank behind the barn with water, using a hand pump. Sometimes it seemed the harder they pumped the more the cows drank.

Every evening when Andy went to bed he would say, "Mom, be sure to wake me early." If she overslept only slightly, Andy was sure his whole day was ruined. In the summer he helped his brother Willie bale hay, because with the war, help was hard to find. In the winter he kept a watchful eye on the sheep. When they lambed, the little lambs needed to be dried to keep them from chilling. He also helped other neighbors with manure hauling or fence building and many other tasks farmers needed to do. With so many young men away in the Service, farmers and neighbors were glad for any help they could get. Andy was strong and could do a man's job; therefore, he was much in demand.

Dannie had also registered when the war began. When he took his examination, he did not pass. He got into the habit of hanging around Chouteau in the evening. Although his mother did not approve, he assured her he was not doing anything wrong. One day when he was fixing some fence at home, Mother saw a carload of girls drive by slowly and stop where Dannie was working. Her suspicions were aroused. When she approached Dannie about it, he acted innocently, "Oh, those were some girls I met in Chouteau, and they were just out for a drive."

In time however, Mother found out that he had been seeing a young girl in Chouteau. She was a senior in high school. She was a Baptist, and her father was a preacher. However, Barbara did not give her approval and encouraged him to date a Mennonite girl. Dannie assured his mother that he was not serious.

Chapter 50
Dan Married - A Trip - New Grandchild

Dannie's friend was named Betty, and she graduated from high school that May. A short time later on the evening of May 28, 1942, Dannie came home at bedtime. He said, "Mother, Betty and I got married this evening. I've come to get some clothes. She is in the car. She is very shy and doesn't want to come in tonight. I will bring her by some other time to meet you."

Barbara did not know how to respond. Finally she said, "I wish you the best." What more could she say?

Fannie and Salina were enthused to learn of Dannie's marriage and could hardly wait to see his bride. Dannie, who was nearly twenty-five, had a truck and hauled milk.

Salina, however, was concerned that her resource of earning money may have ended. Dannie used to pay Salina a nickel to polish his shoes. Fannie's thoughts drifted to places where she would miss Dannie at home. She recalled how she had gathered the eggs and skipped one nest because the hen was setting on it and would peck her if she tried to reach under her to get them. One evening Mother said, "Fannie, you didn't find as many eggs tonight as usual. Did you check every nest?"

"Well," she confessed, "that hen on the one nest wouldn't let me get hers."

"You mean you let that old hen rule you?" Although it was dark by that time, Mother said, "Take a flashlight and get those eggs."

Fannie's heart beat rapidly because she was scared to go out by herself after dark. She thought she could feel that hen pecking her. Dannie heard the whole episode and took heart. He said, "Shall I go with you?" This pleased her. He threw that old broody chicken out, and sure enough, she had a number of eggs. From there on, Fannie would throw her apron over their heads to avoid getting pecked. She was grateful for a brother to help her in time of need.

Another incident came to Fannie's mind. They often got unexpected company. One time her mother had been to help at John Henry's place, and it was after dark by the time the project she was working on was completed. That evening a car from Kansas drove in. In it were Great Uncle Hans and some other visitors. Dannie had been there to welcome them into the house. He explained that his mother would probably come home soon. However, when she did not come as soon as expected, he came out to the kitchen and helped Fannie make some kind of soup he had seen their mother make. Fannie was not very observant when her mother cooked. When Mother got home, the table was set, and supper was ready.

Fannie and Salina went to nearby Mazie school. They normally ran home for dinner. Jean and Norma Parker lived nearby and also went home for dinner. They also had cows to milk. Each evening when they walked home from school together, they stood at the end of Parker's lane and talked. Finally Barbara would call, "Fannie-e-e, come home." Then she would come back to reality and run home. She knew she had better get busy with her chores in order to prevent any further problems.

Barbara and her mother planned a trip to Iowa and Illinois. Barbara took the train and went to Kansas, and from there they went to Kalona, Iowa, and visited some relatives and friends. Next they went to Illinois to visit Joni and Mary Plank. She was Grandma's youngest sister and had lived in Kansas at one time.

They also visited Menno's brother Levi and their family and discussed the fact that nobody knew Menno's whereabouts. Barbara said sometimes she wondered if he might not be living anymore. Levi agreed that could be a possibility. However, they both felt he would get homesick for the children if he was still living. Barbara admired Levi. He had a nice family and was a good father. He treated his wife respectfully, and he helped her with her work because she was often sickly.

Before Barbara came home, John and Mary were blessed with another baby girl, Edna, born on October 23, 1942. She was their fourth child, and Mary was quite busy. When their mother came home, Fannie and Salina met the train in Mazie eager to tell her the news. She was not as surprised as they expected her to be and commented that she thought the baby might get there before she did. Fannie and Salina often helped baby-sit when Mary needed to go help someone else with butchering or other tasks.

Chapter 51
Barbara's Roomers - Grandma Marries - Andy Drafted

With the war continuing, a large parcel of land was bought by Dupont southeast of Pryor, Oklahoma, to make ammunition. They were hiring anyone who was available to work there. Men came over from nearby Arkansas to get jobs. Because housing was a real problem, these men were glad if they could find a place to room and board. Barbara decided with her large house, she could rent out a few rooms to boarders to bring in some extra income.

The first renter was a man named John Robinson from Arkansas. He was a man with high morals and did not smoke or drink which was one thing Barbara required before she rented to them.

Orie Hopkins and Ed Venable were the next arrivals. They said they did not have any bad habits, so Barbara took them in. Each of these men was married and usually went home for the weekend. Barbara rose early every morning to make biscuits, gravy, and coffee for them and to pack their lunch pails. In the evening they enjoyed the supper she cooked for them, and Barbara was glad for the extra income.

Soon after John's arrival his first child was born, so he wanted to find a place to live that had adequate room for his wife and baby. It seemed every shack or brooder house in the area was already rented for families to live. After some consideration, Barbara decided to convert the living room for them, and they did their own cooking. He had a pleasant wife and an adorable baby, and they proved to be good people.

Then a man by the name of Russel Reed came to inquire about room and board, so Barbara took him in. He was a quiet man and never caused any problems. He would, at times, talk about his wife, Maggie, and their little boys and was always eager to go home on weekends to be with them. By and by John found a little larger apartment for his family, and they moved out. Russel then asked to rent the room John's family had vacated. By this time all the other boarders had found housing for their families and moved. Barbara consented, and since the other boarders were gone, she offered to let them rent her dining room as well. She realized that one room would be crowded for a family with four little boys.

The next weekend Russel went home and returned late on Sunday evening with his family. When Barbara met the family she sensed they were very poor. She asked if they had eaten supper, because she thought the children acted hungry. His wife Maggie shyly answered that they had not eaten and said she would accept a little supper for the children. Barbara set out milk and homemade bread, along with some other things. Maggie said, "Look, children, you can have cold bread soup."

Barbara said, "I thought nobody but Amish ate that."

Quietly she answered, "I was once a little Amish girl." Barbara was surprised. Maggie explained that her dad had been in trouble with the law when she was a little girl. One night he hired someone who had a truck to pick up the few belongings they owned and her mother and all the children piled into the pickup and headed for Arkansas from Ohio. Maggie said she remembered wearing a little black bonnet and sitting on her dad's lap. As they were traveling, her dad took her little bonnet off and threw it out the window of the truck. He said, "Maggie, where we are going you will no longer need your bonnet." This made Maggie sad because she cherished her bonnet. When they got to their destination, they saw nothing more of their relatives, and her mother was not allowed to write to her family. Her father changed his name to Yeader instead of Yoder.

Barbara's heart was especially touched, and she developed a genuine friendship with Maggie. The Reed's lived there for quite some time until they found a place with more room.

As time went on, the family got better acquainted with Betty. Fannie and Salina enjoyed when she came with Dan because she played games with them. They were really elated when Dan came one day and announced happily that they had a baby boy named Dannie Joe born May 28, 1943.

Barbara's mother had developed a close friendship with a widower, Jake Miller, a bishop from the Partridge area. Barbara went to Kansas for their wedding on September 12, 1943. They were very happy and moved to his house next to his son Enos in the Partridge area.

A few months later, Andy had his eighteenth birthday and went to Pryor to register. He did not ask to fill out the nonresistant form because others had told them, "Andy won't be drafted because he is needed at home." However, this would not be the case. One of the board members, who saw his name was Chupp, had heard too much about Andy's dad. To take revenge, he was soon drafted. When Andy appeared before the board, he asked for the proper papers to sign that would state his convictions. But he was mocked, and he went home with a heavy heart.

Barbara talked to their neighbor, Mr. Parker, who felt strongly that Andy was indeed needed at home. Because he had a high position in the CCC camps, Barbara hoped that he might be able to help them get Andy deferred. He got up a petition saying that Andy was needed very badly at home to help his mother, and in no time he had fifty signatures. When he presented the petition to the draft board, it was useless. Before long, Andy was called to take his examination, and being a strong, young boy, he passed it without any problem. He was notified to report for training in the Infantry at Camp Chaffee, Arkansas, within a short time.

Andy knew the cows would need to be sold because his mother and younger sisters would be unable to handle all the milking and other chores. Fannie was fourteen and could milk better by this time. Mother and Fannie decided they would keep four milk cows, even though Andy was skeptical that they could handle that many. Word got around, and soon all the cows except four were sold to people from the church. The heifers were also sold, except for the youngest ones, which were still baby calves. They hoped that by the time they would be old enough to calve, the war would be over, and Andy could come home and rebuild his dairy herd from them. One little heifer belonged to Andy, and he had named her Blacky. She was a real pet, and although he hated to part with her, he thought it might be best to sell her, too. His mother and sisters assured him they would give her the best of care while he was gone, to which he finally agreed.

The closer the time drew for Andy to leave, the sadder the whole family became. Every morning as Barbara knelt to pray with her children, Andy, Fannie, and Salina, it seemed like she prayed harder then ever before. During the day she often went to her bedroom and poured out her heart to her precious Lord. Why was the Lord allowing this trial?

Andy had hardly ever been away from home overnight, and now he would need to be gone for who knew how long. He had always felt so responsible for the welfare of his mother and younger sisters. He wondered how they would manage on their own.

By this time Anna was of age and on her own. In the winter she sometimes went to Florida, and in the summer she went to Colorado with other girls. If she was in the area, she was busy doing housework for couples who had a new baby and needed assistance until the mother's strength returned. Sometimes she came home for the weekends. If she had some time between jobs, she came home to sew and help with jobs that were too difficult for her mother and the girls.

The morning of Andy's departure arrived, and he would need to leave before daylight. Barbara fixed a good breakfast, but nobody felt like eating. Then they all knelt to pray. Before long a car drove in, and they bade their good-byes to Andy with tear-filled eyes. Barbara prayed a lot that day. Just as things were looking a little better, she had another trial to face. It seemed her life had so many trials.

She had chickens and found some fulfillment in scattering feed to them each morning, listening to their cheery sounds as they scratched about, eating their feed.

Life went on, and at this time she had no boarders or renters. With the money the cows brought when they were sold, she had finished paying for her eighty acre farm. She still did laundry and ironed for others with the girls' help. The milk from the four cows was separated, and the cream shipped by train from Mazie to Emporia, Kansas. The cream was put in a five gallon can and loaded onto the little wagon. The girls pulled it to the depot in Mazie where the train picked it up later.

Fannie was through the eighth grade, and Barbara saw no need for her to continue her education any further except what she could learn at home such as cooking, sewing, and keeping house. With the chores, Fannie usually had enough to do. They had Amish neighbors, the Mose Coblentz family, who were very industrious people. His wife Lizzie had no girls at home to help her and often asked Fannie to assist her with washing windows, raking yard, or most anything else. Once Fannie helped pluck feathers from their geese to stuff pillows. Lizzie never had any idle moments. She had pretty rows of flowers in her garden, and no weeds were allowed to grow anywhere.

Barbara and the girls often went to John Henry's home to help Mary do her work. With four little children, milking, chickens to feed, eggs to gather, plus the everyday cooking and house work, she could always use extra help. Fannie often baked peanut butter cookies for them. The children liked to be nearby to offer their help, or at least to sample them. Barbara frequently sewed for their children. Salina would play games with the children to keep them occupied.

David went to Mazie school, and every morning and evening on his way to and from school he walked through his grandma's house. He would come in through the front door and walk out through the back. As soon as he was big enough, he gladly helped Fannie and Salina with minor tasks.

Barbara still had sheep, and when they were lambing, she and Fannie would go out and check them and rub the newborn lambs dry with a gunny sack. If it was too cold, they brought the lambs into the brooder house and lit a small kerosene heater to warm them. Sometimes they needed to be checked at night if the weather was cold.

Salina was still in school and loving every minute of it. She always got ahead of the others in her grade, and to keep her busy, the teacher had her coach a boy who had little interest in academics. Salina spoke to him as one in authority and usually got something through his head. In her spare time at home, she often played school with her dolls. When her nieces and nephews came, she also tried to get them to be her pupils. By the time she was twelve, Salina had completed the eighth grade. She had taken two grades in one year.

Chapter 52
Picnic - Barnyard News - Many Problems

Every summer Fannie and Salina would have their nieces, Barbara and Mary, Willie's girls, and Fannie and Edna, John Henry's girls, come over for a night. The next day they would pack a lunch and go down beside the pond for a picnic. Since Edna and Mary were quite young, they put them both on the little wagon and gave them a ride to the pond. They found some shady trees and would spread an old quilt on the ground where they enjoyed their dinner. Sometimes after they ate their lunch, they fished with cane poles using worms for bait. They had to watch Edna and Mary closely, so they would not get in briars and cry.

Barbara and the girls missed Andy very much and guessed he also missed home and the animals. Salina came up with the idea of writing a "Barnyard News" newsletter to send to Andy each week. The girls named each lamb when it was born and enjoyed watching them play. Andy got a full report of each lamb's doings.

One lamb was born with a broken leg, and Barbara did not think it would survive. Fannie had taken a first aid evening course at the local school, just in case Mazie would get bombed (!) or some other catastrophe would happen. With her knowledge and Salina's help, they put a splint on the lamb's leg and wrapped it. This lamb was named Jackie Long Legs. Of course, Andy received a full report of this situation. After a certain time when the splint was removed, the girls were elated to see their little lamb walking. At first, it was rather wobbly, but soon it was running with the others.

Andy was sent to Fort Hood, Texas, for his basic training, which was very rigid. Andy came down with pneumonia and had to be admitted to the Army hospital near the end of training. The others from his division were sent on to California to be sent abroad to fight. While Andy was recuperating in the hospital, his mother became quite concerned when she did not hear from him for a long time. When he was finally able to write again, he wrote he was in the hospital with pneumonia, while the rest of his division were shipped on to California.

Barbara was sorry to hear he was so sick, but she was also grateful that he was not sent overseas to battle. From what she read in the newspapers, the fighting was intense and getting worse all the time. Every day she prayed for the war to end and for Andy's safety, as well as the other boys.

Many were the problems Barbara and the girls faced. One Sunday morning when they went to chore, they heard the pathetic bleating of the sheep. When they checked them, they found that dogs had eaten into the sides of their sheep and nice fat lambs. Barbara said, "One of you girls go and tell Mose Coblentz." Soon he was there and butchered four ewes and one nice fat lamb that were injured. Then he hung them up to cool. Although they were late to church, they had salvaged the meat and put the poor sheep out of their misery.

Other times the cows broke out into the neighbors' fields. Fences needed to be repaired, and some things were too difficult for them to do. They were always glad when Dannie dropped in and lent a hand. They enjoyed when Betty came out with Dan, as they now called him, and their little son Dannie Joe. Willie sent his hired man over occasionally to clean out the chicken house. Sometimes John Henry stopped in and fixed a gate or made other repairs.

Patsy, the old gray mare they hitched to the buggy to go away, caused them considerable problems. At times Fannie could take a bucket with some oats and go down to the pasture, and Patsy would come right to her. Then she would quickly throw the rope of the bridle around her neck, put the bridle on her, and head home with her. Other times she would come close to Fannie, then turn and kick up her heels and gallop away to the other end of the pasture. One Sunday morning, after repeating this trick a number of times, Fannie was about ready to give up. A kind neighbor, Mose Yoder, saw her predicament, jumped on his horse, and rode over. He easily caught Patsy, and Fannie led the horse home. She soon had her harnessed and hitched up, ready for church.

Willie and Amanda were blessed with a baby boy on January 2, 1944. They named him William Jr. Willie was overjoyed to have another son since they had lost their first son. Their daughter Mary had her first birthday on Christmas Day of 1943. Barbara was in the first grade and would have her seventh birthday on February 23. She was quite a helper and could stir up a pan of cornbread in short order, as well as run many errands for her mother.

Chapter 53
Runaway - Atomic Bomb - War Ends - Andy Across

On September 30, 1944, Dan and Betty had another son named Leroy. Fannie went to Chouteau and stayed with them part of the time to help. At the same time, Willie and Amanda and little Mary were on a trip east to Pennsylvania. Anna helped with their chores in their absence. Little William stayed with his grandma and Salina, and Barbara was there for the weekend. Mother Barbara decided to fix some food and drive out to Chouteau to have Sunday dinner with Dan and Betty. She had little William and Barbara and Salina with her. Salina held William and Barbara sat in the middle. Of course, Mother held the reins. When they were almost at Dan's house, they passed a place where barking dogs ran out and bit old Patsy in the legs. She spooked and ran off, dumping all of them out of the buggy. Barbara received a broken arm, and Mom and Salina got by with only a few scratches. William fared the best because he was wrapped in a blanket and had been sleeping. His grandma was most concerned about him. She was relieved to see he was unhurt. The following week Barbara went home with her arm in a cast. Her aunt Anna had to dress her and get her ready for school.

Finally Andy wrote that he had recovered and would be sent to California. He said, "Mom, I could never shoot anyone, even if they put me on the front lines." After being there for some time, the United States dropped the destructive atomic bomb on Hiroshima on August 6, 1945. Plans were made to send a shipload of soldiers to the Philippine Islands to fight under MacArthur. Andy would be in this group. His mother was deeply grieved.

On September 2, 1945, the ship was on dock to take the large group of soldiers overseas. The Army boys stood with their packs, waiting to be loaded. Suddenly bells rang, and whistles blew. The announcement was heard over loud speakers, "The war has ended!" Civilians were grabbing soldiers and hugging them, wishing them well.

The ship was delayed slightly, but it was still loaded. They were on the ship a number of days before it docked in the bay of Manilla, in the Philippines.

Andy was given orders to work night duty in a hospital where many wounded lay. The food was buggy and scarce, but they made the best of what was available. Many booby traps were left behind by the Japanese, and some soldiers were injured by them. It was horrible to see the results of the fighting.

Andy's thoughts often drifted to home and how nice it would be if he could be there with his family. Mail was slow, and the letters were censored. He had to be careful what he wrote, or it would get cut out. If he received a letter from home, it was very special.

Chapter 54
Breaking Heifers - Andy Home - Makes Repairs

The young heifers were starting to calve. Fannie and Salina would manage to get them in the stanchions for milking, often tying a rope around the cow's right hind leg. Salina held onto the rope while Fannie milked. In this way they trained them to stand quietly while they were being milked. They broke six heifers this way. They watched Andy's heifer, Blacky, very closely because she would be the next to calve. But, alas! They did not keep a close enough watch as one evening Blacky did not come up to the barn with the other cows. When Fannie went to look for her, she found her lying dead from calving complications and her calf was dead, too. They hated to write Andy the discouraging news.

Time moved on with very little news from Andy. Mother said, "The war is over. Why don't they send him home?" Others were coming home, but still no word from Andy.

Finally Mother received a letter from Andy he had written in August, 1946. Hastily she opened it, with Fannie and Salina at her side, eagerly waiting to see what he wrote. Barbara read, "Many are now being sent home. The fathers get first priority. Mom, I will come as soon as I can." Tears rolled down Mother's cheeks as she thought what a happy day that would be. Days turned to weeks with no more word from Andy. She prayed fervently for him every day.

One rainy morning Barbara was in good spirits as she went to do her chicken chores. She caught one of her cull hens, came in, got hot water to scald it, and dressed it. She said, "Girls, I'm going to cook a good dinner. Maybe Andy will come home today." The girls hoped her intuition was right. They eagerly helped prepare dinner. They even baked a pie, and the aroma of the chicken baking filled the whole house. Dressing, mashed potatoes, and other home grown food were also on the menu. Time and again Salina would go to the window and gaze to the east, but she saw nothing.

Finally it was eleven o'clock and still pouring down rain. Salina looked out the east window again and said, "There's a car coming down our road." This brought Fannie and her mother to the window, too. Sure enough, it was turning into their lane. They ran to the north kitchen window and looked. "Oh, Mom! It's Andy!" they said excitedly.

Mother quickly opened the door, and Andy popped in, flinging his army bag to the floor. "I'm so glad to be home!" he said.

"We are certainly glad to see you are safe at home, and give you a hearty welcome," Mother and the girls all said at the same time.

"My! I see my little sisters grew up while I was away. I smell something good cooking," Andy said in one breath.

"Yes," Mother replied, "we have dinner nearly ready. I just had a strong feeling this morning that today you might come home. Girls, set the table, and I will make the gravy. Then we shall eat."

Andy had much to tell. He said, "I haven't had a meal like this for a long time."

Mother said, "We heard of others coming home and couldn't understand why you didn't come."

Andy answered, "Everyone was eager to go home. We all had our bags packed and stood in line in the rain for days waiting to get on the ship to come home. When one ship was full, we had to wait for the next one. Then I contracted malaria and had to be in the hospital to recuperate before I could come. I had no way to let you know."

"The main thing is you are here now, and we thank God for keeping you safe," Mother said. The rest of the afternoon was spent reminiscing. Andy marveled that his little sisters had been able to break the heifers for milking. They all told him how sorry they were that Blacky had died. He assured them that he was sure they had done their best.

When the family found out Andy was home, Willies and their children, Barbara, Mary and William; Dan and Betty, with their two boys, Dannie and Leroy; and John and Mary and their children, David, Fannie, Lloyd, and Edna; came over to welcome him. Anna was working for someone in the area and was glad when the weekend came so she, too, could catch up on Andy's experiences. However, Andy preferred not to talk much about them. Instead he wanted to hear what went on at home in his absence. He enjoyed seeing how the nieces and nephews had grown. The younger ones did not remember him.

Andy found many things that were neglected and needed repair. Soon he was busy making repairs and building a new yard fence. Mother mentioned how much she wished for a cellar to store her canned goods and potatoes. Andy assured her that she would get one in time.

Willie was busy building a large barn on the farm he had bought a few years earlier. Jake Helmuth from the Mennonite church was the main carpenter. With the extra work, Amanda needed help with cooking and gardening, so Anna worked there that summer.

One evening a car with two young men came to Mazie and asked where Barbara lived. When they found the right place, one of them came to the door and knocked. Barbara answered the knock, and the young man introduced himself as Levi Yoder from Indiana. He explained that he had met an Anna Chupp in Florida the previous winter and wanted to visit her. Fannie and Salina had been listening in the background and whispered to each other, "Does our sister have a beau, and we didn't know about it?"

Chapter 55
Florida Boys - Willie's Barn - The Fall - Wedding

"She is working at her brother Willie's place," Barbara replied. "I guess Fannie could ride over with you to show you the way." Fannie was glad to assist in any way if her sister had a beau. After all, she had been of age for several years. When they got to Willie's farm, Fannie lost no time dashing into the house to tell the news of the visitors she had escorted there. By this time she had learned that the other boy's name was David, and he came from Pennsylvania. Anna denied knowing much about these fellows. She insisted she had only briefly met them while she was in Florida.

Willie invited them inside and told of his building project, informing them he needed more carpenters. The boys grinned as they exchanged glances. "That is our trade," they said. They explained they really were going on a trip west, but another boy from Indiana was planning to join them in Oklahoma. "It might be a week or more before he comes," they said. They agreed to help build the barn until then. They were equipped with carpenter tools and got right to work the next morning. Their presence meant more cooking for Amanda and Anna. Willie's Mary was a little chatterbox and enjoyed all the attention Levi gave her. She also hoped he would be a suitor for her aunt Anna.

One day Anna was in the garden gathering vegetables for dinner, and the boys were on top of the barn shingling. It was a round roof and really dangerous. Anna glanced up just in time to see Levi fall to the ground. He had a bad break in his arm and was taken to the doctor, where he had a cast put on. Needless to say, his carpenter work came to a halt. He spent most of his time in the house recovering and entertaining Mary and William. Of course, it gave him plenty of time to observe Anna at work too, but she did not act overly enthused.

David kept on working until the other boy from Indiana arrived, then the three boys left for their western trip.

Anna went to Colorado the next summer, and Levi came out and surprised her. Their romance developed, and they set their wedding date for October 21, 1948. Anna's family rejoiced with her. When Mother found out, she decided the inside of the house would need new paper and paint. Anna came home, and the whole family assisted in helping with the redecorating. The cellar was not finished, so Levi applied his skills and helped Andy finish it. When they started to paper the kitchen, some plaster fell off. Levi, with his carpenter abilities, came to the rescue and soon had it patched so they could continue their task.

Andy made many trips to town with his mother to get the things needed for the important day. Women from the church came and helped prepare food or whatever there was to do. Anna had helped many of them when they had new babies. This was one way they could show their gratitude for the help she had been to them. Chickens were butchered, and pies, puddings, cakes, jello salads, and a great deal of other food was prepared for the wedding day.

Grandma and Jake Doddy, as they called her new husband, came from Kansas with Orie and Aunt Edna and Aunt Ida. Levi's brother Orie and family came from Indiana and a sister, the Dan Ottos. Barbara was rather flustered trying to remember everything that needed to be done. Aunts Edna and Ida and daughter Mary and Amanda were also cooks, as well as somemore. With Mary's cooking abilities, Barbara was somewhat relieved. Many of Anna's girlfriends from Indiana and some of Levi's friends came for the occasion. Levi was thirty and Anna twenty-seven. Fannie and a boy from Kansas, Andy Miller, Jr. were witnesses at the wedding. Fannie was eighteen and had been to Kansas that summer working for Enos and Ida Schrock. She had been baptized in the Amish church there. She had struck up a casual acquaintance with Andy Jr., therefore it seemed only right to have him there for this special event.

Levi and Anna bought some cows and other items needed to start farming. Anna had enough money to pay for the furniture and to help pay for the cows they bought. They rented a farm on the south side of 33 highway and were soon busy with farm life. It was quite a contrast to their carefree years of traveling and doing as they pleased.

On November 21, 1948, Willie came over to bring the news that a baby boy, Floyd Ray, was born to them and they needed help. Fannie packed her suitcase and went home with him. The baby clothes needed to be washed, as well as the other laundry. Before long Beatrice, Amanda's sister, came and helped get everything in top shape. She and Fannie even made a few new kimonos for the baby. The next day they went to Pryor with Willie, and he gave them some money to get whatever was needed for the baby. They bought a pretty little shawl and a few other things. The children were thrilled with a baby brother and were quite excited when they brought him and their mother home.

Salina was a very capable young girl by this time and could milk as fast as anyone. Andy went to Indiana that winter and got a job. He made his home with the widow of his uncle Andy Chupp and her children. Their daughter Drucilla was very close to his age. The other children were Dema, Anna, Andrew, Katie, Ben, Emma, and Ike. He enjoyed getting better acquainted with his cousins.

When summer came, he decided to come back home and work on the farm again. Tobie Petershiems from Kansas wrote Barbara to see if Fannie could come and work for them that summer. They had a new baby named Samuel and a little one-year-old girl, Ruby. Barbara thought it might be a good idea. With very few young folks in the church, she feared Fannie would get too friendly with those around the small town of Mazie. Her Aunt Ida and Enos offered to let her stay at their home for weekends.

Fannie was glad to see the friends she had made the previous summer. Enos' children were little, and Fannie enjoyed them. Their Fannie was an ambitious little girl. Robert always had a smile, but his speech was not always too plain. They seemed more like her nieces and nephews than cousins. William and Eli Jay were old enough to milk and chore if they did not get distracted. Sometimes when Fannie helped milk, these boys were discussing ball playing, and then the milking really slowed down. When Enos entered the barn, he would say, "Boys, milk!" With that, they would come back to reality, and the sound of milk hitting the buckets would resume.

Uncle Enos met the girl of his dreams, and her name was Lulu Weaver from Iowa. They got married June 12, 1949, and they worked at a children's home in Kansas City the first year. After that they were hired by a large farmer in Reno County. Their first child, Paul David, was born March 20, 1950, and their second child, a daughter Erna, was born to them September 13, 1951. Lulu was very busy with their two little ones. Enos' sister Fannie often came to her rescue and helped her.

When Fannie finished working for Tobies, she worked in Hutchinson, taking care of a baby named Mark Foy. She pushed him around with his stroller when the weather was nice. Bertha Yoder from Thomas, Oklahoma, came to Kansas and got a job in Hutchinson too. She and Fannie spent a lot of time together. On Saturday they both went to Enos' house, and from there went to church on Sunday. Sunday evenings they went to the youth hymn sings. Monday morning their employers would come to get them again.

Chapter 56
Romance - Marriage - Sad News from Oklahoma

In time, Andy Miller, Jr. struck up a special friendship with Fannie, and Feltie Schrock started seeing Bertha. These two couples double dated and had many happy times together at Enos and Ida's on Sunday evenings. They unknowingly planned their wedding dates for about the same time. Andy and Fannie had chosen October 26, 1950, and then discovered Feltie and Bertha had chosen a week earlier.

Enos and Ida offered to have Andy and Fannie's wedding dinner at their home. Bertha and Feltie planned to get married near Thomas, Oklahoma, since that was where they planned to live. It was common knowledge that Andy was to live on his parents' home place since he was the youngest in the family.

Fannie went home to sew and help her mother quilt and get things ready for the big event. When she broke the news of their plans to her brother Andy, he said, "Isn't he pretty young to be thinking of marriage?"

Fannie answered, "He is nineteen, and has been for a long time."

Andy jokingly replied, "I suppose for a few years." This made her laugh.

Mother rejoiced with Fannie and wished her blessings. She said she knew his family for many years and appreciated them. She went right to work to get her quilts done and helped her choose material for her wedding dress. Fannie chose a moss crepe in royal blue for her own dress, a wine color for the witnesses, and a gray for the girls who would waitress. She stayed busy sewing and helped Salina make her dress. Being the only single sister, Salina would naturally be in the bridal party with Andy's nephew, Andy Fry. She was sixteen and quite excited.

Everything was to be kept a secret until a few weeks before the wedding, when it was announced in the church service in Kansas. By then Barbara, Fannie, and Salina were in Kansas. Fannie had taken all her belongings along and stored them at Andy's place where they would live after their marriage.

The leaves were falling every day. When Andy's sister Polly, her son Orie, his girlfriend Alma, Polly's daughter Lisbet, her boyfriend Ervin, another daughter Ida, and Andy's brother Sam, came from

Indiana the day before the wedding, they were put to work raking leaves. October 26, 1950, dawned with a refreshing little shower that morning. The cooks were busy preparing food for dinner. Andy and Fannie, with their witnesses, Andy Fry and Salina, and Orie and Alma, left early for the home of Sam Schrocks where the ceremony would be performed. The waitresses busied themselves with whatever the cooks found for them to do. Soon the sun came out, and it was a nice fall day.

When they came back to Enos' place after the ceremony, they found everything in order and ready to seat the people at the tables. Andy and Fannie sat at the corner with a set of witnesses on each side. The wedding cake sat right in front of them. They had decorated it the evening before with yellow and blue roses. On both sides of the cake were large pedestaled fruit bowls with fresh fruit. It was indeed the happiest day of their lives. Many aunts, uncles, great aunts, and great uncles were present and gave their best wishes, as well as closer family members and many friends.

The next day when everything was cleared away from the wedding, Andy hitched the team to his dad's rack wagon. They loaded their wedding gifts onto it and took them to his home. All the gifts were stored in a room upstairs. They lived in the same house with his parents the first seven months of their married life. They ate together and helped with whatever his folks had to do.

On November 9, 1950, Anna and Levi were blessed with another son named Mark. Salina was there to assist with the work and help take care of little Paul who was a year old on August 25.

Andy's parents went to Indiana, and Fannie and Andy were alone for a short time. Andy's dad had a catch in his neck when they came home.

On December 9, 1950, Andy's got the sad news that Willie's little Floyd Ray passed away. Fannie went to the funeral with one of her uncles, but Andy had to stay home because his dad was not able to do much. Willie begged Fannie to stay longer than the others, promising they would take her home later. Because the event was such a shock, Amanda needed someone to console her. Floyd Ray had been such a busy little fellow. While Amanda was getting dinner, he had climbed up onto the chest of drawers and found some pills in a bottle. He had taken the bottle and sat behind a big chair and started to eat them. Suddenly Amanda thought it seemed a bit too quiet, so she had gone to check and found him, his mouth all red from the pills he had eaten. She tried to induce vomiting and quickly went to her mother-in-law Barbara's with him. She explained what had happened, and Barbara went with her to Wagoner to the doctor. The doctor read the label on the bottle and said he would probably get pretty sick. They went home and were soon aware that he was indeed a very sick child. Willie said, "We will take him to the hospital in Pryor." There he passed away the next evening. He was the second little son they had seen lowered into a grave.

Chapter 57
Amelia Married - House Fire - Stillborn

Aunt Amelia, who was the baby when Barbara got married, had spent some time in Indiana and met an older single boy, Elton Bontrager, who was caring for his mother. He and Amelia became good friends and got married in December of 1950. She was thirty-seven, and he was forty-five. His mother passed away not long after that. They enjoyed their home. One night they awoke and their house was on fire. Quickly they carried out what they could before the heat was too intense.

On August 16, 1952, a stillborn son was born to them. This was another trial for them. However, the Lord blessed their home with a baby girl December 2, 1953. They named her Anita Faye, and she was their pride and joy. On July 3, 1970, when Anita was sixteen, Amelia died suddenly, leaving her and her father alone. Then he died March 7, 1975, which left Anita all alone. She later married, but still missed her parents.

Andy's folks had a new house built that spring, so Fannie helped cook for the carpenters. Andy was busy helping on the house. On May 24, 1951, the house was completed. This was the day they had long anticipated. Andy's brothers and their families, and Andy's sister, the Harvey Frys, came to help move his parents into their new house and also help get Andy and Fannie get their things in place. It was a pleasure to bring all the pretty new gifts they had received as wedding presents downstairs and place them in the cupboards to put to use. The next day Andy and Fannie went to Hutchinson and bought a chest of drawers and a dinette set. Fannie made new curtains for the dining room and hung them. Although the house was rather scantily furnished, they were happy.

Barbara and Salina went to Oregon the summer of 1951. They stayed in a house with the widow of Uncle Andy Chupp and her children, and all of them worked, picking beans and berries. Salina and her cousin Katie became fast friends. Katie's sister Anna lived in Oregon. The letters from there sounded like the land of milk and honey.

One day Fannie's grandma Fannie and Jake Doddy came to spend the day with Andy and Fannie which meant a lot to Fannie. Without her own mother close, she always welcomed Grandma and the aunts and uncles when they visited.

Jake Doddy had some health problems at times and on December 25, 1951, he passed away. After the funeral was over, Grandma moved back to her house beside her son David who lived on the home place. David and Mary had four children at that time. Twila was ten; Orval, nine; Duane, seven; and Bonnie, two. Bonnie was such a pastime for Grandma. When the other children were at school, she often brought her dolls over and played in Grandma's part of the house.

In the meantime, Barbara's son Andy had developed a friendship with a girl named Lizzie Yoder from Thomas, Oklahoma. She stayed with her sister near Pryor while she cooked for a nearby school. They attended the Mennonite church near Pryor where Andy was a member.

Chapter 58
Andy Married - Barbara Seriously Ill - Babies

Andy and Lizzie got married May 11, 1951. Barbara let them have part of the house because she only had Salina left at home, and she worked for others most of the time. Andy built a new dairy barn and silo and sold grade A milk. By this time he had established a nice herd again.

Barbara pieced quilts and sewed for a pastime. She enjoyed spending a day with her children when they needed help. It was rewarding to see the sparkle in the grandchildren's eyes when she sewed a new garment for them. She was thankful her children were not as poor as she was when her children were small.

Barbara had severe pains, and on February 28, 1952, Andy and Salina took her to the hospital in Pryor. After doing various tests, the doctor advised surgery. She told the doctor how she dreaded the ether. He said, "We can give you a spinal block," and she agreed to that. On March 2 she had surgery for adhesions. However, she was not told the importance of staying flat on her back for a certain period of time.

March 4, 1952, Lizzie gave birth to their first child, a son named Robert. Andy was elated to have a little son.

Salina stayed with her mother in the hospital most of the time. Willie and Mary took turns with Salina to stay with her at night. On March 12 Barbara was released to go home by ambulance. She still had severe headaches however, and on the 26th she had convulsions and was admitted to the hospital again for a few days. On March 31 she went into convulsions at home again, and Andy and Salina took her to the hospital. Her headaches continued. The doctors gave little hope for her recovery.

Through all this they were very careful what they wrote to Fannie, knowing her present condition. However, she suspected they were not writing her the seriousness of her mother's illness. One day she went to spend the day with Aunt Ida and saw a card lying there from Salina. Quickly she read it, and it stated, "Mom is not well, and we don't know how long she can hold out. We don't think she will be with us much longer." This was quite a shock to Fannie. The card continued, "We thought it best not to write Fannie of the seriousness of Mom's illness. We were afraid it would excite her too much in her condition. We don't expect she would attempt to come anymore at this time."

Fannie's thoughts whirled. Dare they go to see her mother? That evening Uncle Andy and Nora came to visit Fannie and Andy and kindly offered to take them to visit her mother yet. Nora said, "If your baby is born while you are there, you will be near your family. Grandma will also go along, and she also feels we should go and take you along."

Early the next morning they, with Andy and Fannie and Grandma, started for Oklahoma and arrived at the hospital that afternoon. When they walked into her room, Barbara said, "Oh, Fannie, did you dare to come?" Nora assured her that they were taking good care of her. They stayed two nights and one day.

Fannie got along fine, and the first evening at home, Enos and Ida came over to get a report of Barbara's condition. A short time after their arrival, Fannie realized the time had come. Andy went to get someone to take them to the hospital. Fannie was grateful for Ida's help and motherly advice. Soon they were at the hospital, but it was a long and difficult delivery. The next evening, April 5, 1952, a son was born, and they named him Earl. She got along very well after his arrival and before long she was at home doing her own work. Both her mother and Salina had wanted to be there for the occasion.

On April 8, Barbara was released from the hospital. However, the severe headaches continued and eight days later she had convulsions again. Andy and Salina took her to the hospital in Pryor. Dr. Werling wanted her to go to Tulsa to a brain specialist, so Willie took her and Salina for the appointment. More tests and x-rays were taken, with no diagnosis.

The doctor recommended surgery on her head, but he did not know what they would find. Surgery was scheduled for April 19. Willie, Dan, Mary, Anna, and Andy came to be near her, as well as Salina who was with her most of the time. Although they found nothing abnormal in her head, from that time on she improved. Three days later she was able to eat and fed herself. She went home on May 3, and her health continued to improve. The doctor said all he could figure out was that she had pressure in her head that was released with the surgery. However, her memory was not as sharp as previously.

When Mom returned home, it was necessary for Salina to work out to help pay the large hospital bill. The church and a few individuals also made generous donations to help with the bill. After Mom's health improved, she and Salina made a trip to Kansas that summer to visit her mother, sisters, and brothers, also Andy, Fannie, and baby Earl.

On October 31, 1952, Levi and Anna were blessed with their third child and son named Harley. Salina was there to help. Paul was three and Mark not quite two, so there was always plenty to do.

That fall, Willie's had some company related to Menno. The conversation drifted to Willie's dad and how strange it was that they had never heard anything from him. Willie said, "Well, he told Mom when he left that she should never let the boys search for him. You know, Great Uncle Hans was once on his way to Florida. He stopped at a gas station somewhere in the South and thought he saw him, but he just suddenly disappeared. When Hans asked someone who that man was, they replied, 'Oh! that was Joe Miller. He is married to a blind man's daughter.' But who knows?" Willie went on, "Sometimes a person hears a lot."

"I know," the visitor remarked. "I suspect he is in the South somewhere. You know he lived in Mississippi when he was little. That makes it possible he may have gone there." The conversation drifted to other things as the evening wore on, but Willie pondered on these things for some time thereafter.

Chapter 59

Search for Menno - Boys to California - Met Dad

Rudy Detweiler asked Willie if he would take them to Florida. He wanted to tow his boat along, too. After much serious thought, Willie said to Amanda, "I think we will take Rudy up on his offer. Maybe we can research some of those rumors we heard about Dad."

Around the first of December they left. First they went to Mississippi to Ananias Schrock's home where they spent a day or so. When Willie inquired about his dad, Ananias said, "Yes, he was here in the winter of 1937. He wasn't here long and I don't know where he went next. He talked of going further south. Also, he talked like he wanted to move his family south." Willie traveled on to Florida, and they helped get Rudy and Deemy settled for the winter.

Willie and Amanda left Florida, going through Minot, Alabama. They had heard a report that he may have been close to that area at one time. Willie went to different courthouses, trying to find some records of Joe Miller, but he learned nothing. Early in the evening, they reserved a motel room for the night. They had a clue that Joe married the daughter of a blind man who used to drill wells. Willie asked the man at the motel if he knew of a blind man who drilled wells at one time. But he did not know anyone like that. A man sitting on a nearby bench overheard Willie's question. When Willie started to walk past him, the man said, "I heard what you asked the manager, and I think you are about seven years too late. There was a blind man by the name of Henry Rolla who used to drill wells, but he died seven years ago."

Willie inquired if any of his family was still in the area. He replied, "You go over to the little town of Brat and inquire there. It is possible that a nephew, Lyle Wiggins, may still be around."

The next morning they headed for Brat. There they found a small convenience store that sold groceries and gas. It appeared to be where the local men gathered to get the morning paper and discuss the latest news. Willie went into the store and inquired where Mr. Wiggins lived. They were given directions, and following them, found a nice dairy farm. After visiting a bit, he invited them to come into the house. He said, "That blind man, Rolla, was my uncle. After he died, the rest of the family moved to California."

"Did he have some children?" asked Willie.

"Yes, he did. One of the girls, Maizie, married Joe Miller, but he was much older than she was. Joe worked for my uncle at one time."

"Would you know where they live in California?" Willie inquired.

"Yes, it's a town by the name of San Marcos, just outside Escadino," replied Mr. Wiggins. They had a pleasant visit with them and were invited to stay for dinner, which they did. After dinner Willie and Amanda thanked them, said good-bye, and started homeward.

They came home December 9, 1952. Andy and Lizzie were butchering a day or so later, and Willie's helped them. The family members that were gathered were interested in the information they had gleaned on their trip. Willie said, "We stopped at numerous places on our way home from Florida. After many stops and no clues, we were about ready to give up. Then we happened on this man in front of the motel. He gave us some clues, and things started to fall in place. We now know the town where Dad lives in California." Everyone was listening eagerly, relieved to hear that he was still living.

Before the day ended, Andy said to Bill, "I will go with you to find him." The trip was planned, and December 14, 1952, Willie and Andy started for California, driving day and night until they got there. First they went to the post office for the street address, but it was illegal for the post office to disclose such information. After inquiring at some other places, they finally found someone who gave them the street address.

When they drove to the house, a young woman came to the door with a little girl at her side. They explained that they were sons of Joe Miller and had come to visit. She welcomed them in and introduced herself as Maizie, his wife. "This is our daughter, Susan," she said. "This is a real surprise. I'm sure Joe will be delighted to see you. He has often told me about his children. Joe is busy building houses in a new division in San Diego. Susan and I can ride over with you to direct you, if you would like."

"That would be nice of you, if you don't mind," Willie and Andy agreed.

"My Grandmother lives near there. I will point him out to you, then Susan and I will get off at my Grandma's house. That way he will be all the more surprised."

When they were close, she pointed out the place where he was working, and she and Susan stayed back. Willie immediately recognized his dad, although he no longer had a beard. At first he was occupied with his work and did not notice them. The boys walked over to him and shook hands with him. Willie said, "Well, how are you, Menno?"

He said, "You must be on the wrong track because that is not my name."

Willie said, "Aren't you Menno Chupp?"

He answered, "I never knew the man."

"Dad, I see you still have your scar where you were burned, and your arm is still crooked."

He looked quite surprised, then said, "You aren't my boys, are you?"

They answered, "We certainly are."

Tears streamed down his face, and he said, "How did you ever find me here?"

"Your wife came over with us and gave directions."

"Then you know I'm married again."

"Sure, and we also met our little sister."

House Menno was building when boys found him.

"I want you to understand that you are not to mention your last name in my wife's presence. All she needs to know is that you are my boys. I legally changed my name in the South to Joe Miller. You know my mother was a Miller, so I am as much a Miller as a Chupp. By the way, how is my little mongoloid son, Levi?"

"He died in 1940," they answered.

"I have often thought of him."

They helped him for awhile, then picked up Maizie and little Susan and went to their home. Maizie prepared a tasty supper for them and remarked, "Joe, how could you stay away from your boys all these years? They seem like such fine young men."

"I raised them right," he answered jokingly.

When supper was over, their dad had many questions about his own siblings and also his other children. "Your brothers have all died, but your sister Millie is still living. She has heart problems and is often not well," they informed him.

The boys helped him with his building project a day or two which he enjoyed. They said, "We need to return home to our own families." The morning of their departure came, and they bid their dad good-bye. He went to work early, telling them to come again.

As the boys were preparing to leave, Maizie followed them to the car. She said, "I have some questions, if you don't mind answering them. What was the cause of your mother's death?"

Because the boys could not lie, they answered, "Our mother is alive and pretty well at this point."

"Really! Your father told me he spent all his money on medical bills for her before she died. He said he was so heartbroken after losing her, he just needed to get away. When I inquired about his children, he told me they had a rich grandpa who would provide well for them if he was not there."

The boys answered, "Our mother has worked very hard to make ends meet, and we children helped in any way we could." Maizie looked amazed, but said little more.

When the boys returned to Oklahoma, the ones at home had many questions.

In the evening of December 23, Fannie, Andy, and baby Earl boarded the train at Hutchinson for Wagoner, Oklahoma, and rode all night. The next morning as the day was dawning, they arrived at their destination. Willie was at the depot to meet them and took them home to Mother and Salina. Andy, Lizzie, and little Robert lived in one part of the house. It was good to see everyone. They were at John and Mary's one day, and their children had grown so much. On the twenty-ninth the whole Chupp family was at Willie and Amanda's house for the day and had a delicious dinner. Each family had contributed something. Much was discussed about the miracle of finally knowing the whereabouts of their father. Fannie and Salina tried to visualize him because they were too young to remember many details about him.

Willie said he hoped to take his family to see him that next summer. He mentioned that Susan had some distinctive Chupp features.

Andy, Fannie, and their baby returned home. Fannie thought she would like to meet her father, but California sounded too far away. In her mind, she wondered if that would ever happen. Being young and trying to get a start in farming was not easy, and she knew they could not afford a trip to California. Before long, she wrote her father and received an answer.

Chapter 60
Fannie's Letter - Salina's New Job - Deaths 1954

His letter was dated February 13, 1953. He wrote,

"Dear beloved Daughter and Family,

I will answer your kind and welcome letter I received. Greetings in Jesus' Holy Name, from whom all blessings flow. I was so glad to see my boys. Nobody knows what I went through the last sixteen years. But thank God for what good has befallen me. I had been very sick for a year and last February I was operated on and very near lost my life. Am glad for better health. I had kidney stones. I'm busy building houses. They are very pretty. I think you married a fine young man as I knew his parents. I prayed often that God would watch over my children. Now they are all grown except Susan. She is quite a daddy's girl. She is a smart little girl and talks about her brothers since the boys were here. I wish you could see her. She asked who I was writing. I said your sister Fannie. I hope someday, if it is the Lord's will, I can see all my children again. So you have a baby. I bet he is cute. Tell Leffs hello for me. I will sign off wishing you all God's blessings. Think of us in your prayers.

Your unworthy, Dad"

Andy and Lizzie had their second child, a daughter, Roberta, on April 16, 1953. Barbara enjoyed little Robert very much and was glad that he now had a little sister. Salina helped with the work there.

About this time Salina received a letter from her great aunt Mary Ann in Thomas, Oklahoma, to ask if Salina would please come and work for her daughter Bertha and Johnny Yoder. They had a new baby, and she was not doing too well. With her poor health and the other youngsters, she had trouble keeping up with her obligations. The latter part of May, 1953, Salina started working there. She enjoyed her work and the children, although they were sometimes mischievous. As she got acquainted with the youth in that area, she attracted the attention of a young man by the name of Joe Bontrager. After her job was completed and she returned home, they communicated by letters.

On August 9, 1953, Willie and Amanda were blessed with a baby girl named Ruby. With Barbara sixteen and Mary almost ten, the household duties were well under control. Grandma Barbara sometimes helped for a day because Salina was still in Thomas.

In 1954, Andy's parents and sister Lisbet and Harvey Fry bought a farm in Indiana and moved early that spring. That left their new house empty. Earl was two and missed his grandparents very much.

Grandma Fannie was living on her home place. David's wife, Mary, had many health problems. She was frequently admitted to the hospital. Bonnie found security with her grandma at these times. David found it necessary to have a *maud* (maid) to help them occasionally. Mary did her work when her health permitted. In spite of the efforts the doctors put forth to help her, she passed away on April 21, 1954, a sad day for her family. Twila was twelve; Orval, eleven; Duane, nine; and little Bonnie was five. Grandma felt a real closeness to these four motherless children. Aunt Fannie, as well as others, came frequently during the week to offer their assistance.

Uncle Will's son Billy, was a good ballplayer, and many evenings found him playing ball with his friends. One evening, he came home earlier then usual. He told his parents that he did not feel very well. He was only eighteen and had never complained much. They were really shocked when he died that night, July 27, 1954. This brought many of the Bontrager family together again to pay their last respects for one so young.

Andy and Lizzie welcomed another daughter into their home August 10, 1954. They named her Betty Jean. She was their third child. Mother enjoyed these little ones.

Kansas had a severe drought, and very little grew that summer. Andy and Fannie felt it keenly since they were just trying to get started in farming. Dust storms blew the freshly sown oats right out of the ground. In order to provide groceries and other needs for the family, Andy needed to find work. He went with two other young men to shear sheep that spring. That fall, the town of Yoder started to build a new schoolhouse, so Andy found a job there as mud boy. It was hard work, but with another baby on the way, he was glad to get it.

The morning of October 26, 1954, Aunt Fannie came and took them to the hospital in Hutchinson. Salina was there with little Earl. That evening another son, Omar, was born to them. Mother was also in Kansas and helped when she was not with her mother, sisters, and brothers. Andy continued his job at the Yoder school until it was done.

Soon after Mother and Salina went home, Salina went to Thomas, Oklahoma, to work for Johnny and Bertha Yoder again. They had a new baby, and Bertha had many complications and was unable to care for her family of little children.

Chapter 61
Voluntary Service - Wedding - On Willie's Dairy Farm

Salina enjoyed her work, and being nearer her special friend, as well as other friends, was indeed a pleasure. Their romance progressed, and when Joe proposed, she did not need much time to think about it before she gave her answer. When she went home, the letters kept mail trains busy. There were also some visits in between. In December, 1954, Joe went to Kansas City to do his two years of Voluntary Service. They were married on May 26, 1955, on Joe's twentieth birthday, while he was on leave. The wedding was held at John and Mary's place. The ceremony was in the walk-in haymow, and the dinner was served in the house. It was a nice day, and many relatives came from Thomas, Oklahoma, and Kansas, as well as Andy and Fannie with their two little boys. His brother Eldon and his wife Mary Ellen and Salina's nephew David and Vera Stutzman were their witnesses.

The day after the wedding, Joe and Salina were busy deciding what to take along to Kansas City and what to store at her mother's house until they came home to stay. The following day, Joe was back on the job, and Salina was busy arranging things in their tiny little apartment. They had a nice landlady. After Salina had their small home arranged, she also got a job in a hospital. More young married couples were doing their Voluntary Service there, so they socialized with each other.

Andy and Lizzie were blessed with another baby girl January 4, 1956. They named her Mary Jane as they both had a sister by that name. Andy and Lizzie bought a place north of Pryor where they built a new house and moved into it.

The drought had been so severe the last few years in Kansas that Andy and Fannie did not see how they could survive much longer. Andy's father occasionally sent them ten dollars to help pay for groceries. About this time Andy's nephew Eli, and Katie Miller, got married and offered to move onto the old home place where Andy's lived. Andy and Fannie had a public auction and then moved to Oklahoma onto her brother Willie's dairy in February of 1956. It was a lovely day, and Fannie's sisters and brothers came to help unload the truck and get them settled. By this time Anna and Levi had bought a farm only a mile west of them.

Willie owned a Purina Feed Store in Pryor and the elevator in Chouteau. They lived a quarter mile north of the farm where Andy and Fannie lived. He was busy with his businesses at both towns. Their daughter Barbara left for college in Virginia. Mary and William attended the country school across from the dairy. Ruby loved to sneak over to the dairy farm to play with Earl and Omar, her cousins.

Andy and Lizzie moved into their new house north of Pryor that summer with their four little children. This left mother Barbara alone until Joe and Salina would return in December. So Barbara had an older sister from the church, Fannie Yutzy, come and stay with her. She still took care of her chickens. The two women enjoyed each other's company and spent their time quilting or piecing quilts and visiting.

On October 26, 1956, Joe and Salina were blessed with their first baby, a boy named Merle. Barbara went to Kansas City to help them until Salina had her strength again.

December soon arrived, and Joe and Salina came back from Kansas City. They bought some dairy cows and did some farming on her mother's eighty acres. The house was divided, so each had their own part.

Chapter 62
Dan's Family Visits Dad - Babies - Moves

Dan, Betty, and their boys went to visit his father, who had moved to Las Vegas by that time. When Maizie had learned that his first wife was still living, she had divorced Joe. He now hauled the garbage for Las Vegas and fed it to his hogs. Willie and his family also visited him a few times while he lived there. At times, he had a black housekeeper.

Finally he moved to a farm near Aguila, Arizona, which he got as a government claim. He had some animals and lived in an old trailer house. He started to build a new house with high hopes of making his fortune there.

On November 28, 1957, John and Mary's oldest son David, got married to Vera Stutzman. He was the first of Barbara's grandchildren to get married. Barbara's mother from Kansas came for the event. She stayed with Barbara for some time, and Barbara sewed for her as she generally did when she came. On December 5, Amanda picked up Mom, Grandma, and Salina to go to Andy and Lizzie's for dinner. On their way there, they stopped at the birthing clinic in Pryor to see Fannie. Willie had taken her and Andy in early that morning. The doctor said, "It's a slow process." Andy walked out to the car to see all of them, and when he came in, he heard the baby's hearty cry. It was a girl, and they named her Carol since it was the month of Christmas.

Joe and Salina had a little girl born to them February 28, 1958. They named her Mary Arlene. These were busy years for Fannie and Salina with their young families.

On October 10, 1959, Andy and Lizzie were blessed with another son named Andy Ray. He was their fifth child, and with four older siblings, he didn't lack for attention.

In 1959, Willie decided to sell the farm, and gave Andy and Fannie the first chance. It had two barns and some newer buildings with a well-kept appearance. Andy and Fannie felt it was a bigger debt load then they wanted to carry. Instead, the farm was sold to Sam Chupps from Indiana. In the meantime, a run-down farm south of Mazie came up for sale. They decided it would fit their budget better, so they bought it.

On November 5, 1959, John and Mary had a big wedding for their oldest daughter Fannie and Norman Miller. John had a small house moved to the west side of their big house for them.

On December 20, another daughter was born to Andy and Fannie. They named her Darla. John and Mary's daughter Edna and Grandma Barbara assisted with the work until Fannie regained her strength. Andys were in the process of building a one hundred foot long chicken house on the place they bought. Every morning for days, Fannie loaded her four little children and the food into the buggy, then drove to the place they had bought which was about six miles away to serve dinner to the men working there.

In February, the chicken house was finally done, and neighbors helped move the one thousand pullets into it. There was a little shanty with four small rooms on the farm, and Andy and Fannie and their growing family moved into it. The house was so cold they kept the baby in a basket in front of the stove to keep her warm.

Before long, they butchered a beef and Johns, Joes, and her mother helped them. The next day Fannie canned a lot of meat. She set the jars on the kitchen floor to cool when she took them out of the pressure cooker. The next morning when they got up, she discovered many of the jars of meat were frozen, and some jars had cracked.

It was soon evident that little Darla would need to be moved to the crib in their bedroom and Carol to the small youth bed where the boys had slept. The weather was getting warmer, so the little boys were moved to a small lean-to room that leaked badly.

They had a small little outside cave where they kept the eggs. The first year they hauled them to Chouteau for a hatchery, but that was not too profitable. The next year they moved a house onto the farm, did some remodeling on it, and moved in there. They also filled the big chicken house with layers but no roosters. A sign on the 69 highway brought some customers to the door. The rest of the eggs were taken to Wagoner to a cafe or to the lake area where they had customers. They also supplied one grocery store in Wagoner. To meet specifications, the eggs needed to be weighed and graded each evening and put into cartons according to size. This job was usually done after the children were in bed in the evening.

Chapter 63
Mother's New House - Levi's Move to Missouri

By this time, Barbara had a small house built a short distance south of the big house and lived in it. Joe, Salina, and their children occupied the entire farmhouse.

In 1960, Levi and Anna decided to move to Jamesport, Missouri. They sold their farm in Oklahoma and bought one southeast of Jamesport. They had a public auction in Oklahoma and moved that same year. Barbara hated to see them move away since she enjoyed having all her children in the same area.

A new member was added to Joe and Salina's family January 24, 1962. It was a girl, and they named her Barbara Karen as a namesake for her grandma. This pleased Barbara very much.

That year Andy and Fannie read in the Budget that a new settlement had started in Leon, Iowa. "Sounds like land prices are cheap there," they mused. This made them enthused, although they did not personally know anybody that lived there. They, with their children, boarded the train out of Tulsa one day and went to Kansas to visit. While there, they met Mose and Cora Yoder and found out they lived in the Leon area. Moses invited them to visit, which gave them something to think about. From Kansas they went by train to Trenton, Missouri. From there they got a taxi to take them out to visit Levi, Anna, and their boys in their new home. After spending some time with them, they hired a taxi and left for Leon, Iowa, to the Mose Yoder home. After seeing many hills, they questioned if a person could make a living there. However, they enjoyed the hospitality they received. They stayed a day and a night, then went to the Kalona area where they saw more hills. They visited some cousins there, then the next morning they boarded the train in Iowa City for Indiana. In Goshen they got a bus that took them to Topeka, where Andy's dad met them with the buggy. The four children, Earl, Omar, Carol, and Darla, were glad to get to Grandpa Miller's where Mommie had a good supper prepared. Grandpa and Grandma Miller were excited to again see their youngest son's offspring.

After they got back home to Oklahoma, Andy and Fannie discussed the area they had seen in Leon, Iowa, and decided to go back that spring and take the little girls along. Grandma Chupp stayed with the boys and someone helped them chore. After shopping around for a farm, they decided on 120 acres northeast of Leon. They bought it, then went home, sold their farm, and had an auction. August 1, 1962, they arrived at their new home in Leon. The trucker, who arrived before they did, had already unloaded the cows when Andys and the children drove in early that morning. The other four families who lived in the area came and helped to get their belongings unloaded and into place. Earl and Omar soon had new friends, as well as Carol and Darla. The girls were four and two, and the boys were ten and seven years old.

September 9, 1962, Anna and Levi were blessed with another son, Daniel. Harley, the youngest, was nearly ten, so a baby was most welcome.

Two years later Joe, Salina, and their three little children, along with her mother, Barbara, moved to Kalona, Iowa, on the farm they bought northwest of Kalona. They had a small house moved next to theirs for Barbara. It joined their big house. Barbara hated to leave Oklahoma because she had called that home for so many years. But she wanted to be near her youngest daughter Salina and her family.

Chapter 64
Mother Sells Farm - Move to Kalona - Much Sickness

Barbara sold her eighty acre farm to John and Mary. Their son David, and Vera and their children, Linda, Jerry, Calvin, Roger, and James then moved there. Barbara was glad it would remain in the family.

By this time Uncle Enos and Lulu lived in Indiana, and a son Glen was born to them February 13, 1953; and a special child, Mary Lou, born September 3, 1955; a son, Marlin Ray, born February 1, 1958; and their last child, Dale, born February 17, 1960.

Uncle Will's wife, Martha, died July 12, 1956. He was very lonely in their new house. His daughter Fannie Alice and youngest son David were still single, which helped to ease the loneliness. He later married an older single girl.

Grandma Fannie was happy for her son David, when he announced that he was planning to get married. He met a young widow, Ilva, from Archbold, Ohio. She had two daughters from her first marriage. They got married February 27, 1959, in the Mennonite church near Archbold, Ohio. Then she with her two little girls, came to the home farm in Kansas to live. She was very considerate of David's mother who lived in the west end of the house and was getting up in years.

Ilva detected that David's daughter Bonnie had some health problems. After getting medical help, they found a severe kidney disease which was incurable. Her condition worsened as her kidneys deteriorated, and she died June 27, 1969.

They were told by specialists that it was a genetic disease, and after some research, they thought it was possible that it might have been the cause of the deaths of two of Uncle Will's sons.

Aunt Fannie's son Donald was in the Service and had some ailments that had never been diagnosed. After some tests, it was found that he had the same disease, but it was in earlier stages.

He bravely faced the consequences and worked at jobs that he could handle until his health no longer permitted. Fannie had married Oliver Troyer July 22, 1966. Donald had lost his father shortly before his sixth birthday. He was glad when his mother remarried.

On December 28, 1970, at the age of twenty-five, Donald went to be with the Lord. To know him was to love him, and his mother missed him so much.

Andrew had to part with his wife, Nora, Jan. 29, 1966. She had battled cancer for quite some time. She had surgery and chemotherapy, doing everything the doctors recommended. In spite of all their efforts, her health declined, and the time came for her to tell her husband and children good-bye. She had a radiant testimony and kept a positive outlook as long as possible. Her death left Andrew alone on his farm, and he had many lonely days.

Eventually, he went to Kalona to visit his sister Barbara, knowing she had faced many trials in her life. While there, he met a single girl, Elizabeth Mast. They struck up a friendship and corresponded for a time, then got married July 16, 1967. She moved to Kansas, and they later moved into a new house on the west end of Yoder. This is where they still live in 1997, and they have shared many happy years together.

February 13, 1966, Anna and Levi were blessed with their fifth son. They named him Andy. Paul was sixteen by then, and Mark was also out of school, so the boys were a good help with the work. Harley was in the eighth grade. Daniel was three and could talk like a grown person.

At times, Barbara would get very ill with extreme pain. Sometimes after vomiting, she would get some relief. She had this problem for years and had been on numerous diets for gall stones. A special diet often helped her pass some stones which brought her some relief.

In October, Salina grew more concerned about her mother because she had many days when she did not feel well. When Mary and Fannie heard about it, they decided to go visit their mother. Maybe she needed encouragement. She was glad for the girls' visit, but on October 13, 1969, she became extremely ill. Salina, Mary and Fannie followed the ambulance to the hospital in Washington.

After the doctor ran some tests, he said she would immediately need surgery for gall stones. Mary and Fannie stayed at the hospital all night, but Salina went home to care for her family. She came back early the next day.

By this time, Andy and Fannie were well established in their new community in Iowa. They got acquainted with the local people and liked their new home. Before long, Fannie had health problems. For many months, she was in constant pain, finding some relief from pain pills. Finally they were advised to see a doctor in Kirksville, Missouri. After numerous tests, she was admitted to the hospital there, where tests continued. Finally exploratory surgery was performed, and cysts were found and removed. One had ruptured and poisoned her whole body. As she lay recovering, her thoughts often went to her father in his lost condition. She prayed if the Lord would restore her health, she would put forth every effort to go to visit her father and speak to him about his soul. The Lord healed, and time went on. She had never mentioned her promise to Andy because she thought they could not afford a such a distant trip.

In 1968, Fannie started having health problems again, and she was reminded of her promise to the Lord. She told Andy, and he said, "Why didn't you tell me sooner?"

"Because I thought we couldn't afford a trip like that," she answered.

Andy said, "I'm sure the Lord will provide somehow." They made plans to go, and Wayne and Bernice Miller offered to go along and help with expenses. Bernice had two sisters living out West that they wanted to visit.

Chapter 65
Trip to Arizona - Confession - Cousins Meet

At two o'clock on the morning of March 4, Andy and Fannie, with their little girls Carol and Darla, and Waynes started out. By seven o'clock that evening, they were in Albuquerque, New Mexico, at Bernice's sister's place. They spent a day and two nights there, then headed for Phoenix. After spending a night there with friends, they headed further west to Aguila. They found Fannie's father's very shabby trailer house. Nearby a new house was being constructed. A man emerged from another trailer home parked nearby and asked, "Are you Joe's daughter?"

"Yes, I am," she answered.

"He went to Wickenburg and said for you to make yourself at home until he comes home." They went into his trailer house. Fannie had taken groceries along to prepare for supper. She had stirred up a chocolate cake and peeled potatoes when the fellow that stayed there announced, "Here comes your father in his station wagon." Fannie's heart beat fast as she anticipated their first meeting. She was thirty-eight years old at that time and had not seen him since she was six. He stopped his station wagon and slowly got out of it. Fannie ran out to meet him, threw her arms around his neck, and said, "Dad!" through her tear-filled eyes. His eyes also filled with tears as they embraced. When he got his composure, he said, "Are my other girls as big as you?" She tried to answer his questions while her thoughts drifted. In her heart, she would not have known him from any tramp on the street. He was thrilled to meet his son-in-law and his two little granddaughters.

Fannie said, "Dad, I stirred up a cake and am getting supper ready, but I can't light your oven."

"Oh," he said, "it doesn't work, but some folks a little ways from here are nice folks. I'm sure that lady would let you use her oven."

While Dad showed Andy and the girls his pigs, chickens, donkey, and other animals, Fannie went to bake the cake. These neighbors proved very helpful, and seeing her plain garb, they also had many questions. Fannie explained some of the situation to them. She told them how, for many years, the family had known nothing of his whereabouts, often fearing he might not be alive. The lady was very understanding. Fannie said, "By the way, let me give you our phone number. Should anything ever happen to my dad, would you please call us collect?" She assured Fannie that they surely would. When the cake was done, Fannie thanked her for her kindness and went back and finished the rest of the meal. Dad had a small garden and had nice head lettuce, so that was also on the menu.

After supper, it started to rain, but they visited some more. Dad just opened up to them, and with his head bowed with emotion, he said, "You have two young boys at home. Do be careful what they read. My life could have been so different had my mother been more careful what I read as a young boy. I loved to read, and my young mind took in all of it. Once, when I was quite young, I saw an advertisement for some books." Then he cleared his throat again. "Well, I ordered them. They came one day when my mother was spending the day with one of the married children. My mind soon absorbed what I read, and knowing my mother would not approve, I hid them in the attic. I often got them out to read when she was gone. Through these books, I learned to read people's minds and know what they thought of me." With tears running down his cheeks, he said, "My life could have been so different had I never read them. Do be careful what your children read."

Trailer where Dad lived and house he was building near Aguila, Arizona. Trailer in back where hired man lived. Dad's station wagon.

Because the time was getting late, they told him they would go to a motel in Aguila to sleep and return to visit him the next morning. He said, "You won't be able to get to town. When it rains here on the desert, you get stuck in this sand."

"Well, what should we do? You don't have room for us here."

He answered, "I always sleep on the couch, and there is a small bedroom where your girls can sleep." He found some clean sheets, and Fannie soon had the girls tucked between them. "Now this fellow that lives in the other trailer always sleeps on his couch, so you could sleep in his bedroom." Dad told the man about the situation, and he assured them that would be fine with him. When Andy and Fannie entered his trailer, he looked like such a rough character and had his gun by his side. The radio blared most of the night. They went to bed, but slept very little as they thought of the events of the day, and how they were now here in this rough-looking man's trailer. Would they still be alive by morning??

Morning dawned bright and clear, and they were unharmed. They went over to Dad's trailer and found the girls well rested and ready to start the day. Fannie said, "Dad, on Sunday, we will take you along with us to the church in Phoenix."

He answered, "I'm sorry, but I can't go. I don't have clothes fit to go to church."

"Dad, you can't let me down when we came this far to see you," Fannie said. "I only remember twice when you were still at home that you went to church. I will look in your closet and see what clothes you have." With that, she opened the closet door. "Dad, here is a suit coat." She held it out. "We will get you a new shirt and pants today."

After breakfast, Dad went along to see an old gold mine near Wickenburg. They ate dinner together at a nice restaurant in Wickenburg. Dad was happy to introduce them to anyone he knew. They went to a clothing store and found a nice white shirt and a pair of pants for him. He was as thrilled as a child with a new toy. That evening they took him to his home, and Fannie said, "We will see you at the motel, early in the morning, to go to church with us."

Later, at the motel, Andy asked, "Do you look for him?"

"Sure," Fannie answered. Although Andy wasn't so certain, he did not say much.

At six o'clock the next morning, a knock was heard on the door of their motel. When Andy answered the door, there was Dad, all cleaned up, shaved, and dressed in his new clothes.

He said, "I will drive on to where we ate dinner in Wickenburg yesterday and drink coffee until you stop there to get me." They scurried around to get ready, and soon they were on their way. When they arrived at the restaurant, Joe met them, and they continued on their way to Phoenix. Andy and Fannie felt very strange in this church since they knew nobody. But the true Word was preached, and they listened attentively.

When church was dismissed, people were very friendly. One young lady came and invited them for dinner. She had heard through others that they were in the area. Her name was Millie Ann, and she explained that Fannie's father was an uncle to her father, Dan Borntrager, in Mississippi. She had been named in honor of her grandma. She had lived in that area many years for the sake of her health.

Before long, she had a tasty meal on the table and got everyone seated. Dad asked Millie Ann about her grandma. "Oh, she lives in Mississippi close to my parents," she answered. "She would be delighted to hear from you."

After dinner Millie Ann called her parents, and her father, Dan answered.

"Is Grandma there?"

"No," he answered, "she went to Florida."

Millie Ann said, "Uncle Menno is here and ate dinner with me."

"What? You say Uncle Menno! I must talk to him, too."

After they hung up, Millie Ann called to Florida and talked to her aunt Ida and said, "Uncle Menno is here and would like to talk to Grandma."

"Really! I can hardly believe it. I also want to talk to him." After a short time, she put her mother, who was a sister to Menno, on the line. It was a very emotional time for both of them.

After that Millie Ann said, "Menno, you have a cousin here. His name is also Menno, and I will call him and tell him you are here."

In a short time Cousin Menno and his wife arrived and extended greetings to everyone. This Menno was six years older than Dad, and his northern home was still in Newton County, Indiana. He told Dad, "I remember when your folks moved to Mississippi, and you were a tiny baby." The afternoon passed quickly. After they left, Andy's stopped for Wayne's at some friends and started back to Aguila for the night. The next day, they planned to drive to California where Fannie's aunt Anna and Fred lived.

It was rather crowded in the car until they got to Wickenburg where Dad had left his car that morning. As Dad climbed out, he thanked them heartily for everything. Fannie asked, "Dad, I will ride back to Aguila to the motel with you." This pleased him.

As they were riding along, Fannie said, "Dad, why did you leave my mother?"

He answered, "It was not her fault. She was the best woman I ever knew, and you children owe everything to her. You owe me nothing."

At the motel, Fannie got out. As she bid her father good-bye, she could not help but notice the tears in his eyes. She felt sorry for him as she thought of what he had made of his life. She encouraged him to go to church and live for the Lord. What else could she say? Early the next morning they started for California, but still her thoughts drifted to her father.

Chapter 66
More Visits With Dad - Grandma's and Dad's Deaths

After they returned home Fannie wrote her dad and received some letters in return. Andy and Fannie made another trip to visit her dad in February 1970, taking John and Mary along. They arrived at his place on the nineteenth, and he went with them to the old gold mine. They bought groceries, prepared supper in his small trailer, and ate with him. They stayed in a motel in Aguila that night, and the next day they drove to Phoenix. Their father also drove down and met them. That evening Millie Ann and Dad went with them to Rudy Borntrager's home for supper. He was a cousin to Andy. All of them went to Millie Ann's house for the night. The next day was Sunday, and they attended church with Millie Ann. Again they met Dad's cousin Menno Chupp and were all at his daughter's house, the Clayton Yoders, for supper. Monday morning, Andys and Johns left for home after bidding farewell to their father. He left for his home on the desert with fond memories of their visit.

When they noticed the effort it took for him to walk, Fannie had suggested he could come and stay with them. He thanked her and said, "Son Andy offered me a home, too, but I have this land and some animals I need to take care of. I'd like to find somebody to help me since that other fellow left." It was hard to see what he had made of his life.

On January 1, 1971, Fannie received a phone call from the hospital in Wickenburg. A nurse said, "Your father is a patient here and had a heart attack. His condition is not good. He gave me your number to call." Fannie thanked the nurse, then called her sister, Salina.

Salina said, "We are butchering and quite busy, but I would desire to see my father yet because I don't remember him at all." Later Salina called back and said, "Joe's parents are here and encourage us to go see Dad while we can. They offered to help the children in our absence. Mom has also consented to go along. We will come to your place this evening and be ready to drive until we get there."

Andy arranged his work, and Fannie packed. That afternoon at two-thirty, Joe, Salina, and Mother came, and Andy and Fannie joined them. They drove and drove, not knowing if they would still see him alive. At midnight, they stopped at a motel in Texoma on the border of Oklahoma and the Texas panhandle. After a few hours of sleep, they were back on the road to Arizona. When they finally got as far as Millie Ann's house, she said she had been to the hospital to visit him that day and he was released.

The next day they drove out to Aguila and rented a motel room. Joe and Andy drove out to get Menno, and he spent the day with them in the motel room. They bought some food and ate it in the room. It proved to be an emotional experience for their parents. They had not seen each other for forty years and were like strangers to each other. He said, "I'm now an old man."

She answered, "And I'm an old woman." That was about the extent of their conversation.

The stay in Arizona was short because Joe's needed to get home to their young family. Marlin was born to them after moving to Kalona on March 30, 1967, and Gary was born April 14, 1970. A kind sister from their church offered to take care of them in their absence. Merle, Mary, and Karen were old enough to do the chores for a short time.

After they returned home, Fannie wrote her dad and received a letter from him that he had mailed January 26, 1971. He wrote,

"Dear Daughter and Family,

Greet you in Jesus' Holy name. I'm not feeling well. Hope you are all well. Good health is such a blessing.

I think I'm getting my place sold. If the man comes up with the money. I have a big rupture I need to have fixed before I do any traveling. The doctor says it won't be a bad operation. I have suffered a lot the past year but don't want to complain. Rather suffer here than in the hereafter. Pray for me. If all works out I may see you about March. I will keep you informed. May God be with you until we meet again. Gracious heavenly father have mercy on me.

Your humble well wishing father, Joe D. Miller"

When Fannie read the letter, she hoped that it would work out for him to come and stay with his children. The boys had offered to care for him in Oklahoma when they had visited him the last time. His children realized he was really not able to be alone any longer. He had no phone, was all alone, could get around so poorly, and lived far away from his neighbors.

The other children wrote to him and occasionally received a short letter from him in return, too.

Grandma Fannie sometimes had heart spells, and her children would be summoned to her bedside. Every time she would rally out of it, and soon she would be on the go again. The morning of July 8, 1971, when her son David checked on her, she was not well. She said, "I think the Lord will call me home today. Please don't call the children home as it will hinder me." They did call Andrew because he was a minister. He and his wife Elizabeth arrived soon and were still able to speak a little to his mother. Her mind was clear. She eagerly looked forward to meeting her Maker and before long, took her last breath. If she had lived a few more months, she would have been ninety-six. She was survived by thirteen children, sixty-six grandchildren, one hundred seventy-nine great-grandchildren, and twenty-eight great-great-grandchildren.

At nine-thirty in the evening of July 20, 1971, Andy and the children had just gone to bed, and Fannie was preparing to go also, when the phone rang. When Fannie answered, it was a collect call from the woman who had let Fannie use her oven on the first visit to see her dad. She explained who she was and said, "You told me if anything ever happened to your dad to call you." Yes, Fannie remembered. "We no longer live close to your father because we moved our trailer to Aguila. However, my husband went to check on Joe every day. Our temperature here has been hovering at 120 degrees during the day, and we knew your father's refrigerator didn't work. Jim has been taking some ice to him in a chest every day. Today he found your father face down in the house he never finished, and life was gone. He apparently had a heart attack. My husband called the funeral home in Prescott, which is our county seat. It is about sixty miles away. I will give you their number."

Now what should she do? Andy got up, and they called Salina and Joe, Andy and Lizzie, and tried to call Willie and Dan. They then learned that the same woman had called Dan, and he and Willie were ready to leave to go out to Arizona to bury their dad. Finally about midnight, Fannie reached the funeral home and told them to embalm him. She said she would call again the next morning. She was told that if she had not called, his body would have been put in a plastic bag and buried as a pauper. They explained that with the tremendous heat, his body showed some skin slippage. However, they assured her they would do their best to embalm him if that was what the family desired.

The next morning Salina broke the news to her mother. Her reaction was, "Let's give him a decent burial." After more phone calls, it was decided to fly the body to Des Moines, Iowa. The funeral would be held at the Salem Mennonite Church near Leon, where Andy and Fannie attended. Many relatives and friends came for the funeral. He was buried in the cemetery by the old Franklin Brethren Church. Barbara wanted his tombstone to bear his birth name. The children and Barbara shared the burial expenses. Willie and Dan did not make it back in time, but they saw to it that he had decent clothes for burial. They went out to his place and picked up his Bible and some mementos. With letters he had lying there from radio ministers, it was evident that he had been seeking help for his troubled soul.

Buried N.E. of Leon, Iowa, in the old Franklin Dunkard Cemetery.

The day after word of his death was received, Fannie received a letter from her father. It was dated July 19, and postmarked the day before his death. It read as follows:

> "I wish to thank you for the times you visited me. Also want to thank you so much for the prayers you offered in my behalf. I don't think my time is much longer on this earth. I have suffered much but don't want to complain. I just pray the Lord can forgive me that I can enter heaven when my time is up here. I will also write Salina, then I will go to the post office to mail this.
>
> Your humble loving father, Joe Miller"

The words he spoke some years before rang in Fannie's ears, "If I had never read those books when I was a young boy, my life could have been so different." What was his destination? The Scripture says in 1 John 1:9, "If we confess our sins, he is faithful and just to forgive us our sins, and to cleanse us from all unrighteousness." It is our prayer that he found peace.

Barbara felt a satisfaction in knowing that Menno had a decent burial. She trusted he had found peace with the Lord in his last days. The letters that Salina and Fannie had received after his death were evidence that he had been seeking, and this brought comfort to the family.

Chapter 67
Quilt Friends - Visits - 1973 - 1974 - 1975 - Joys and Sorrow

Barbara had made many friends in Iowa by this time. Through her quilt piecing, she had met many people. She was swamped with piecing to do for others. As time allowed, she pieced for herself and sold many lovely tops. People came from quite a distance to see and buy the quilts she had made from many colorful scraps. Typical to her characteristic of thriftiness, she used some very tiny quilt blocks. With her friendly disposition and clear memory, it was a pleasure for people to visit with her.

After Andy and Fannie had met her father's cousin, Menno Chupp, from Newton County, Indiana, in Arizona, and had heard of the history of her paternal grandmother, Fannie had a desire to go visit that area. They took this opportunity August 18, 1972. They ate lunch with Menno and his wife. In the afternoon, Menno and his wife took them to the cemetery where Menno's grandparents, Nathan and Mattie Chupp, were buried. They were also privileged to see the farm where Mattie, Menno's mother, lived when her first husband, David Yoder, passed away. Later she married Isaac Chupp who worked for her on that same place. Although Fannie never met her paternal grandmother because she died before Fannie was born, she perceived that she had been a courageous person. She must have experienced many trials and triumphs in life.

Barbara had a chance to go to Leon on July 21, 1973, with grandson Merle and his cousin. She was glad for the offer and readily accepted. This would give her a chance to spend time with Fannie's family. Their children were almost grown by this time. Their daughter Carol had painted a state quilt, and she thought this would be great to have her grandma set the blocks together for her with stars in the corner of each block. This idea was an original of Grandma's. She was delighted to do this for Carol.

One day Fannie, Carol, and Darla took Grandma to Jamesport, Missouri, to visit Annie and Levi and their boys. The two oldest, Paul and Mark, were on their own and worked in other states. Harley would soon be twenty-one. Daniel and little Andy were glad for their grandma's visit. A few days later, Fannie took her mother back to Kalona. She commented to Salina what a nice little trip she had. She was glad to be home again and back to her quilt piecing. Marlin and

Gary, the youngest of Joe's children, enjoyed playing on the floor in Grandma's house. This made time go faster for her.

Andy and Lizzie's oldest daughter, Roberta, planned her wedding for September 1, 1973, to Arlis Unrua. Since Joe and Salina did not go, Andy and Fannie took Barbara. They stayed a few days and visited at the homes of Barbara's children and grandchildren.

Barbara was happy when her aunt Mary Plank, her mother's youngest sister from Illinois, came to visit her on September 19, 1973. They seldom got to see each other and could hardly get done reminiscing of times gone by. Barbara's daughters, Mary and husband John from Oklahoma, and Fannie from Leon, Iowa, were also there at the same time. It was interesting for them to listen to their visiting. Since her aunt Mary was very hard of hearing, they sat close together to converse. She was only six years older then Barbara.

Barbara's paternal aunt, Mary Ann and Benedict, lived only a few miles away, and many times they came to visit Barbara, or she went to visit them. Mary Ann was a good cook and often invited Barbara for a meal. They enjoyed reminiscing of their childhood days. They spoke of many things, including how the Indians had come to water their horses.

On February 9, 1974, another son, Lavon, was born to Salina and Joe. He was their fourth son, and they had two girls. He had dark, curly hair like Merle and Gary. Once a visitor remarked that Marlin's hair was not curly like the others. Marlin heard it and piped up, "Oh, sometime it will be."

Barbara's brother Ed was often very lonely after the death of his first wife. He lived near Hazelton until he met and married Cora Yoder, an older girl from the Kalona community. She was a cheerful person and did much quilting. Barbara enjoyed being with her, and they would often converse about quilts. Since they lived near the edge of Kalona, they often came to visit Barbara, or she went there if she had the opportunity.

On July 11, 1974, Barbara got the sad news that her brother Enos and Lulu's oldest boy had been killed in a motorcycle accident at the entrance of Interstate 80 near Middlebury, Indiana. Barbara did not feel able to go to the funeral. However, she encouraged Salina and Joe to go. Andy and Fannie went to Kalona, then they all went together for the funeral.

Barbara was shocked when she received word that Ed, her brother, died in the hospital in Iowa City on August 27, 1974. She had not realized that he had been that sick. His son Perry was at his bedside at the time of his passing. Barbara would miss him very much. He was next to her in age of her siblings, and they had many happy times together growing up. She cherished the few years that he had lived close by so they could be together more in their sunset years.

On March 7, 1975, Barbara got word from Indiana that Elton Bontrager, her sister Amelia's husband, had passed away. Her heart went out to their young daughter Anita. Amelia had died suddenly on June 3, 1970, when Anita was sixteen, and now five years later she had to part with her father. Being an only child, she had a heavy load on her young shoulders.

On Barbara's birthday, women came from every direction to visit, bringing cake and ice cream. This cheered her to have so many friends. Usually they brought some handwork to do while they chatted. She exchanged quilt patterns with them and gave instructions for patterns that were difficult to understand. When she had her eightieth birthday on July 12, 1975, her daughter Fannie and husband Andy and their children, Darla, Earl, and his wife came from Leon to spend the day with her. These were highlights in her life when the children or grandchildren came to visit. Her nephew Perry Bontrager and his family also came that evening and brought a freezer of homemade ice cream. They lived nearby and made frequent visits which Barbara cherished so much.

Barbara always enjoyed attending the weddings of her grandchildren. She made sure she had a quilt pieced for each one when that time came. She got an invitation to the wedding of Ruby, the youngest daughter of Willie and Amanda, for August 31, 1975. She found a way to go to Oklahoma about ten days earlier which gave her an opportunity to visit with her children and grandchildren that lived there before the wedding. The great-grandchildren were on the scene by this time, and on each visit to Oklahoma she eagerly looked forward to seeing the new additions. Willie's daughters, Barbara and Mary, were both married as were Dan's boys, Dannie Joe and Leroy. Mary and John's children, David, Fannie, Lloyd, and Edna, all had their own homes and little ones. It brought back many memories when she visited David and Vera and their children as they lived on the place she had lived for many years before moving to Kalona. My, how hard she and the children had worked to pay for that eighty acre farm. John and Mary had bought the place when Barbara moved to Kalona with Joe and Salina. Roberta was the only one married yet of Andy and Lizzie's children. Barbara thought time had passed by quickly. It seemed such a short time to her when they had been babies.

Andy and Fannie came for the wedding and took her mother along home. Barbara had much to tell on the way home. She had enjoyed her visit and seeing many of her old-time friends. The closer they got to Iowa, the more eager she was to get home. She missed Joe and Salina's children so much. She mentioned that she wondered what they would have to tell her when she got home. They often played in her house while she was busy piecing quilts which made the time pass faster for her. The innocent chatter of these little ones often brought a smile to her face. Sometimes she would invite them to eat a meal with her which was really a treat for them.

Chapter 68
Twins - Travels - Modern Convenience - 1977 - Reunion

March 17, 1976, was an exciting day because that was the day Salina and Joe were blessed with twins. When Joe brought the news home, he said they had a good-sized boy named Wayne and a tiny baby girl named Wanda. The children were so excited, they dashed to Grandma's small house. Each wanted to be first to tell her the news. She rejoiced with them. She did have some concern for the little girl since she weighed only a little over four pounds. The older children Merle, nineteen; Mary, eighteen; and Karen, fourteen; were a big help. Of course, Barbara helped some to prepare meals and other light jobs. When they brought the babies home, Salina would feed one baby while one of the girls fed the other one. It took a lot of patience to feed little Wanda since she preferred sleeping over eating. They were a happy family, and Barbara often came over to their house to offer her assistance.

That summer Salina and her girls cooked dinners for large tour groups. Mother usually made it her duty to peel the potatoes. The twins often sat in their infant seats, enjoying each other's company, and Barbara loved to watch them. When the tour groups arrived, they always commented on the babies. Wayne was much bigger then Wanda, but that did not hinder Wanda from getting what she wanted. She was a gritty little person.

When garden vegetables were ready, Barbara would sit and shell peas, snap beans, or clean sweet corn for Salina. It made her mother feel needed to help when she could if it did not demand being on her feet which seemed to be her main weakness. Salina made sure that her mother had plenty of vegetables to eat, too.

Helping Salina brought back memories of the time her own children were little. She was glad none of them were as destitute as she was when they were young. She had prayed often for her children when they were growing up, and now she also prayed for her grandchildren.

Aunt Mary Ann and Benedict were getting to the point where their children felt they needed to live closer to one of them. Their youngest daughter Bertha and her husband Johnny lived in Garnett, Kansas, and in September, 1976, their children moved them to a few rooms of Bertha's house. This way she could help with the needs of her parents. Since they had often visited her in years gone by, Barbara knew she would miss them very much.

When Barbara received the message from Indiana that Eli Yoder, the son of Noah and Deemy, had passed away after a battle with cancer, she longed to go to his funeral. With Salina and Joe's little ones, they felt it was best not to go, so daughter Fannie and Andy from Leon, Iowa consented to take her. The funeral was August 27, 1976. Barbara had many fond memories of him when he was a baby and growing up in Garnett, Kansas. Many times he had played with their children when Barbara and Deemy worked together. Andy and Lizzie from Oklahoma were also at the funeral. Fannie ended up in the Lagrange hospital for minor surgery. Son Andy and Lizzie then took Mother back to her home in Kalona while Fannie recuperated a few days. Mother enjoyed their short visit.

When Barbara found out that Mark, son of Anna and Levi, would get married in Clark, Missouri, on March 10, 1977, to Lydia Beachy, she said, "I hope to go. I knew Lydia's grandparents years ago when we lived in Garnett, Kansas." She found a way with some friends, going there a few days before the wedding, which pleased her. She would have time to spend with her sister Mary and John Y. and her sister Mattie and Eli Gingerich that way. To be able to visit with these sisters meant so much to her as she seldom had this opportunity. She enjoyed her visit with them, and they took her to visit their married children.

When the day arrived for the wedding, she again met many people she had not seen for years. From there, she went to Jamesport, Missouri, and spent two weeks with Anna and Levi. She was glad to help Anna with patching or other small tasks. It also gave her a chance to see their young sons as they grew and had chores to do. They enjoyed showing her around the barnyard to see the calves and other animals.

When she was ready to go home, she wrote daughter Fannie in Leon to come get her, and she would be with them for awhile. So on March 23, Fannie, Darla, and two of their little foster children went to get her and spent most of the day there. Since it was only a two hour drive, they came home that evening. Darla helped with the chores but complained of pain in her side. This alarmed Grandma as she vividly recalled how her dear son Leroy had died from appendicitis. By ten o'clock Darla's pain was severe. Andy and Fannie took her to the hospital where she was soon in surgery for appendicitis.

In a few days, Mother was ready to go home as she felt she had been gone long enough. She had a chance to go home with somebody from Leon. She was in for a surprise when she walked into her house; she could hardly believe it was the same place. Salina had painted the walls and cleaned her house thoroughly while she was gone. They had even put a new rug down in her house so she would not be so apt to fall. The kerosene lamps had also been put away, and the house now had electric lights instead. Barbara did not like that too well. They explained that since her house was joined to theirs, she had at times put them in danger. Sometimes her lamps would smoke, and she did not notice until they came over and told her. They explained that this could have easily caused a fire. Barbara knew this was a fact, but she had not meant to do this. Oh, these modern things she could do without!

Salina and Joe saw Barbara was aging, so they planned a reunion for July 29, 1977. They invited her children, grandchildren, and their children, as well as Barbara's sisters and brothers. They also welcomed her nieces and nephews. Her daughter Fannie had major surgery a short time previously, but with some persuasion, the doctor gave his consent for her to attend if she took some precautions. Joe had a tent set up in the yard where they could sit and visit. A grandson, Bill Jr., flew overhead to let them know that someone should come meet him at the airport. Soon a few were on their way to fetch him and were also privileged to get a ride on his plane. Barbara was now eighty-two. The day passed quickly, and everyone had an enjoyable time.

A granddaughter, Karen, wrote the following account of the day:

"The Bontrager Reunion"

On Friday, July 29 of '77, was a big day.
"The day of the Bontrager Reunion has finally arrived," we would say.
We got up that morning, looking to the day with great anticipation,
Many from other states considered it their vacation.
Those that had been here for the night included Uncles Bill and Dan,
Uncle Andy and Lizzie, and Aunt Mary and John, all in the

Oklahoma clan.
Also having been here were Great Uncle Enos and Lulu from Indiana.
Cereal, rolls, and coffee was the breakfast that morning served by Salina.
About 9:15, more relatives started arriving.
First, was a van of Kansas folks with Great Aunt Edna and Orie driving,
With them they brought cousins Freda and Glen, Great Aunt Anna and Fred.
Also on the load Great Aunt Fannie and Oliver, "Well, we're finally here," they said.
It wasn't long until Great Uncle Andy and Elizabeth were driving in the lane,
They weren't alone 'cause Great Aunt Ida and Enos with them came.
That makes twelve Kansas folks in all that were here for the day.
Coming from Ohio were Great Uncle David, Ilva, and Kay.
With them they brought Betty Jo and Rol, the newlyweds.
"We're planning to live in Oregon and make that our home at the present," they said.
From Wisconsin, cousin Edna and Emanuel were the only ones that came.
From Leon, Iowa, were Aunt Fannie and Andy, and each child mentioned by name
Is Earl and Fannie, Omar, Carol, and Darla Fern.
Next in line is cousin Sarah, from Jamesport, Missouri's, turn,
And Aunt Anna and Levi, Daniel and Andy, were also along we learn.
'Ere long, an airplane was circling above our tent, we wondered, "Who could be there?"
Then we came to the conclusion that cousin Bill from Oklahoma was here,
So Cousin Perry with his pick-up headed for the Kalona airport, which is quite near.
Cousin Mark and Lydia from Clark, Missouri, arrived soon after noon.
They were the last ones from out-of-state to come – the tent still had lots of room.

And of course we Iowa Bontragers didn't want to miss out on the fun,
So naturally cousin Perry and Gertie and their girls – five is the sum,
Laura, Rosella, Viola, Loretta, and Linda were here with us.
And of course, Grandma Chupp – over her everyone made a fuss.
Since being the oldest of fourteen children, she was the oldest one here.
She turned eighty-two this summer and everyone thought she was a dear.
Because of Grandma the reunion was planned;
I trust we all enjoyed the day; at least, I thought it was grand.
And of course, Joe and Salina were there since it was in their front yard,
And Merle, Mary, Karen, Marlin, Gary, and Lavon even in it had a part,
Even the twins – Wayne and Wanda, who were sixteen-and-a-half-months old.
About mid-forenoon, Mrs. Alvin L. Miller, Norma and Delila came as they had been told,
They mostly prepared the noon meal which consisted of lots of good things to eat,
Bread, jelly, ice-tea, corn, scalloped potatoes with ham for the meat,
Tapioca, fresh tomatoes, muskmelons, coleslaw, and cheese,
Also applesauce, pie for dessert – we had plenty of all of these.
The afternoon was spent in a very pleasant way,
With uncles and great uncles getting up and saying what they had to say,
Even a couple of great aunts and in-laws got in a word or two,
How Ida wrapped a dead bird, and hid it in the woodbox, and other things she'd do!
How Edna, Amelia, and David prayed about the locked attic door,
The innocent faith they had, if we only had more.
How Anna got scared and cried and begged Fannie to cry
When a motorcycle went whizzing by.
Well, I'll just tell you, that by day's end, we all had a hunch,
That this Bontrager Family was one happy, talkative bunch.
About mid-afternoon, other entertainment entered our mind,
Some went on plane rides with cousin Bill, bike rides, and all else

they could find.
Awhile before supper, cousin Leroy, Fannie and Denise had yet come.
Merle brought Fern Swartzentruber, so in counting all the relation sixty-four was the sum.
About twenty others made stops in and out during the day,
Just to visit with someone they knew or see who all was here, they'd say.
Henry, Lydia Mae, Laverta and Loretta Bontrager came to help serve supper,
Which consisted of lemonade, tapioca, and sandwiches in a big Tupper,
Cheese, potato chips, tomatoes, ice cream, and strawberries, cake and pie.
Oh, no, the day was nearing an end, we thought with a sigh.
After supper we decided to go back out.
We all knew we had a good day without a doubt.
May God keep us close to Him each day,
As together we journey the rest of the way.

- By Karen Bontrager

Barbara kept in contact with her aunt Mary Ann, and she knew it was for their good that they had moved where they had help. On September 7, 1977, she received the message that Benedict passed on to his reward at the age of ninety-one. She felt sorry for Mary Ann. She knew they spent many happy years together.

Chapter 69
Wedding - Aunt Dies - Christmas in Leon - Merle Weds

Barbara had an invitation to the wedding of Harley, son of Anna and Levi. He was getting married in Illinois. Joe and Salina consented to take her which made her happy. Joe sowed oats yet May 3, 1978. That afternoon Fannie came from Leon and by two-thirty Barbara and Fannie left with Joe and Salina for Illinois. The next day was the wedding of Harley and Lena Beachey. It was a rainy day, but Barbara was so glad she could be there. She rejoiced to again have a short visit with her maternal Aunt Mary who was up in years and lived in that area. Barbara, John, Mary, Levi, Anna, Joe, Salina, and Fannie ate supper with their cousin Fannie and Sylvanus Yoder in Arthur. She was the daughter of Uncle Levi Chupp. Her sister Sarah and husband Henry Beachy also came over for supper. Fannie and Salina had never been with these cousins much. They all enjoyed the evening there and stayed for the night, leaving for home early the next morning.

On May 9, 1978, Mother, Salina and the girls and Gary, and the twins came to Andy and Fannie's place for supper. Gary had a weakness in his legs and was taken to Des Moines for treatments frequently, so they came on to Leon from there. The next day they and Fannie and her girls and daughter-in-law Fannie all went to Jamesport, Missouri, to spend the day with sister Anna and family. Mother did not feel too well and laid down part of the time. They returned home that evening, and Salina took her mother along home. She took her to the doctor the next day, and he said it was her heart. He gave her medication and recommended she take it easy.

The next day, Mom got word that her dear paternal Aunt Mary Ann passed away. She rested a lot, and on the twelfth, Joe and Salina took her to the funeral, which was the next day.

On July 12, 1978, Barbara sat at her sewing machine, merrily piecing a quilt when she heard footsteps. She looked up from her work to see Fannie, Carol, and Darla come to surprise her for her eighty-third birthday. They all enjoyed a scrumptious dinner at Salina's house. In the afternoon, Salina and Fannie took their mother along to the country stores and did some shopping in Kalona. That evening, they enjoyed homemade ice cream. Fannie and the girls stayed for the night, and the next day they and Salina and her girls cleaned the large china cabinet for their mother. They washed all the dishes. It was interesting for the granddaughters to hear where she got each dish. Some had been wedding gifts. They thought it so interesting that they put tape on the bottom of many pieces to say where she got them. Barbara decided to mark some pieces of who was to have them when she passed on. When that job was done, they washed all her windows. That evening Fannie and her girls left for home.

On December 24, 1978, Joe and Salina and their five youngest children and Mother arrived at Andy and Fannie's in Leon and were there for the night. The next forenoon Merle, his girlfriend Fern, and Mary and Karen came and were at Andy's for Christmas dinner and the day. Earl and Fannie were also there, and everyone enjoyed the day. Barbara enjoyed watching as the children played games and tried to make the most of their time together. The day passed quickly, and they departed for home.

On July 11, 1979, Anna had a good chance to go to Leon to her sister Fannie's and was there for the night. The next day was their mother's eighty-fourth birthday. Andy, Fannie, and Anna drove to Kalona to be with their mother for her birthday. A number of women came in the afternoon and brought cake and ice cream to celebrate Barbara's birthday. Barbara enjoyed all the activities very much.

Merle, the oldest of Joe and Salina's children, was courting Fern Swartzentruber. He often brought her home and over to see his grandmother in her cozy little house. When he broke the news of their engagement to Grandma, she was not too surprised. They planned to get married September 8, 1979.

Merle and Fern's wedding day arrived. Andy and Lizzie and their daughter Roberta and her baby Amy and Bill Jr. came from Oklahoma. Andy and Fannie from Leon, Iowa, and their children, Earl and his wife Fannie, Omar, Darla and her boyfriend Ivan Stoltzfus from Maryland, also attended. Barbara enjoyed each one's visit. Fannie helped look after her mother's needs that day so Salina could enjoy visiting with the guests.

The next day Barbara's children and grandchildren who had stayed enjoyed a visit and a snack at her house before they left for home.

Chapter 70
1980 Three Weddings - Ailments - Family Visits

Merle's sister Mary soon announced her engagement to Willis Schrock. Darla, daughter of Fannie and Andy, and Ivan Stoltzfus from Maryland announced their engagement about the same time. Time went fast, and these grandchildren were setting up homes of their own. Fannie and Andy's daughter Carol was teaching school in Pennsylvania and had met the man of her dreams there. Barbara mused about these things in her heart, thinking that she had never been that far away from home. She hoped her health would permit her to attend all the weddings.

March 29, 1980, was the wedding day of Mary to Willis Schrock. This brought Barbara's brother Andy and his wife from Kansas, John and Mary from Oklahoma, Andy and Fannie, Omar, Darla and her fiancé from Maryland, Carol and her special friend, Noah Yoder from Pennsylvania, Earl, Fannie, and son Matthew from Florida. Carol and Noah were privileged to be in the bridal party, as were Mary's sister Karen, and a brother of Willis'. John and Mary stayed a few days, and Salina took them to visit in various homes.

On April 3, Barbara's brother Andrew and his wife took Barbara, John, and Mary to Leon for Darla and Ivan's wedding. Barbara enjoyed it all, though it did tire her.

April 4, 1980, Good Friday, dawned bright and clear. This was the day of Darla and Ivan's wedding. Many relatives and friends came from far and near for the occasion. Barbara enjoyed meeting Ivan's relatives from far away Pennsylvania and Maryland.

This was also the time Carol and Noah chose to make their engagement known. Fannie was really in a dither trying to make sure that everything was well taken care of.

Joe, with his heart condition, was sick the next day, so Salina took him to the doctor. When Joe did not improve much, Salina took him to the doctor again the seventh of April, 1980. Still Joe did not show much improvement, so April 22, 1980, Joe and Salina went to Kansas City to consult a specialist. He was given chelation treatments. They went home the 26th. Some days he felt better, but many days he was not well. Joe's health concerned Mother much, and as a result, she often felt ill.

Fannie went to Kalona on May 23, 1980, and washed walls,

ceilings, and cupboards in her mother's kitchen. School was over, so Noah brought Carol home from her teaching job. They stopped to visit her grandma and Joe's family, then Fannie went with them to Willis and Mary's home for dinner. It was quite evident that Mary did not lack in cooking skills. She had learned that well from helping her mother cook for large groups of people at home.

Barbara had mentioned to Salina that she would like to visit some of her old friends at the Pleasant View Home. On June 17, 1980, Salina told her she would take her. This really pleased her mother. She was slow in getting around, but it made her day. Her old friends were so glad for her visit.

Barbara had a chance to go to Fannie's in Leon a few days in June, 1980. She thought it would be nice to help Fannie in preparing for Carol's wedding. They put her to work cutting quilt blocks for a quilt for Carol in greens. It would be a Log Cabin that she could use for everyday.

Barbara was pleased that Carol and Noah would get married on her birthday. When she arrived at daughter Fannie's the evening before the wedding, she got acquainted with Noah's relatives from Pennsylvania. A big bus brought most of his family. John and Mary came by bus from Oklahoma that evening. Enos and Ida came from Kansas. Anna and Levi's son Paul and his wife Linda and daughter Joanne came from Florida. After supper, guests went to various homes for the night.

The next day was a very warm day for the wedding. Dinner was served in the church basement. The colors were mint green and peach. These colors were evident in the dresses of all who had part, as well as on the bridal table. That evening an early supper was given at Andy's, and afterward the family was out to bid farewell to Noah and Carol as they left for their wedding trip.

John, Mary, Barbara, Ida, and Enos left after supper to go to Kalona and spend more time with Barbara. On July 14, 1980, they went to near Hazelton, Iowa, with Perry Bontragers, Barbara's nephew, to attend the funeral of a friend.

On August 4, 1980, Barbara was happy to have Sylvanus and Fannie Yoder from Illinois as visitors. She was the daughter of Menno's brother Levi. Since Barbara did not get to see them much, this was special. Barbara had a good memory which made it interesting for visitors to converse with her.

It was August 12, 1980, when Salina informed Fannie that Joe's health was not good. His heartbeat was very slow, and he felt worn out all the time. Andy and Fannie knew their son Omar was very capable to take care of their work, so they left that afternoon to help out at Joe's. Andy hauled manure, and Marlin mowed hay. Willis also helped with Joe's work. Fannie, Salina's girls, and a few of Salina's sisters-in-law butchered fryers for them and got them into the freezer while Joe and Salina were consulting with his doctor. On the fourteenth, Joe was admitted to the hospital, and Andy helped Marlin some more. Andy and Fannie left for home that evening. The next day Joe had surgery to put a Pacemaker in to help his heart. Joe's health was heavy on Barbara's mind. She felt his family needed him so much. She prayed much that his health would be restored. Their children were as dear to her as her own had been.

On August 30, 1980, Salina informed Fannie that Mother was not well. Her sons Bill and Dan from Oklahoma were there. Knowing the doctor had earlier warned her about her heart, Andy and Fannie went to be with her. The next day was Sunday, and Bill and Dan offered to stay with Mother and encouraged Andy's and Joe's to go to church, which they did. Though these boys were men now and not in the Amish faith, Barbara requested that they read to her from her well-worn German Bible. To her, the German was much plainer. So Bill read to her in German, and he could still read quite fluently. Dan admitted he had forgotten how, so he just listened. At noon, Merle's and Willis' and the rest ate dinner at Salina's table.

Joe was able to help along with the work again since he had the Pacemaker. On September 1, Bill and Dan bade good-bye to their mother and left for home. She was ready to rest, although she did enjoy their visit.

October 7, 1980, Andy and Lizzie, John and Mary, and their daughter Edna and three little girls came to spend some time with Barbara. The next day, Salina had a tour group for dinner, so the women helped her serve. Mother enjoyed their visit so much.

November 19, Barbara's brother Andrew and his wife stopped by to visit. They came frequently to visit her mother and always visited Barbara, too. A few days later, Fannie and Andy came to attend a funeral of Andy's cousin, and they took her mother along also. They left for home that evening. She enjoyed all her visitors, although she often wished they would stay longer.

December 12, 1980, Barbara's brother Andrew and his wife and her sister Ida and Enos Schrock came from Kansas. They ate supper and stayed for the night.

On April 24, 1981, Fannie went to Kalona. There was an annual quilt show going on in that area. Late in the afternoon, Salina and Fannie took their mother to see all the pretty quilts. It almost wore her out, but she enjoyed every minute of it.

Chapter 71
To Oklahoma - Wedding Visits - Reunion in Leon

On April 28, 1981, Barbara had a chance to go to Leon to visit Fannie and Andy. She wanted to help, so Fannie let her pick out nuts the next day. The thirtieth Andys took her along to Oklahoma. They took her to her son Bill's for supper and to John and Mary's for the night. The next day they took her to visit John's children. They ate dinner at Fannie and Norman's, and Barbara enjoyed seeing this granddaughter's children. The oldest was nearly twenty-one. My, how time did fly! Her oldest great-grandchild was Linda, daughter of David and Vera. She was nearly twenty-three and married to Eli Burkholder. They had a son who was a year old.

That evening was the wedding of Mary Jane, youngest daughter of Andy and Lizzie, to Paul Miller. Barbara was so thankful to be able to be there. The next day Andy and Fannie took her to son Dan and Betty's for dinner. Their son Leroy and children, Danelle, Barry, and Perry, the twins, were also there. Barbara watched as these children rode their unicycles. She thought it looked rather dangerous. It reminded her of the time her Dannie would ride a goat to go for the mail when they lived in Garnett, Kansas. She used to think that was dangerous, too.

May 3 was Sunday, and she was glad to attend the Amish church she had called home for so many years. That evening grandson David and Vera, who now lived on Barbara's old place, had most of the Chupp clan for supper. This brought back many memories of when she had lived there and struggled to make ends meet. That night she and Andy's were to her son Andy and Lizzie's for the night. The next day they headed for home. Barbara lay in the back seat most of the way. They stopped at Jamesport, Missouri, for early supper at her daughter Anna and Levi's. By the time they got back to Andy and Fannie's, it was bedtime.

The next morning, Barbara did not feel well and rested all forenoon. But by the next day, she wanted something to do again. Fannie let her cut quilt blocks, which made her forget her ills. That evening Salina, Mary, Wayne, and Wanda came in time for supper and stayed overnight. Early the next morning, they and Grandma went home.

On April 15, 1981, Anna came by bus to spend some time with

her mother. This was a chance for Joe and Salina to be gone a few days knowing Mother would be well taken care of. They decided to go to Leon as they were having very inspiring meetings in that church. They returned home the morning of the 18th. That afternoon Anna returned home by bus.

On June 4, 1981, Barbara was pleased to have her granddaughter Betty and Jim and little son Nathan from Pennsylvania come to visit her. She seldom got to see Betty and remembered her better as a little girl when she lived in Oklahoma.

June 27, John and Mary from Oklahoma came to visit with Barbara and Joe's family. They also visited John's sister. One evening, Joe's took John's and Mother to Joe's parents for supper. Barbara was glad to be able to go along.

July 11, 1981, Andy and Fannie planned a reunion at their home near Leon, Iowa. Barbara came and most of her children and a number of grandchildren. Her sisters Anna and Fred, Edna and Orie, Ida and Enos and a brother Andrew and Elizabeth, all from Kansas, came. It was a lovely day and while some enjoyed visiting and reminiscing, the younger generation played volley ball. The number attending was sixty-four. Ivan and Darla and their baby Juanita from Maryland, Noah and Carol from Pennsylvania, Levi and Anna's son Paul and Linda and their little daughter Joanne from Florida came the farthest. It was held in Andy's shed, and a rocking chair was taken out for Barbara to sit on. She held out well and enjoyed it all very much.

Salina gave Mother's kitchen two coats of paint in October. A week later Barbara's leg pained so much that she was just in bed. Joe's had fixed an intercom by Mother's bed so she could call them in the other house if she needed anything. The twins were often in her house to play, and Mom could have them run errands. After being in bed three days, her leg was some better so that she could sit on a chair with her leg elevated.

John and Mary's retirement sale was October 31, 1981, in Oklahoma, but Barbara decided not to go since traveling tired her. She encouraged Joe and Salina to go, and Andy and Fannie went along, too.

Barbara's prayers and thoughts were with her daughter Fannie as she was to have surgery on December 1, 1981, for possible kidney stones. However, after Fannie was under anesthesia, the surgeon did one more test and found a growth. He decided it was a case for a specialist in Des Moines. When Fannie regained consciousness and heard the diagnosis, she felt rather depressed. Three days later, Mary and Karen brought Salina to be with Fannie a day. Barbara knew she would tire out too much to be of much help, so she encouraged Salina to go. Fannie had been anointed the evening before and felt at peace, having committed everything into the Lord's hands. Darla, Ivan, and little Juanita came from Maryland on the fifth to help out. Many prayers were offered, and December 8, Fannie had surgery. A large bladder stone was removed, but the Lord had miraculously removed the growth.

Chapter 72
Ill Health - Girls Visit - More Visits - Reunion

On March 27, 1982, Fannie and Andy went to visit her mother because her legs were giving her problems. Her daughter Mary was also there, and Anna came by bus that afternoon. Salina was sick, so the sisters looked after their mother. The next day was Sunday, so Mary and Anna stayed with their mother. Salina was feeling better again, too. Mother enjoyed having all four of her girls there. Andy's left for home that evening. Anna returned home by bus.

With Joe's health a constant concern, Salina had a lot of responsibility to see after her family's needs. Fannie felt it her duty to help out when she could with Mother. She had a good chance to be with her a few days June 9 and 10, 1982. Salina was busy picking strawberries, and Mother would stem. Fannie cleaned out cupboards for Mother while she was there. She went home that evening taking Gary along.

John's sister, who lived in Kalona, died of cancer, so June 13, John, Mary and their son David and Vera, daughters Fannie and Norman, and Edna and Cristie came from Oklahoma and were with Mother and Joe's. Barbara's oldest great-grandchild Linda and her husband Eli also came. The next day they attended the funeral.

June 30th, 1982, was the funeral of Barbara's nephew Willie's wife near Hazelton, so Barbara and Salina attended with Perry and Gertie.

Since Barbara had so much trouble with her legs, it was decided that a recliner might be a big help to her. July 10, 1982, Andy and Fannie bought a new recliner in Leon and took it to Kalona for her. They stayed, and the next day they took her to the Amish church and afterward to visit her nephew Perry and Gertie. She was pretty tired by evening, so Fannie and Salina stayed with her while the rest went to church. Monday was Mother's birthday, and she wanted to go and visit some who were sick in bed. So Andy's took her, along with Wayne and Wanda, to visit, then returned to Joe's for dinner. Andy's went home that afternoon, and Barbara rested.

On July 19, Salina saw that Barbara did not feel well, so she took her to the doctor. He gave her medication and warned her to take it easy.

The morning of August 20, 1982, Andy and Fannie left early and stopped at her mother's where they picked up her sister Anna and son Daniel. They then proceeded on to Indiana for a reunion of the descendants of Isaac and Mattie Chupp on August 22. It was hosted by Uncle Andy Chupp's family. Most of Fannie's siblings were there. Since it was Sunday, the forenoon was spent in singing and a sermon. The older grandchildren of Isaac and Mattie told of their memories or what they had heard about their family's roots. Too soon the day was over.

Barbara's grandson Paul and Linda and family from Florida came to visit the 26th. They had also attended the reunion in Indiana. They spent a few days, and Barbara enjoyed visiting with them. She did not often get the chance.

Wayne and Wanda proudly showed Grandma their new pencils, paper, and crayons as they would start to school on September 1, 1982. It was hard to tell who would miss their merry chatter and play the most, but Grandma knew it would be more lonely for her.

On September 3, 1982, Salina decided to paint Mom's bathroom, and knowing it would weary her, she took her to spend the day with Susan Bender. Lena Mast from Kalona and Anna Mast from Oklahoma would also be there. She looked forward to the day with great anticipation as both were old friends from years long gone.

On October 4, Barbara's son Dan and his son Leroy came to visit a few days. She felt so sorry for Leroy as he had been in a serious truck accident a few years earlier and would never be the same. He was fortunate to have gotten out alive. It was always a real treat when her children and grandchildren came to visit.

November 22, 1982, Barbara was glad to have her daughter Fannie drop in for the night and the next day. Other visitors the next day were her brother Andrew and his wife from Kansas. Then her sister Mattie and Eli Gingerich and their son Urie and his wife all came to visit, too. How she enjoyed the day!

Andy and Fannie met their son Earl and his wife and their two little boys at the airport on December 16, 1982, as they flew in from Florida. A few days later, they took them to Kalona to visit their grandmother and Salina, Joe, and family. Ivan, Darla, and Juanita also came for the day.

On March 25, 1983, Andy and Fannie took two widows, Barbara Stutzman and Bernice Miller, to Kalona. That evening they enjoyed a nice visit with Mother, Joe, Salina, and family. The next day they attended the M.C.C. relief sale in Iowa City.

On April 9, 1983, Andy and Fannie stopped by for a short visit on their way home from a trip to Pennsylvania to visit Carol and Noah. She always enjoyed hearing about their trip and how Carol and her family were faring.

One nice day in May, Salina took her mother to visit shut-ins and people who could not get out much.

On June 8, 1983, Salina took Mother to the doctor, and a week later she took her again. Her health was not good.

July 11, John and Mary came to be with Mother while Salina prepared for the reunion. The twelfth was Mother's birthday. However, she didn't feel well, so Salina took her for a treatment hoping for an improvement before the reunion.

On July 16, 1983, was a Chupp Reunion at the home of Joe and Salina in a tent in the yard. Close to one hundred attended. There was a program in the afternoon, and everyone enjoyed the day. Joe had made sure that a comfortable rocking chair was in the tent for Mother. She remarked that she enjoyed the day very much, although she did not understand everything. Her hearing was not too sharp anymore.

Those that stayed for Sunday had their own church service at Joe's in the tent. Barbara's brother Andrew preached a sermon and her granddaughter Mary Jane from Oklahoma led the songs. Those that were there ate dinner and left for their homes in the afternoon.

August 31, 1983, Barbara's sister Fannie and Oliver Troyer from Kansas came to visit. They ate supper in Joe and Salina's house and stayed for the night. This lifted Mother's spirits as her sister Fannie was such a jolly person. She had seen her share of sorrow when her first husband Ammon passed away, and later her son Donald was laid to rest from a rare kidney ailment. Oliver had also lost his first wife, and they enjoyed their sunset years together.

October 1, 1983, Salina took her mother for a flu shot. Mother could hardly get around, so Salina helped her walk.

Barbara was glad when her daughter Mary and her granddaughter Lorene came October 19 and stayed until the twenty-third.

October 20, 1983, Fannie went to Kalona to be with her mother while her sister Mary was there. They cooked dinner in Mother's little house. The next day Fannie took her mother and sister Mary visiting in different homes. They ate dinner at the home of Ivan and Alma Swartzentruber. Alma was a niece to Menno. Barbara enjoyed the day immensely.

December 12, 1983, Andy and Fannie were on the way home from Indiana and stopped to see her mother. Fannie thought this would be a chance for her to do Mother's weekly cleaning. She knew Salina usually did it, but with her family to see after and Joe's poor health, she wanted to give her a break. Sometimes it was nearly more then Salina could handle. Salina usually sent one hot meal to Mother every day.

On March 18, 1984, Merle and Fern had their first baby, a girl named Danelle. Barbara was happy for them. Merle seemed to have a special bond with his grandma. "Now Salina you are already a Grandma," she said. "Time goes so fast." March 30 was a shower for this little Miss. Barbara even braced up and went with Salina. She had a little quilt ready for the occasion, which was her practice with all of her grandchildren's first babies.

April 11, 1984, Dan left for home after spending a few days with his mother. That afternoon, Anna came to spend a few days with her. This gave Salina a break. Anna cooked in Mother's house. One meal she invited Joe's family over to eat in Mom's house which was special. Since Mother was not able to cook, they missed never eating in her house. Anna left for home the thirteenth. April 28, son Andy and Lizzie came to be with Barbara a few days. They ate their meals in Salina's home.

Barbara felt a bit of loneliness after Andy's left. The twins and Lavon often came over after school and filled her in on the happenings at school. She looked forward to these times, too. They were delighted when she saw their work and complimented them.

Barbara received a card from her sister Mattie that she was coming to visit her. This brought a smile to her face. May 23, 1984, she came, and they enjoyed their day together. A few days later son Bill, wife, and their daughter Annie came. She had not seen this little granddaughter very much since she did not travel anymore. Bill often came with Dan, and their wives stayed at home.

Bills left, and a few days later, on May 29, daughter Mary came to be with Mother. Since Mother was not feeling well, Mary's visit relieved Salina of looking after her. Mary also helped Salina cook for a tour group. Sunday evening, June 3, Salina and Mary both stayed with their mother as she was not feeling well. Mary left for home the next evening.

Chapter 73
Twin Girls - Eighty-ninth Birthday - Joe sick

On June 18, Salina received a phone call from her excited sister Fannie informing Mother that Darla and Ivan had twin girls born to them the night before. They named them Jessica and Janice. Carol and Noah had a little girl born three days earlier named Jana. Barbara said, "I don't understand it," as she could think of very few twins in her family, and this was the fourth set of great-grandchildren. A few months earlier, she had a set of twin great-great-granddaughters born to a grandson of Mary and John Henry's. Well, her main concern was that they were all healthy and would grow up to serve the Lord.

On July 11th, Salina washed windows in her mother's house. That afternoon Barbara's oldest granddaughter Barbara drove in and brought her mother Amanda, and her aunts Mary, Anna, and Fannie along. They almost filled Barbara's living room. Mother enjoyed every bit of it. The next day was Mother's eighty-ninth birthday. They all enjoyed the day, and that evening Fannie's husband Andy came, too. Of course, Fannie had plenty to tell about these new grandchildren she had. Early the next morning, Andy and Fannie left for Pennsylvania to visit their daughter Carol and family. They would get acquainted with their new baby girl. The others all left that afternoon, and Mother's house was extra quiet again.

July 28, 1984, a van from Missouri drove in. In it were Eli and Mattie Gingerich, Barbara's sister, and their sons Andy and Jakie and their wives, also Ezra and Edna Miller. He was the son of Barbara's sister Mary and John Y. This was really a pleasant surprise for Barbara. They brought dinner along and ate in her little house. Too soon the day was over, and Barbara sat musing over the day's happenings.

On August 4, son Dan and his twin grandsons from Oklahoma came. She could not tell which was Barry or which was Perry; they looked so much alike. They were raised in town; therefore, the farm was an adventure to them. They played with Gary and Lavon and helped them with their chores. They were there a few days, and Dan spent most of his time with Mother in her little house. Salina prepared all the meals in her house for them. Mother enjoyed their visit so much, and tears came to her eyes as they bid her good-bye.

August 24, Barbara was elated when her sister Edna came from Kansas. She informed Barbara she would stay a week. Edna also had her lonely times since her husband Orie had so suddenly passed away in front of their Florida home on March 2, 1983. Orie and Edna had already made plans to celebrate their fiftieth anniversary that summer. It had left Edna in a state of shock because she thought his health was good. The visit was good for both sisters. They cut and sewed some quilt blocks and shared their feelings. August 31, Edna bid Barbara good-bye and left for her home in Kansas.

Barbara had much to think about after she left. In Barbara's eyes, her sister Edna had always been so happy. Orie and Edna had traveled much and shared nearly fifty happy years together. They raised three boys and one daughter Freda. They used to take the children along on their travels when they were still at home. Many times they had visited Barbara. Now those children were married, and with Orie gone, Edna had her lonely days. Such is life with its trials. Of one thing Barbara was sure: she had a Heavenly Father who always saw her through.

October 1, Salina took Mother to the doctor, and she got a flu shot. Salina had to help her walk as she could hardly get around by herself. Salina took her to visit another shut-in since they were out anyhow. There were times that Barbara could hardly treadle her sewing machine. With her legs causing her so much trouble, Salina had done Mother's cleaning every week for quite some time.

Barbara peeled potatoes for Salina's tour groups if she was able. She was thankful to be able to help out that much. She could no longer cut them up as her hands had so little strength.

November 8, 1984, Noah and Carol and their little girls from Pennsylvania stopped by to visit her grandma. They ate dinner in Salina's house. They left soon afterward for Leon to visit her parents Fannie and Andy.

November 20, Joe and Salina went to Jamesport to attend the sale of her cousin. They were at her sister Anna and Levi's overnight, then left for home the next day. Barbara was glad they could go, but her own days of traveling were over.

January 4, 1985, Barbara received word that her sister Mary's husband passed away. Barbara's thoughts were with the family, but she knew her health would not permit her to go. Since Joe was also sick and coughing, it was not possible for Joe and Salina to go either.

She was glad to hear that Fannie and Andy went. She often prayed that Joe's health would improve.

January 8, Barbara's brother David and his wife and her sister Ida and Enos came to visit. They ate supper at Joe and Salina's house, then slept at the motel in Kalona. With Joe's health like it was, they did not want to burden them more then necessary. They came to visit with Barbara again the next forenoon, then went on to Buchanan County to visit more relatives.

Salina took Joe to the doctor after they left, and he said he had a start of pneumonia. He was given medication, and in a few days he felt some better. But by the fourteenth, he was worse again. Andy and Fannie came and were with Mother a few days. Fannie, Salina, and the twins stayed with Mother Sunday evening as she did not feel well. Andys went home Monday afternoon.

On January 16, some neighbors brought dinner in for Barbara and spent the afternoon with her. This cheered her up some. Often when Joe was sick, Mother did not feel well either.

Anna and Levi came on February 5 and were there until evening.

On February 7, Barbara got out some quilt blocks and sewed them together. At times, Salina cut blocks, and her mother sewed them. A week later, Joe was sick again and had to go to the doctor. It seemed he just could not regain his strength and often forced himself to work or to help his young sons as they struggled with the work.

Barbara's sons, Bill and Dan, came to visit her on February 18 which brightened her day. They left again the twentieth. On March 4, Mom sewed some quilt blocks again. On March 9, Fannie came and spent the day with Mother. The next day was Sunday, and Mom had quite a few visitors which she enjoyed.

March 20, Barbara's little house was almost full as her sister Mary and her son Ezra and his wife and their son John Henry's from Clark, Missouri, came to visit. This brought cheer to Barbara. Too soon the day was over, and they again bid good-bye. They marveled at Barbara's keen memory.

March 26, Salina helped Mother set quilt blocks together as sometimes she could not figure out how they belonged anymore. It was getting to the place that Salina did not want to leave Mother alone. At times, Lavon and Wayne would stay with her and play in her house in case she needed something.

Chapter 74
Corn Planted - Sudden Departure - Blackout

With such nice spring weather, Joe was eager to plant corn. Marlin and Gary were old enough to get the ground ready and helped as much as they could. There were times when Joe felt so sickly that he would let Marlin plant while he laid on the pick-up seat and rested. However, on April 22, he felt well enough to plant corn late into the evening. On the twenty-fourth, he felt really sick but kept on planting. The next day Salina took him to the doctor, and he said he had a start of pneumonia again. He gave him a shot and some medication. The next day Joe said he felt better and went out to plant again. With the boys' help, he was able to keep working. Late in the evening of May fourth, he came in and said, "Well, the corn is all planted. I was never done this early other years."

Salina said, "I hope you didn't overdo yourself, no better then you felt."

"I don't think so," he answered with a smile.

May fifth was Sunday, and Joe and the family all went to church. Salina said, "I think this afternoon you had better rest."

"Oh, I thought we'd go listen to the Gospel Echoes sing. That isn't work," he chuckled. Mother had visitors so they felt safe to leave about her. They sat close to Merle and Fern, and Joe could not resist holding his only granddaughter a bit. When they got home, the boys went to milk while Joe did get a short nap. One of the boys came in and said, "Dad, we have a sick cow."

Joe said, "I'll be right out and give her a shot."

Salina set supper out for the family, then went over to check on Mother and sat down to visit with her company a little. As she saw the clock moving right along, she went over to her house to see if the family was done eating supper. She reminded the children that it was time to get ready for church. The boys were showering, and Salina saw Joe had not yet returned to the house. She asked, "Where is Daddy?"

"Oh, he hasn't come in yet," they answered.

Salina and the twins went out and called for him, but they received no answer. After searching the barn in vain, Salina called Mary and Willis. "We can't find Joe," she said.

"We were just ready to leave for church, but we'll come right away," they said. When they arrived, Salina told them where she had looked. Willis, with Gary and Lavon, went to the brood shed. There he lay with a scraper in his hands, his life gone.

This was a great tragedy, and when they told Barbara, she said, "Oh, why couldn't it have been me instead. Joe was still needed so much to raise his family. I have lived my life, and I'm old and can't work." Friends tried to encourage her, telling her the Lord still had something for her to do. Salina was too full of grief to offer much support to her mother. Joe had always treated his mother-in-law with respect, and she would miss him so much.

The days that followed were a blur. Barbara's children and grandchildren and many other relatives arrived from many other states to show their last respects to one who was loved by all that knew him. May seventh, over eight hundred people filed through at the funeral home to extend their sympathy. The next day was the funeral, and again, many friends and relatives attended. Fannie and Andy made it their responsibility to take Barbara to the funeral and see to her needs. The morning after the funeral, Salina's siblings stopped in for a light breakfast with her and her children. Then one by one they bid good-bye and left for their homes. Merle and Fern and Willis and Mary came and spent the day with the family. They reminisced and tried to comfort each other.

On May 14, Fannie came to relieve Salina a few days, helping to care for Mother. Mother often said, "Oh, why couldn't it have been me instead of Joe?" Still, she did not want to doubt the Lord's will.

On the evening of May 30, Salina and her children were together discussing plans for the future. Perry and Gertie, Barbara's nephew, came to spend the evening with Barbara. When they entered Barbara's house, they found Barbara on the floor, unable to get up. She had already been lying there four hours. After helping her up, she said she must have blacked out, then came to again after she fell.

John and Mary came from Oklahoma on June 7 to spend some time with Mother. On Sunday, John went to church, but Mary stayed with Mother. Salina also stayed at home because she had severe back pain. June 11, Andy and Fannie came for dinner on their way home from Indiana. They were with her mother most of the afternoon. June 22, Anna came to be with Mother. That evening Enos, Barbara's brother from Indiana, came to visit Barbara and Salina and her family. He left again the twenty-sixth. Anna stayed and helped out until the twenty-ninth. The neighbor women often came and stayed with Barbara to relieve Salina.

July 12, 1985, Barbara's ninetieth birthday, her granddaughter Barbara from Oklahoma came and brought her mother Amanda and Al Troyers. Mattie and Eli Gingerich from Clark, Missouri, and Fannie and her daughter Darla and her little girls from Leon were there, too. Barbara enjoyed each one's visit. That evening they all enjoyed a fish fry provided by the Oklahoma folks. Everyone left for home the next day except the Oklahoma folks, who stayed until the fifteenth.

August 6, Barbara's cousins Eli Miller and his wife and Feltie and Lydia Yoder from Indiana came and spent two days with Barbara. She enjoyed their visit very much.

August 10, Mother's nephew Perry and Gertie brought his brother Joe's from Wisconsin to visit Barbara, and they all ate dinner with Salina. On August 11, the older girls from the community brought supper in and spent the evening with Barbara. She felt really unworthy of everything people did for her. Her mind was clear, and she enjoyed visiting with anyone that came.

Chapter 75
Isaac Chupp Reunion - Tragedy - Poor Health

On August 16, John and Mary and their daughters, Norman and Fannie, Cristie and Edna; Barbara's son Andy and Lizzie and their girls, Roberta and Arlis, Betty and Jim; Bill Jr. and his sister Barbara; and Levi and Anna and sons, Daniel and Andy from Missouri; and Andy and Fannie from Leon and their son Earl from Florida came. The next day was a reunion at the Kalona Park for the descendants of Mattie (Yoder) and Isaac Chupp. This was a hard day for Salina's family so soon after Joe's death. It had been planned earlier so Andy and Fannie helped Ivan and Alma Swartzentruber host it in Joe and Salina's place.

Those that stayed for Sunday were at Salina's farm for worship service. Calvin Yoder preached. After dinner most everyone left for home.

Barbara helped Salina cut up some apples to can on August 28. She did not have much strength in her hands anymore, but she still wanted to help what she could.

A granddaughter, Carol and Noah Yoder, from Pennsylvania stopped in September 7 to visit and eat dinner in Salina's house. They left in the afternoon to go to Leon.

On September 9, Barbara snapped and cleaned beans for Salina. She was glad if she was able to help sometimes. She seemed better at this time. On September 27, Barbara's sister, Ida and Enos, came for supper and stayed for the night. They lived in Kansas, and Barbara was always glad to hear news from there.

October 9, Barbara could hardly walk without help as her legs were giving out on her. October 31, daughter Fannie came to spend a few days. She helped Salina make a lot of noodles and did extra cleaning for Mother.

November 5, 1985, son Dan and his wife Betty came. They were there two days, then left again for home.

December 30, Levi and Anna came to stay a few days. Barbara's brother, Andrew and Elizabeth, also came and stayed there for the night. Elizabeth's mother passed away, which was their main reason for coming. The next day was her funeral so Levi's and Salina went, too. Barbara was not well, and the nurse came to check on her.

During this time, they received word from Kansas that Alvin

Miller, Enos and Ida's son-in-law, was in serious condition due to electrical shock while making repairs. Salina's heart was really touched as her cousin Fannie also had a young family at home. She could well identify with her trials.

January 1, 1986, Anna and Levi left for home by bus in the afternoon. January 3, the nurse came to check on Barbara again and helped bathe her. The message came from Kansas that Alvin had passed away. Salina made arrangements for someone to look after her mother, and though the roads were icy, she and son Gary went to Leon. They arrived in time for supper and stayed overnight. The morning of January 5, they went with Andy and Fannie to Kansas to attend Alvin's funeral which was the next day. It was a very sad day. The morning after the funeral, they returned to Leon with Andys and drove on home yet that evening.

In January, 1986, Mother's health was declining. January 22, Fannie came to help out with Mother's care. Salina and Fannie sorted through some of their mother's quilt patterns and pieces and put them away. It was evident that Mother would not be able to do much piecing anymore. Fannie left for home the twenty-fourth. January 28 and 29, Barbara's brother David and Ilva and niece Freda came to visit. This gave Barbara a slight moral boost. After they were gone, she pieced a doll quilt, which proved to be almost too much for her. The thirty-first, the nurse checked on her again and bathed her.

February 4, Willis brought their boys to Salina's, and that afternoon a little girl, Sara, was born to them. Salina was happy for them. Mother reminisced how this was like her own family had been, as she also had two boys first, then a girl.

February 6, John and Mary came to help care for Mother. They stayed until the ninth, then left for Jamesport to visit Levi's. February 12, the nurse came again, but Mother was not well. February 19, a neighbor stayed with Mother. March 6, she was not well, and the 7, the nurse came to check on her again. Salina often sent one of the children over to see how their grandma was doing. March 10, Salina was with Mother most of the day as she was worse. A few days later, Salina saw she was noticeably worse. When the nurse came, she advised Mother to stay off her feet.

The evening of the twelfth, Andy and Fannie came. The next day, Salina went with them to Iowa City to get a hospital bed for Mother. They helped move some furniture and get the bed situated in the living room so she would be able to see out of the window. Andys left that evening for home. Mother stayed in bed day and night. She was getting worse all the time. The nurse came and verified that she was losing out. In the afternoon of the seventeenth, her children, Dan and Mary, came from Oklahoma to be with Mother. The next day Mother's sister, Mary, and her daughter, Susie, and her husband came to spend the day. Daughter Mary cooked dinner for them in Mother's little house. They left again that evening. Mary stayed with Mother, and Dan left for home. Sunday the twenty-third, Mary stayed with Mother while the others went to church. She had quite a bit of company that afternoon. On the twenty-fourth, Mary had a chance to go to Leon and then went on home from there. Sometimes the neighbor women took turns to come and care for Barbara. The twenty-eighth, Salina slept close to Mother in case she got any worse as she was losing out. March thirtieth, Karen stayed with her grandma in the evening.

Chapter 76
Mother's Maud - Ninety-one Now - Family Visitors

Salina realized the time had come when she could no longer give her mother the adequate care she needed. So on March 31, 1986, Emma Beachey came to stay with her. When Emma went home for the weekend, Salina and Wanda slept in Mother's house to care for her. When there were days that Emma had other plans, neighbors and others helped out. April 15, Andy and Lizzie from Oklahoma, and Anna and Levi from Jamesport, Missouri, came. They left again on the eighteenth. May 13, Fannie, Darla, and her little girls came and left for home the next day.

May 16, Son Bill from Oklahoma came and stayed a few days. He stayed with Mother on Sunday so the others could go to church. Barbara asked him to read to her out of her German Testament again.

May 31, Enos and Ida, with their sons, Floyd and Robert, and their wives came to visit Barbara. Enos and Ida slept in Barbara's house and looked after her needs that night. They left June 2. On the fifth, Anna and Enos Sarah from Jamesport, Missouri, came and visited Barbara.

June 27, Mother's brother Enos and wife Lulu from Indiana came and were there for the night and the next day. Barbara enjoyed their visit. Enos was her youngest brother, and Barbara was married and had a few children of her own when he was born. He enjoyed hearing her tell of family happenings he did not remember. As Barbara's mind was clear, she could tell much that happened long ago better then what happened a short time ago.

July 3, Noah and Carol and their children from Pennsylvania, and Daniel, son of Anna and Levi, and his girlfriend from Indiana, came to visit their grandma. They marveled at how clear her mind seemed.

July 5, Barbara's cousin Edna, daughter of her paternal aunt Mary Ann, and her husband Amos came and took care of Barbara two days. Their visit brought back memories to Barbara of her aunt who had been a close friend to her and had passed on to her reward.

July 10, John, Mary, and Dan from Oklahoma, came to be with Mother. They were there for Mother's ninety-first birthday. The next day was Sunday, and Dan and Mary stayed with their mother while the others went to church. Dan left that afternoon for home, but Johns stayed a day longer.

Barbara received a greeting and a letter from her oldest grandchild, Barbara, that made her feel she had left an indelible impression on her life. Her letter follows:

Dear Grandma, July 10, 1986

Greetings of love and "Happy Birthday"! Ninety-one years is certainly an accomplishment. Your life has been filled with many things - hardships as well as the good things - life has to offer. One thing that always impressed me is your deep-rooted faith in God and the courage you had to keep going.

There are times I just close my eyes and think about spending the night at your house. I can hear you reading the Bible passages and prayers in German. These are precious memories I will always remember about you. Isn't that a nice thing for one to remember about their grandma?

Of course, your quilt piecing is another thing I remember. You could take the tiniest scraps and make something beautiful and useful. Being a Grandma myself now, I hope someday my grandchildren will have such good memories of me. Your birthdays have always been times your family shared in.

Many other things come to my mind as I think back. We children always cheered when we saw your buggy and old Patsy coming a long way off. There were times your sisters and bothers came to Oklahoma from Kansas for your birthday and often just to visit. Through this, I grew up with a closeness to them. I still enjoy to go visit them. Hope to see you before long.

With love, Barbara

Then the sixteenth, Fannie came from Leon and brought Barbara Diener from Indiana along. She was the little girl that was raised by Menno's sister Sarah and Eli Beachey. They left again after dinner on the eighteenth. Mother enjoyed very much to see Barbara again whom she remembered as the little girl with the pretty blue eyes.

July 31, Mother was worse again, and August 1, Salina saw she was losing out. She was glad for Emma's help with Mother. August 2, granddaughter Barbara and her mother, Amanda, and Mother's daughter, Mary, all from Oklahoma, and Fannie from Leon came to visit. The next day was Sunday, and Amanda and Mary stayed with Mother while the others went to church. Everyone ate dinner with Salina and her family. The next day they helped Salina work up corn and can peaches. Mother had severe pains, and Mary and Fannie were with Mother all night. They all left for home the next day, and Mother was so sick she hardly talked. August 6, Merle and Fern came over to visit Grandma and saw she was very sick.

August 7, Barbara was in severe pain and looked bloated. The next afternoon, Karen came home from Arkansas where she was serving at Hillcrest Home and went right over to see her grandma. She felt a little better but was very weak. Grandson Omar and Rose also came to visit her that day.

August 10, son Andy and Lizzie from Oklahoma came and were glad to find her feeling a bit better. The next day her brother Andrew and his wife and her sister Edna came from Kansas to visit her. The thirteenth, Andy and Lizzie left for Indiana. The nurse was out to check on her. She was very sick by evening, which was another concern for Salina.

August 16, Andy and Fannie and their son Earls came. Willis and Mary brought supper in and spent the evening. The next day was Sunday, and Fannie stayed with her mother while the others went to church. The eighteenth, Andys left for home and took Wayne and Wanda along. They had a chance to go home again in a few days.

August 23, son Bill, wife and daughter Annie, and granddaughter Heather and her brother Seth came to visit. They rented rooms in the motel in Kalona and were with Barbara during the day. They left for their home in Oklahoma two days later.

September 10, Barbara's nephew Ezra and his wife from Clark, Missouri, along with some others, stopped in for a visit with Barbara as they were passing through the area. Visits like this always lifted Barbara's spirits.

Sunday evening the fourteenth, Karen stayed with her grandmother while the others went to church. She enjoyed visiting with her grandma of happenings in her life long ago. She jotted down things of special interest which were contributed for this book.

Chapter 77
Very Sick - Children Come and Go - To Hospital

September 18, Barbara was very sick, and Salina and Emma were up with her most of the night. The nurse came out to check on her the next day and felt she had suffered a heart attack. Her daughter Fannie and Andy came that evening and stayed up with her most of the night to relieve Salina and Emma.

September 20, her granddaughter Fannie and Norman and their children, Lorene, Polly, twins Earl and Erma, and Jay, and another granddaughter Edna, Cristie and their daughter Miriam, Jerry Beachy, and Dean Knepp, all from Oklahoma, came. Mother was not well and tired easily. Salina stayed with her overnight. Andy and Fannie left for home that evening.

September 24, Mother's sister, Mary, and Mrs. Jake Beachy came from Riceville, Iowa, to visit.

September 27, Bill Jr. brought another grandson, Lloyd, and his wife Esther and their girls, Mary and Barbara, from Oklahoma. They visited Mother and some other relatives, then left for home after dinner the next day.

September 30, Mother breathed so hard and the nurse was out with her four hours. Because of this, she decided to put oxygen there for Mother to use when necessary.

October 1, Mother was really sick. October 2, Fannie came in the afternoon to help care for her. October 3, Mother could hardly breathe, so oxygen was used. The next day, Fannie went home, and Dan came from Oklahoma. The next day was Sunday, and Emma went home. Salina and Dan stayed with Mother. In the afternoon, John Henry and Mary came from Oklahoma, and also their daughter Edna and Cristie. Johns stayed with Mother that night. October 6, Dan left for home. The next day John and Cristies left for home, and Mary stayed to help care for Mother. October 10, Mother was very sick, and Salina stayed with her until midnight. October 11 and 12, Mary stayed with Mother, and she seemed a bit better. The next day she was worse, and the nurse came out again. The fourteenth, Mother was very sick again. Mary cared for Mother the fifteenth and sixteenth. Mary left for home the evening of the seventeenth. The twentieth Emma was gone, so Salina cared for Mother.

October 25, grandson David and Vera and granddaughter Fannie and Norman from Oklahoma, came to visit and ate dinner at Salina's house. The next day was Sunday and those from Oklahoma stayed with Mother. They said she was quite talkative. After eating dinner at Salina's, they left for home.

November 7, Fannie came from Leon and was there for the night and helped care for Mother. She helped Salina make doughnuts the next day. That afternoon a load of Mother's nephews came to visit her from Clark, Missouri. Mother did not feel too well that evening. Andy came too, for the weekend. Fannie and Salina were both up with their mother most of the night. The next day was Sunday, and Fannie stayed with her mother while the others went to church. She had many visitors in the afternoon. Andy and Fannie left for home that evening.

November 20, Gertie Bontrager stayed with Mother as Emma wanted some time off. Mother had a bad day. Salina cared for Mother the next day, and she seemed some better.

December 5, Mother had a weak spell, and Willis had to help Salina and Emma get her to bed. Salina was up with her until midnight. December 6, Andy and Fannie stopped by for dinner on the way home from Indiana and visited Mother. December 10, Mother had another bad day.

January 2, 1987, Bill and Dan from Oklahoma came to visit their Mother a few days. That evening, Fannie and Andy came from Leon. The next day Fannie, Bill, and Dan stayed with Mother while the others went to church. Andys left for home that evening, and Bill and Dan left the next morning.

January 5, Barbara's sister Mary and her girls and their husbands came for a short visit. They were on their way home from Indiana where they had attended the funeral of Barbara's cousin Dan. Barbara wanted to hear the details of his death and funeral. She was glad her sister Mary was so able to go yet.

January 6, daughter Anna came to help with Mother's care. The next day Mother was in pain. Salina called Fannie on the eighth and told her Mom was suffering much again. Salina went to the doctor and got more medicine for Mother. The next day she seemed more comfortable. January 13, the nurse was out to check Mother. She said she had fluid on her lungs. Salina was with Mother all day. She seemed much improved in a few days. January 16, her daughter Mary came from Oklahoma and cared for her a few days.

January 18, Barbara's brother, David, and his wife and daughter, Twila, from Ohio, stopped in to visit. They were on their way home from Kansas where they had attended the funeral of Oliver Troyer, their sister Fannie's husband. With Fannie's loss, Barbara's thoughts were with her at this time.

January 20, Barbara had severe pain again. The problem seemed to be her bowels. Karen left for Arkansas to work that very day. This was also hard on her grandma as Karen could cheer her up when no one else could. She would miss her so much. The next day, Salina talked to the doctor, and he gave her more medication. Since she was so miserable, Salina and Emma were up with her most of the night. Salina called the doctor again the next day, and he gave her pain pills. On the twenty-sixth, she was in so much pain again, and it seemed to be her bowels. The nurse came to check on her again the next day and brought more medication. The evening of January 30, her daughter Fannie came to help care for her. Sunday, February 1, Andy came and took Fannie home that evening.

February 3, Salina took care of her mother, and her son Lavon was also sick. She was kept very busy. On the fifth, Mom finally felt better. She was better for about twelve days, then she did not feel well again. The nurse came to check on her. This went on until the night of February 24. Mom was so miserable that Salina was up most of the night with her. She was not well the rest of the month.

March 1 and 2, Mother suffered so much that the nurse came out again and gave her an enema. The next day Mother was so sick, the nurse came out and brought more pain killers and Valium. The next day she was more restful but very weak. The fifth, she again had a very bad day. On the sixth, John and Mary came from Oklahoma. The doctor gave Demoral to relax her. The night of the seventh, Salina was up with Mother from one o'clock on. She was so restless and still had pain. Finally she went to sleep at six o'clock, and Salina felt exhausted, too. Mother slept most of the day, but again had a rough night. Mary and John were up with her much of the night.

The next day was Sunday, and Mrs. Leon Helmuth came to help care for her. Salina also stayed, and at one point, they thought she was gone. But she revived again. Fannie came that evening from Leon because they felt their Mother would not hold out much longer. The next day she was worse, so the ambulance was called, and Mother was taken to the hospital in Washington. John, Mary, Salina, and Fannie followed the ambulance. They took x-rays, did more tests, then gave her a shot, and she rested better. Fannie left for home that afternoon. Johns left for home the next morning, and Salina stayed with Mother. She would waken and talk some but was confused. The next night, Emma stayed with her, and Salina went home. Salina and Wanda went to see her the next evening. The doctor released her on March 12, and she went home that afternoon by ambulance.

Chapter 78
Home - Wedding - Ninety-two Now - Karen Home

March 14, at six in the evening, was the wedding of Andy and Fannie's son Omar to Rose Stoll in Daviess County, Indiana. Mother seemed better, so early that morning, Salina, Gary, and Wanda left for the wedding. Emma was with Mother, and friends offered their help if needed. Salina and the children came home late the next evening. The next day, Salina updated Mother on the wedding. Mother was glad Salina could go.

Neighbors and friends came to visit at times, and she was better but still weak. March 20, her nephew Perry and Gertie and their daughter Laura and husband came to visit. They found her very depressed. At times, she questioned why she was still living. April 3, Mother did not feel well again, so Salina got more medicine for her. She had her better days, and again those days when she was not well.

May 2, her son, Andy and Lizzie, and her daughter Mary came from Oklahoma. They spent a few days and then went home again. Mary was glad to see her feeling better than she was the last time she had seen her.

In the afternoon of May 28, Barbara's brother Enos came from Indiana. Salina was also with Mother when twenty Amish young folks came and sang for Barbara which really cheered her up.

May 31, her grandson Omar and his wife Rose came to visit. She was glad to see them as she had not been able to attend their wedding. She gave them her best wishes. It was always a pleasure for her to see her grandchildren marry Christian companions.

June 11, Barbara counted it a privilege when her cousin Susie from Indiana and three of her children stopped by to visit her on their way to Kansas.

June 16, her niece Freda and Glen Kauffman brought Barbara's sister Anna and Fred from Kansas to visit. They ate dinner and supper in Salina's house, then came to her little house to visit. Nephew Perry and Gertie also came to spend the evening. She enjoyed every bit of it, although she was very tired by bedtime.

July 2, daughter Anna and Levi from Jamesport, Missouri, came in time for dinner. After dinner, Levi went on to Indiana, and Anna stayed with Mother. July 6, Levi came back from Indiana, and that afternoon they left by bus for home. Those few days that Anna was there meant much to Barbara.

July 10, granddaughter Barbara from Oklahoma brought her mother Amanda to visit, and her sister Mary from Colorado flew in to visit. They all stayed in a motel in Kalona. The next day Fannie and Andy from Leon came in time for supper. Sunday the twelfth was Mother's ninety-second birthday. Everyone went to church except Amanda and her daughter Mary. They ate dinner at Salina's house and were with Mother in the afternoon. Andy and Fannie went home that evening. The next day, they planned to leave on an extended western trip in their motor home. Their daughter Darla, Ivan, and three little girls and Ivan's parents from Maryland would go along.

July 14, son Dan and wife Betty from Oklahoma came to visit and spend a few days. Barbara always questioned them about their son Leroy who was injured so badly some years earlier as he was trucking in Arkansas. He had a young family that needed him so much, but he was hardly able to work. This concerned Barbara. She was glad to hear he kept a positive outlook, and hopefully in time he would get well.

July 24, Mother complained of not feeling well. Fannie called from Las Vegas the next day to check on Mother. They were now on their homeward way.

Andy and Fannie got home from their western trip July 30. Sweet corn was ready, as well as other garden vegetables. Fannie was busy catching up, but by August 6, she took her three little granddaughters and went to Kalona to visit Mother. Salina was glad for Fannie's help with Mother as she had a group of people from France to feed. Ivan and Darla were working nearby on a job and came through there in the afternoon. They took the girls home, and Fannie stayed for the night. Mom was feeling better that evening, so Fannie left for home the next forenoon. Later that day, Barbara's son Bill and his wife and their daughter Annie and granddaughter Heather came to spend a few days.

September 1, Salina helped Mother over to her house, and she lay on Salina's couch. Some ceiling tile had fallen down in Mother's house earlier, and this was the day carpenters came to replace them.

September 18, Barbara was happy when her youngest sister Ida and Enos from Kansas came. Other visitors that day were her nephew Enos' widow, Sarah Bontrager, from Jamesport, Missouri, and her two oldest children and their partners. Enos and Ida stayed a few days and slept in Barbara's house and took care of her while they were there.

October 10, Salina cared for Mother and also took care of Willis and Mary's children. The next day was Sunday, and Mother did not feel well, so Salina stayed at home with her. That evening Leon Helmuths came and took care of her so Salina could go to church.

October 13, son Andy and his wife Lizzie came and were there a few days. They left for home the sixteenth. October 19 through 23, Karen took care of her grandmother. Mrs. Leon Helmuth was so kind to come and take care of Mother October 25, and again the thirty-first, so Salina and her children could go to church.

November 3, daughter Mary came to be with Mother. This relieved Salina as she knew Mary gave her the best of care. Mother had her good days and her bad days. Mary was still with her the tenth, and late that evening, Fannie and Andy came from Leon. The next day, Andy helped Willis remodel the barn on the farm they bought and planned to move onto soon. Fannie stayed with Mother. The nurse was out as Mother was worse. Her nephew, Ezra, from Clark, Missouri, stopped by to visit. Andy and Fannie went home the next day, and Mom had a hard day.

November 23, Andy and Fannie were with Mother for the night, and the next day they helped Willis and Mary move onto the farm they bought.

Between the neighbors and Salina and Emma, someone was always with Mother. December 7, Karen came home from Hillcrest, and she helped out when the need arose. December 13, Karen stayed with Mother so the others could go to church. Salina had slept in Mother's house the night before.

December 19, Willis' children were with Salina. That was the day their second daughter, Naomi, joined their family. She was their fourth child. These were Barbara's great-grandchildren.

December 28, Andy and Fannie and their children Earls and their three boys, Noah and Carol and their three children, Ivan and Darla and their three children all braved the slick roads to come to Kalona. They ate dinner in Salina's house, and all visited in Mother's small house.

Chapter 79
1988 Maud Quits - February in Leon - Improves and Visits

January 1988, Emma informed Salina that she wanted to have off from caring for Barbara during the month of February. Salina called Fannie and told her the predicament they were in. Andy and Fannie offered to take her to their home near Leon. Salina was not sure how they could move her since she could no longer walk. They said they would figure out a way. When Salina broke the news to Mother, she was very upset. In the meantime, Andys got a hospital bed set up for her. January 30, Andy and Fannie came with a borrowed van with a bed in the back. With the help of Salina's boys, they got Mother loaded and were on their way by one-thirty in the afternoon. When they got home with her, their son Earl came and helped unload her and get her to bed. She was pretty tired from the trip.

The next day was Sunday, and Fannie stayed at home with Mother. They had some visitors in the afternoon to visit Mom. The next few days, Fannie devoted most of her time to bathe and care for Mother. She borrowed a wheelchair for her. On the third, she baked a big batch of cookies and put Mother on the wheelchair and brought her to the kitchen where she could watch. For dinner, she pushed her to the table. By afternoon she was ready to rest again. She seemed to enjoy being in the kitchen with her wheelchair. Often after her bath, Fannie pushed her to the window where she could watch the pretty cardinals on the pine tree north of the house. With a blanket of snow, this was indeed a lovely sight.

Some days Fannie would get out quilt blocks to work on. This interested Mother so much, she even helped cut some. It was a slow process and took real effort on Mother's part, but it did interest her. Saturday the thirteenth, Leon and Mary Helmuth and Wanda came from Kalona to visit Mother. This was a real highlight for her. One day, Darla and her little girls stayed with Mother so Andy and Fannie could do their tax work.

Mother seemed to be improving, so on the twenty-first, Mother was alone while Fannie went to church an hour. Quite a few people stopped to visit. Once the school children came and sang for her, which she enjoyed. Although she was showing improvement, she was counting the days when the month would be up, and she would be taken to her home. February 23, Levi, Anna, and their Andy came to spend the day from Jamesport, Missouri. Mother enjoyed their visit very much.

Earls brought pecans over, and Mother picked them out while sitting on her wheelchair. February 27, Earl helped load Mother, and Andys took her to Earls for dinner which was a pleasure for her. The next day, Sunday, they took her to Ivan and Darla's for dinner. Earls and their boys and Omar and Rose were also there. She enjoyed it very much. On Monday, they took her to Omar's place for dinner, and she enjoyed that, too. The next day, Tuesday, Mom's things were packed, and Andys took her home that afternoon in the car. She walked into her house with a little help. Emma was there to help care for her again. Andy and Fannie stayed for the night. The next morning, Mother wanted to get dressed and was on her wheelchair most of the day. Andys left for home that afternoon.

March 9, her son Dan came and ate dinner in Salina's house. Mom and Emma also ate there. Dan left the next afternoon for home.

Chapter 80

To Hospital - Home Again - Ninety-three Now - Chupp Reunion

March 11, Mother complained of pain in her side. The doctor thought she might have cracked a rib. March 13, Andy and Fannie came for an ordination at Salina's church. A sister from the Amish church stayed with Mother. She called the church and said Mother was in terrible pain. Andy, Fannie, and Salina went home immediately and called the ambulance as they saw her pain was nearly unbearable. They followed the ambulance to the hospital and stayed until church time that evening. Emma stayed with her that evening. Andy went home with others Sunday evening.

Fannie and Salina arrived at the hospital by eight o'clock Monday morning. Salina took Emma home, and Fannie stayed. When Salina came back in the afternoon, and the doctor said Mother might need surgery, but they would wait at least a few days, so Fannie went home. The shots Mother received gave her some relief. Salina stayed for the night, and Karen was with her the next day.

March 16, Mother was very restless and seemed confused at times. Fannie came again the next afternoon and stayed with her all night. She seemed more calm after they changed medication. They had her on I.V. and gave her nothing by mouth. Salina was with Mother the next night. She had much pain and many shots. Then Fannie was with her again the next day, and she and Emma both stayed for the night. John and Mary came from Oklahoma the evening of the nineteenth. Salina brought them to the hospital the next morning, and Salina and Mary stayed that night. Fannie brought John and Bishop Henry Bender to the hospital the morning of the twenty-first. Mother seemed so listless but was given a little liquid by mouth. Fannie left for home that afternoon, and Karen stayed with Mother that night. Salina and Johns went to the hospital the next day, and Karen went home. John and Mary stayed that night with Mother. March 23, Mom showed improvement and was given solid food to eat. The morning of the twenty-fourth, John went home to Oklahoma, and Mary stayed. Mother was so much better that the doctor released her, and she went home by ambulance that afternoon.

That evening, her son Andy and Lizzie came. They also visited Lizzie's brother and his wife but spent most of the time with Mother.

Sunday the twenty-seventh, Andy, Lizzie, and Mary stayed with Mother while the others went to church. About four o'clock that afternoon, Andys and Mary left for Leon to spend the night and then went on home from there the next day. Mother was tired out after having so much company that day.

March 29, Salina took care of Mother as Emma wanted the day off. She seemed so listless and tired out. She was just up and down. April 6 and 14, she was worse and then the fifteenth, she felt better again. April 30, her daughter Fannie came and was with her for the night and the next day so Salina's family could all go to Communion. Mother seemed better that day, and Fannie left for home that evening.

May 3, Mother's brother Enos from Indiana came and brought cousin Susie and her husband, Jonas. They visited with Mother and ate supper in Salina's house. Mother was so glad to see them as she did not see her cousins often.

May 10, son Bill came from Oklahoma to visit his mother. He rented a motel room in Kalona. The next day he encouraged Mother, and he took her to visit her granddaughter Mary and Willis and their young family and also to visit Mother's cousin Edna and husband. Mother enjoyed the visit from her firstborn so much. He left again for home the fourteenth.

May 19, Barbara enjoyed a visit from her nephew Joe from Wisconsin. He reminded her so much of his father, Ed, who was her oldest brother.

May 27, Andy and Fannie drove a car to Kalona for someone else and visited Mother and ate dinner at Salina's. That afternoon, Barbara had more visitors when her brother Andrew and his wife, her sisters Edna and Ida and Enos came from Kansas. She felt her cup running over and was overjoyed to have these siblings visit. Andy and Fannie left for home, and the others took Salina's family out to eat that evening. The next afternoon, Enos and Ida went to Hazelton. Edna stayed with Barbara, and they had a nice time visiting. May 29, Edna stayed with Barbara while the others went to church. In the evening, her brother Andrew and his wife stayed with her while the others attended church.

June 2, Emma took another job so this meant more responsibility for Salina. The twins were with her often in case she needed anything. Salina slept in Mother's house at times. June 8 and 9, Mother complained of not feeling well. On the tenth, she complained of severe backache. The eleventh, the nurse came to check on her. She felt better again the next few days. It kept Salina busy to check on her and try to keep up at her own house. The sixteenth, Andy and Fannie stopped in for a short visit on their way home from Pennsylvania. Emma sometimes stayed with Mother at night. Neighbors were so good to come stay with her on Sundays so Salina could go to church with her children.

June 20, Salina picked peas, and Mother helped her shell them which was an accomplishment for her. The twenty-fourth, Mother did not feel well again, which was always an extra concern for Salina.

June 27, granddaughter Barbara from Oklahoma came and brought her mother, Amanda, along. They stayed in Kalona at the motel to make less work for Salina. They left for Leon in the afternoon of the twenty-ninth and were at Andy and Fannie's for supper and overnight. Karen helped with Mother's care when she was not at her job. Wanda often ran the sweeper and dusted for Mother.

July 9, a granddaughter Betty and her husband Jim Gieb, flew out to visit. Andy Ray, Betty's brother from Oklahoma, came at the same time. They left again the eleventh. Then the twelfth, Andy and Fannie came from Leon to help Mother celebrate her ninety-third birthday. They helped her over to Salina's house for dinner. She seemed to enjoy the day. They left for home again that evening.

July 20, Levi and Anna's son Paul and his family from Florida, came for a short visit with his grandmother. They were enroute to Oklahoma for the reunion of the descendants of Isaac and Mattie (Yoder) Chupp. It was held at the Mazie School on the twenty-third, with approximately two hundred present. Salina had made arrangements for Mother's care during her absence.

Susan Pointer from Washington state, the daughter of Menno Chupp, was also at the reunion and got acquainted with her Chupp relation. She is a half sister to Barbara's children, and only a few years earlier, she had discovered she had so many siblings. She was quite intrigued with her relatives, and the Amish way of life was all very new to her.

Since Emma could no longer care for Barbara, it proved to be more then Salina could do with all her other responsibilities. August 4, Fannie visited her mother, then she and Salina went to Wellman to make arrangements for Mother to enter Parkview Manor at Wellman, Iowa.

Chapter 81
Hot Weather - Move to Parkview - Cousins Visit

August 13, Salina cared for Mother until afternoon when Mary and her granddaughters, Rachel and Esther, from Oklahoma came, and then Mary took care of Mother. The weather had been up to one hundred degrees on some days which was hard on Mother. Salina did put a fan in her room which gave her some relief. Mary stayed with Mother on Sunday while the others were to church. August 15, Mary and the girls left for home. Salina slept in Mother's house the sixteenth. The next day, Salina and Karen marked Mother's clothes, and Emma came to be with Mother for the night.

On the eighteenth, Andy and Fannie came and helped move Mother to Parkview Manor at Wellman. This was hard for all concerned. Mother said, "You will take me home when my house is all cleaned." They told her they could not promise. The Manor was air conditioned and much more comfortable. Salina and Andys ate dinner with her at the Manor and helped put her things in place there. At three o'clock, they bid her good-bye, and Andys went home. Salina stayed a while longer.

The next day, Karen and Wanda went to visit Mother, and she was glad to see them. Salina did not go to see her for a few days, and when she did, Mother was not in a good mood. The twenty-fifth, Salina took Mrs. Leon Helmuth along to visit Mother. A few days later Salina and Wanda went to visit Mother, and she was happier. Sunday, the twenty-ninth, Lavon was baptized so Andy and Fannie came from Leon for the occasion. They came to the Manor early and wheeled Mother out for the church services there, and when that was over, they wheeled her back to her room and went to Sharon Bethel Church in time for the baptism. They stayed there for the fellowship dinner.

Afterward they went back to the Manor and visited with Mother and stayed to eat supper with her. They had a table alone with Mother which she seemed to enjoy. They drove on home that evening.

September 3, Dan came from Oklahoma to visit his mother, and she was glad to see him. Wanda went with him to the Manor to visit. The next day was Sunday, and Dan was with Mother most of the time. He did go to Salina's for dinner and again for supper as Salina had her children there for dinner, too. The next day, Salina and Dan both ate dinner with Mother at the Manor and visited her. Dan left for home that afternoon.

The next day, Salina, Lavon, Wayne, and Wanda all went to visit Mother.

September 19, John and Mary came from Oklahoma to visit Mother. They slept at Salina's house and spent most of their days at the Manor. They left for home the twenty-first, and Andy and Lizzie came from Oklahoma. The next day, Salina went with Andys to visit Mother. She was always glad when her children came to visit. They were there a few days, then left again for home.

October 8, Mother's brother David, his wife Ilva, their daughter Kay, and her husband Jamie from Ohio, came to visit Mother. She was glad to see them and to meet Kay's husband, and they had a nice visit.

October 14, Andy and Fannie came to visit Mother and got cheese to take back for Earl's bulk food store.

October 17, Salina went to visit Mother, and she seemed happier than usual. Two days later, Wanda went to the Manor and spent the whole day with her grandmother. This cheered her up as Wanda looked at letters and greetings she had received. She ate dinner with her and wheeled her around. Salina went after her that evening and talked with Mother, filling her in on what was happening at home. She was always so busy with feeding groups of people and running errands for the boys.

The twenty-second, Salina went in again and told Mother that she got her old hens butchered the day before and canned most of them. How Mother wished she could still work like that! "Did you have help?" she asked.

"Oh, yes, Gertie and sister-in-law Ruby helped."

"I'm glad you had help. I've dressed many chickens in my younger years."

December 1, Andy and Fannie stopped to visit Mother on the way to Indiana. Salina was there, too, so they got to see her also. From Indiana, they would go on to Pennsylvania to visit Noah and Carol and children.

December 9, Bill came from Oklahoma to visit his mother. He spent the nights at Salina's. Bill left again the eleventh for home. Salina went to visit her mother the next day and passed out in

Mother's room. The nurse called Marlin, and he came and took Salina to the hospital in Washington. She was very sick and requested anointing. Late that evening, her wish was granted, and she felt much better afterward. Fern came to see Salina the next day and took her home. The fourteenth, Andy and Fannie stopped in on their way home from Pennsylvania. Salina had gone for a CAT scan and stopped at the Manor a little on her way home. Mother was glad to see she was able to be up and going some again. The fifteenth, Marlin's special friend, Becky Stoltzfus from New York, came, and Marlin took her to the Manor to see his grandmother. She was glad to meet Becky. It seemed only a short time that he was a little boy playing on her floor.

The nineteenth, Becky flew home, and Salina went to see Mom. It was such a busy time. Lavon got his driver's permit, Karen came home from Indiana, and they were baking cookies and making candy. The twenty-third was the Christmas party at the Manor so Salina, Karen, and Wanda went. The twenty-sixth, Willis and Marlin dressed some hogs. The next day, some fat hogs fell into the manure pit, and the boys worked hard to get them out. Salina stopped to visit Mother, and when she told her what had been going on, she thought it couldn't be. Marlin would leave for New York at midnight, so they had helped him get packed.

January 4, Karen left again for her teaching job in Indiana. Salina felt she would have a little time to go see Mother, so she asked Emma to go along. Mother was glad to see them.

Salina tried to go to see Mother a few times every week and often took the twins along.

January 15, Mother's cousin Susie and Jonas from Indiana came to Salina's and wanted to visit Mother. Jonas was sick when they got there, so Salina turned Mother's little house over to them. The next day, Jonas was taken to the doctor and got some medicine. Salina took Susie in to visit Mom almost every day. The evening of the seventeenth, Jonas was so sick, Susie and Salina fixed an onion poultice to put on him. The next morning, he seemed better, but he was worse again by evening. The nineteenth, Salina took him to the doctor again.

Chapter 82

Mother's Outing - Triumph at Last - Funeral

January 20, Andy and Fannie picked Mother up at the Manor and brought her to Willis and Mary's for dinner. Fannie sewed a housecoat for Mother, and Mother asked Mary if she could do something for her. She let her sew buttons on some little dresses. This pleased her very much. Salina was also there and did some handwork. Andys took her back to the Manor in time for a short rest before suppertime, then left for home.

The twenty-first, Salina and Susie went to visit Mother again. Jonas seemed some better. He was able to come over to Salina's house for supper that evening. The next day, Salina took them to the Amish church. The next few days, Jonas felt better but was still weak. Salina and Susie went to visit Mother every day.

January 30, Marlin and Becky announced their engagement. Salina went to visit Mother a bit. When she got home, she put a Lone Star quilt in frame for Marlin. The next day she had a quilting, and the weather was so nice.

February 2, it turned cold, and Salina picked the twins up at school. From there, they went to Harold Dean Miller's for a party. Afterward she planned to take them to visit Mother and tell her of Marlin and Becky's engagement. But the Lord had other plans. She was not at the party long when she got a call that Mother had passed away. It was such a shock as she seemed to be in fair health. She had wheeled herself to the table for dinner, then returned to her room. Later a nurse came in to bring her some juice and found her sitting on her chair, and life had fled.

Mother had a special interest in the romance of Marlin and Becky. That very day, Salina and the twins had planned to tell her of their engagement. But now it was too late. Her sudden passing was a real shock, but still, they could not wish her back from her triumphal entry into Heaven's glories. So many times she had been sick to the point of death. This time, she had not been sick and had eaten her lunch in the dining room with the other guests as usual. After wheeling herself back to her room, she had apparently fallen asleep in the Lord.

Salina called her children, and as the word spread, neighbors came to her house to help out in any way they could. She called each of her brothers and sisters, as well as Mother's sisters and brothers. Those from Oklahoma informed her that they were having freezing rain, and the roads were hazardous. They were unsure when they could come, but they would start as soon as it was safe. Dan was not feeling able to come at this time but expressed his regrets.

Fannie and Andy came at nine-thirty the next morning. Salina was glad to have at least one of her siblings to help with more funeral arrangements and whatever came up.

Amish neighbors, Neal Bontragers, offered to have the funeral in their home. They also offered to have the wake the evening before the funeral. Mother had made most of the arrangements earlier. She had earlier made a request to daughter Fannie that she wanted one minister to preach in English for the benefit of those who could not understand the German. So Delmar Bontrager consented to take that part.

Early the morning of February 4, Mother's body was brought to the Sharon Bethel Church. Salina, Fannie, and Andy were there. That afternoon, Mother's sister Edna, and Levi and Anna's oldest son Paul and his daughter Joanne arrived by plane from Florida. Levi and Anna and sons, Mark and Andy, and their daughter-in-law, Lena, came from Missouri. Just as they were getting ready to eat supper, Bill Jr. and Noah Ray Chupp came from Oklahoma, each bringing a van. On them were Barbara's sons, Bill and Andy, and his wife Lizzie, and their girls, Roberta, Mrs. Arlis Unruh, Mary, Mrs. Paul Miller; Bill's oldest daughter Barbara; John and Mary and their children David, Fannie and her husband Norman, and Edna, Mrs. Cristie Miller. They reported very hazardous driving. It was snowing and bitterly cold in the Kalona area. Noah and Carol came from Pennsylvania. Karen, Uncle Enos, and Levi and Anna's son Daniel and his wife arrived from Indiana. Later that evening, Mother's brother Andrew and his wife Elizabeth, her sister Ida and Enos Schrock, and her sister Fannie, all from Kansas, came. The next day was Sunday and, after a short service at Sharon Bethel, they ate dinner there. In the afternoon, some of Mother's nieces and nephews from Michigan and Wisconsin came. Many local people came and went all afternoon to extend their sympathy to the family. Many expressed their appreciation of her courage in her many trials, and many mentioned how she had pieced so many quilts while she was able.

After supper, the body was moved to the Neal Bontrager home for the wake. The Amish young folks were there and sang.

Monday morning, more relatives arrived in time for the funeral from Clark, and Jamesport, Missouri. Mother's sisters and brothers were all there except two. A great nephew, Edward Bontrager, from Jamesport, Missouri, preached at the funeral, as well as her home bishop, Henry Bender.

The oldest grandson from each family was pallbearer. They were Bill Jr. Chupp and David Yoder from Oklahoma, Paul Yoder from Florida, Earl Miller from Leon, and Merle and Marlin Bontrager from Kalona. She was buried in the cemetery a short distance south of Neal's residence where the funeral was held.

Following is the obituary:

Barbara Chupp was the oldest child and daughter of Andrew F. and Fannie (Bontrager) Bontrager. She was born July 12, 1895, near Haven, Kansas, and died February 2, 1989. She reached the age of 93 years, 6 months, and 20 days. She joined the Amish church at a young age and remained faithful to the end. She married Menno I. Chupp February 26, 1914. He died July 20, 1971, near Aguila, Arizona.

To this union were born 9 children: William Claremore, Oklahoma; Daniel; and Mary (Mrs. John H. Yoder) Chouteau, Oklahoma; Anna (Mrs. Levi J. Yoder) Windsor, Missouri; Leroy (deceased); Andy of Adair, Oklahoma; Levi (deceased); Fannie (Mrs. Andy A. Miller) Leon, Iowa; Salina, widow of Joe Bontrager Kalona, Iowa. She left at her departure 34 grandchildren, 90 great-grandchildren, 21 great-great-grandchildren; 3 brothers and 6 sisters, Andrew of Kansas; David of Ohio; Enos of Indiana; Mary widow of John Y. Miller of Riceville, Iowa; Anna (Mrs. Fred Yoder); Fannie, widow of Oliver Troyer, both of Hutchinson, Kansas; Mattie (Mrs. Eli J. Gingerich) Edgewood, Iowa; Edna, widow of Orie W. Yoder, Ida (Mrs. Enos E. Schrock) both of Yoder, Kansas. Barbara was preceded in death by 2 sons, 2 grandsons, 1 great-grandson, 1 great-great-grandson, 3 brothers, 1 sister, and her parents.

She lived in Kansas until after the birth of 7 children, when the family moved near Chouteau, Oklahoma, where 2 more children were born. She lived in Oklahoma 35 years. In February, 1964, she moved to Kalona, Iowa with her daughter Salina, the Joe Bontragers. She lived in her little house beside Salina and family until last August when she moved to Parkview Manor in Wellman, where she passed away February 2, 1989. She had many friends who visited and also helped with her care the last few years. The following poem was found in her prayer book.

Mother Has Fallen Asleep

Mother was tired and weary,
Weary with toil and pain;
Put by her glasses and rocker,
She will not need them again.
Into heaven's mansions she entered,
Never to sigh nor to weep;
After long years with life's struggles,
Mother has fallen asleep.
Near other loved ones we laid her,
Low in the graveyard to lie;
Although our hearts are near broken,
Yet we would not question "Why."
She does not rest 'neath the grasses,
Tho' o'er her dear grave they creep;
She has gone into the kingdom,
Mother has fallen asleep.
Rest the tired feet forever,
Dear wrinkled hands are so still;
Blast of the earth shall no longer
Throw o'er our loved one a chill.
Angels through heaven will guide her,
Jesus will bless and keep;
Not for the world would we wake her,
Mother has fallen asleep.
Beautiful rest for the weary,
Well deserved rest for the true;
When our life's journey is ended,
We shall again be with you.
This helps to quiet our weeping,
Hark! Angel music so sweet!
He giveth to his beloved,
Beautiful, beautiful sleep.

Chapter 83
Memories and Tribute to Mother

Barbara experienced many trials in her time. She worked hard to provide for her family when her health permitted. For the past few years, she had longed to depart from this life and to be with the Lord. Often she questioned why she was still here on this earth. We children reminded her that we still needed her prayers. Her mind was usually clear, and she was faithful in praying until the Lord called her home.

Following is a memorandum selected by her daughter Anna:

Mother dear, of you I'm thinking
Since you've left us here below.
While our hearts indeed are saddened,
We know you are happy, dear.
Many years you have been with us;
Now we miss you, Oh, we do!
But you've longed to go to Heaven,
Now the Lord has called for you.
Many are your own dear loved ones,
Who have gone the way before:
Now with outstretched arms they greet you
On that happy golden shore.
Now you've gone to a better world
Where you'll never know a care.
How you loved your dear old Bible
And those sacred songs of love!
And you loved your Heavenly Father
And have wished for joys above.
You were always kind and loving,
Dear to all who have known you
But repay you – we can never –
That the blessed Lord will do.
Yes, dear Mother we will greatly
Miss your kindness and your cheer.
But we're glad to know that you are
Where their never is a tear.
Here we never will forget you.
But this life will not be long,
Soon we hope we all may meet you
With that bright Angelic throng.

Her descendants have had a few reunions since she made her triumphant departure.

One song that has been sung each time was:

"Thank You, Mama"

Somebody somewhere was praying that night,
When Jesus came in, and I saw the light,
It must have been Mama, I heard her before,
As she knelt by her bedside, her tears touched the floor.

Chorus:
Thank you, Mama, for praying for me,
If you had not prayed then where would I be?
They called you old fashioned, but you loved the Lord,
And your prayers touched the Master
as your tears touched the floor.

She held to the altar and wouldn't give in,
'Til she knew all her children had been born again.
Just an old fashioned Mama, but she loved the Lord.
And her prayers touched the Master,
as her tears touched the floor.

She left many precious memories for us all. She never wasted anything. Tiny scraps of fabric were turned into beautiful quilts. Some great-granddaughters have in their possession little doll quilts she made.

On July 12, 1983, when we as a family were together for a family reunion, a grandson, William Chupp, Jr., read a nice tribute to his grandmother, Barbara A. Bontrager Chupp, which he composed. It reads as follows:

Grandma was born near Yoder, Kansas, July 12, 1895, to Andrew F. and Fannie D. Bontrager. She was the oldest child and was able to experience all the trials, hardships, and joys of this family, growing up in the Amish church to which she has remained faithful all her life.

The rigors of life at the last of the nineteenth century were probably a good preparation for the long, hard life she was to face in her lifetime.

Abraham Lincoln once said, "Man cannot escape history, we will be remembered in spite of ourselves!"

Through her constant smile, we can see the lines in her face, her stooped shoulders, her wrinkled hands - all of which cannot deny her age - a good long life that has been given of God to enjoy on earth. From an early age, I can remember the excitement we as grandchildren had of "going to Grandma's house," or of her coming to our house. Usually daytime visits were for work. I know of no other person that enjoyed work more than Grandma.

During the summer months, she came to help with the canning - sweet corn and all the fruits and vegetables. Then in the fall, it was butcher day. The biggest need I can remember that made Grandma so necessary that day was to be in charge of cleaning the sausage casings and the hog heads. She never minded doing the hardest or the dirtiest work. And I always knew if Grandma was there that things would get done right!

During the early spring was the time for repapering the plastered walls and getting things ready for church. Paper hanging was mostly women's work, and they did it with a fury that will never be forgotten. They made their own paste, hanging each strip perfectly in place. But the thing I remember best was all the talking that went on when these women got together. There was always more news to be told than could ever be published in a newspaper: what young people were sparking, how many eggs the chickens were laying, how much milk the cows were giving, how many noodles they made yesterday, what the neighbors were doing, who got a telephone or electricity, how many loads of manure that were hauled on the corn ground, etc., etc., etc. No gossip - just facts!!

The only thing that came near to that kind of gab session was a family "Blow-Out" which was an evening of homemade ice cream, cake, sandwiches, and all the fixings. But this included the menfolks also. Grandma's east porch swing was a favorite pastime for us grandchildren. We always had room for one more!

The time our parents left on a trip and Grandma came to stay at our house was a real time of learning more about her deep faith. God was first in her life, and each morning we had family devotions. Since there were no grown men there, Grandma led the Scripture reading and prayer. A lot of people today may never hear their grandma pray, but, though I couldn't understand the old German prayer she prayed each morning, I knew God understood that Grandma wanted Him to guide and protect our lives!

"A penny saved is a penny earned" must have been my Grandma's favorite saying. She was the thriftiest person I know, which brings me to what we all know was the work she enjoyed the most. I never will forget how many empty spools there were in her toybox. Quilting was more than a hobby with her; it was a lifelong obsession!! She took the tiniest piece of scrap and put it into a thing of beauty.

Yes, my grandma could have been one of the great women in the Bible. She could have been Ruth - gleaning in the fields of Boaz, or Dorcas - making her fine linen, or Hannah - who gave her son Samuel to God's work! She could have been a great woman of secular history, Margaret Thatcher, Prime Minister of England or Indira Ghandi of India, or come through the concentration camp with Corrie Ten Boom. But really I'm glad she wasn't any of these famous people. I'm just glad she was my grandma!

To me, my Grandma's life has been a big quilt that God put into His frame long ago. He took each scrap - each small piece of her life - and made it into a thing of beauty. Each one of us who has been involved in her life will be there, too!! Won't that be the prettiest thing in Heaven! Yes, I think that all the time Grandma thought she was living through each day, one at a time here on earth. Each time she went through times of trials and sorrow, God was right there telling her "Seek first the kingdom of God and all these things will be added unto you."

Grandma - We, your children, grandchildren, great-grandchildren, great-great-grandchildren, and all your earthly family and friends tell you today, July 16, 1983, that we love you - God bless you forever - May we look forward to Eternity together.

Written by your grandson, William Chupp, Jr.

It may be of interest to some people to see how she earned her money in her sunset years when she was still able. When we girls went through Mother's things, I got a small book where she kept a record of some of her quilt piecing. I will give some examples:

July, 1969, I made 10 quilt tops in all for Mrs. Cora Yoder and got $28 total.

November 19, 1971, pieced 3 big Heart and Gizzard quilts for

Mrs. Jacob Gingerich. She paid me $18.

Mrs. Eash paid $10 for 2 large quilt tops December 17, 1971. February 5, 1972, Pauline got 9 big quilt tops, blocks for 3 quilts, and 6 cushion tops. Paid $50.50 for all. Sold 6 big quilt tops and 3 crib size to Beachey sewing. Paid $30.

I pieced a big 90 by 108 Old Maid's Puzzle for Mrs. Vernon Bontrager, December, 1972, and she paid me $9. I didn't ask for that much. In 1973, I took 5 quilt tops to the Amish sewing, and they gave me $10. Pieced for my granddaughter Mrs. Cristie Miller in Oklahoma in 1973, 7 big quilts, 1 crib quilt, blocks for 4 quilts, 3 cushion tops, 2 doll quilts. She paid me $35. Pieced for Mrs. Holzhauser in Oxford, Iowa, in February, 1974, one Old Maid's Puzzle, and three others and sold 2 quilt tops, Log Cabins, and a crib quilt, and 4 cushion tops. She paid $75 total. Pieced 8 quilts for Mrs. Morris Swarzentruber. She got them in January, 1975, and paid $75.

I didn't find much record any later. I know the last few years of her life she did very little quilt piecing.

In Mother's sunset years, she did not write many letters anymore. She said she could not think of anything to write, so she often wrote nice verses or poems. Here is one she wrote on a letter to her daughter Fannie:

A Mother builded a temple,
With loving and infinite care,
Planning each arch with patience,
Laying each stone with prayer,
None praised her unceasing efforts,
None knew of her wondrous plan,
For the temple the Mother builded,
Was unseen by the eyes of man.
Gone is the builder's temple –
Crumpled into the dust.
Low lies each stately pillar,
Food for consuming rust.
But the temple the Mother builded,
Will last while the ages roll.
For the beautiful unseen temple,
Was a child's immortal soul.

Author unknown

In September, 1990, Andy and I went to Phoenix, Arizona, to visit Andy's nephew who had Lou Gehrigs disease.

I had a desire to drive to Aguila and on out to the country where my father, Menno, had lived the last years of his life, and also where he died. My cousin, Millie Ann Borntrager, consented to go with us.

We had a bit of a problem to locate the place. The new house he had started to build some years previously lay in splinters on the ground. The fences were down, lying in a heap and all twisted up. When we had visited him the first time, he had nice fenced lots for his hogs and other animals. Parts of a washer lay scattered. The v-shaped hog trough was there in the midst of all the debris. As tears streamed down my face, the question came to me, "What had really taken place?" Perhaps a storm. Everything was so mixed up and in shambles, much as his life must have been.

How thankful we are for the promise we have in 1 John 1:9! "If we confess our sins, he is faithful and just to forgive us our sins, and to cleanse us from all unrighteousness."

Foundation of Dad's house, Aguila, Arizona

Dad's home remains in Arizona. Remains of his hog pens.